Road Trip:
Conversations With Writers

Road Trip:
Conversations With Writers

Shelly Clark and Marjorie Saiser
Editors

The Backwaters Press
Omaha

First Printing, 1000 copies, April 2003

The Backwaters Press
Greg Kosmicki, Editor/Publisher
3502 North 52nd Street
Omaha, Nebraska 68104-3506
Gkosm62735@AOL.com
www.thebackwaterspress.homestead.com

ISBN: 0-9726187-0-8

SPECIAL THANKS

We are grateful to the writers who gave so generously of their time.

We thank reference librarian Sue Ladehoff. Thank you to photographers Randy Barger and Matt Riley, and to designer Chris Bristol.

Special thanks to editor, publisher, and friend, Greg Kosmicki.

For our children:

Elizabeth and Haley

Paul and Susan

and for all the children who are writing their first stories

[Writing is] like driving a car at night. You never see further than your headlights. But you can make the whole trip that way.

— E.L. Doctorow

TABLE OF CONTENTS

Road Trip

Road Trip

SHELLY CLARK received an MA in journalism at the University of Nebraska-Lincoln and her BA from University of Nebraska-Kearney. She taught for 15 years in Imperial, Nebraska. During her tenure at Chase County High School she was a recipient of the Peter Keiwit Teacher Achievement Award for Excellence in Classroom Teaching and two-time winner of a Cooper Foundation Excellence in Teaching Award. She was an instructor in the Journalism Department at Midland Lutheran College in Fremont, Nebraska. Her poems have appeared in *Nebraska Territory, Nebraska English Journal* and *Plains Song Review.* Her work has been anthologized in *Times of Sorrow/Times of Grace.*

MARJORIE SAISER received an MA in creative writing at the University of Nebraska-Lincoln, winning the Vreelands Award and the Academy of American Poets competition. Her work has been published in literary journals including *Prairie Schooner, Georgia Review, Zone 3,* and *Cream City Review.* Poems of hers have been nominated for the Pushcart Prize. She is a recipient of the Merit Award from the Nebraska Arts Council, and in 1999 received the Literary Heritage Award. Saiser is a speaker for the Nebraska Humanities Council. Her first full-length collection, *Bones of a Very Fine Hand,* won the Nebraska Book Award for poetry in 2000. Her other books are *Lost in Seward County* (Backwaters Press, 2001) and *Moving On* (Lone Willow Press, 2002). She is co-editor of an anthology of writing by women of the Great Plains, *Times of Sorrow/Times of Grace* (Backwaters Press, 2002).

Shelly and I are in the car, driving south, heading home to Nebraska after a poetry workshop at the University of Minnesota-Duluth. We crane our necks, taking one last look at Lake Superior, the inland sea that has fascinated us all week—mornings with fog, nights with a gold smear from the full moon, afternoons when we've waded briefly in its incredibly cold waters.

For our last look, there are sail boats, appearing small on the huge painting of the lake. We turn away; it's a long road home. We are writers, so we talk about writing. We also talk about family, the price of latté, the number of white vans on the road, the cute professor, our mothers, our daughters, our old loves, our broken hearts, the family dogs. There's a lot of windshield time from Duluth to Lincoln. As the soda cans and pretzel sacks pile up on the floor, our ideas get wilder, and we hatch the concept for a book:

Let's do a book of interviews with writers. Let's talk to writers about their childhoods and about their writing habits and their teaching ideas. It'll be fun. Let's tape dozens of people; let's type up the interviews. (Reality sets in later.) We are so excited we almost forget to turn right at Des Moines. We talk about our own writing habits and influences:

MARGE: I like the idea of being part of a community. When I write alone on the couch in the morning before sunrise, I think of pajama-clad writers all over this country doing their morning pages. I'm part of a horde of writers who are trying to make sure the day doesn't get away from them without some writing. I like to write in the half-dark, to be writing when the crows make that fuss that means the sun is coming up, to get some writing done before the demands of the day take over. I don't always do that, of course, but it's a goal. I fall off regularly, but I figure gaps are OK, as long as not writing doesn't become a habit.

Poetry can deal with the daily things of living, and when it does, it seems to be saying that ordinary people count. Ordinary lives, day to day. You can write poorly about this, as you can write poorly and sentimentally about any other topic, but you can also reach out to the edges of what you know and find the insights that occur to you.

SHELLY: What kinds of things in your childhood do you see as influences on your writing?

MARGE: Oh, I think the subtleties of grassland. The Niobrara and the Keya Paha, those rivers I splashed in when I was a kid. The farmers talking about rain and the government. The Saturday night dances in my little town, Naper. Hundreds of people dancing, my friends at intermission walking main street, some kids driving cars, making U-turns at the edge of town, driving up and down. My parents ran a cafe, and we had our living quarters in the back. I waited tables when I got big enough, washed dishes, fried hamburgers.

My parents had several pool tables in the basement of the cafe, and also two bowling lanes. My sister Kathy and I set pins, jumping up and sitting on the side, as the bowling balls rolled down the alley toward us. I played pool and snooker. I learned my math facts by playing cribbage with my mother. Cribbage teaches you very fast all the combinations that do and do not make fifteen.

Besides the cafe, my parents ran the theater, so sometimes I sold tickets, popped popcorn, and then went upstairs into the projection booth where my dad was operating the machines. I'd watch the movie—a western or a comedy—with him, or I'd turn around and lean out the window and look down on main street. We ran the same movie on Wednesday and Friday, and then a new one on Saturday and Sunday. I saw two movies per week, two times each.

I heard stories in the cafe, farmers talking. My mother is a great storyteller; that was an influence on me, the way she always loved to tell stories.

Birds figure in my poems, as they figured in my growing up. The hawks and the kingbirds and larks. There is no sound quite like a lark on the prairie in the springtime. I am stopped stockstill by the song of a cardinal. When I hear a cardinal, I equate it with my father. The kingbird, as well, I connect with him, because a kingbird is a silent, watchful, graceful bird.

Growing up in a small town, having the run of the place, I think that was an influence. Biking on country roads, playing softball on summer nights until it was so dark you couldn't see the ball coming toward you—the freedom of that was important, as well as spending so much time outdoors. Having a great deal of solitude also had an effect.

SHELLY: Did your teachers have an effect?

MARGE: I had a teacher in grade school who influenced me. Mrs. Fischer loved learning, she loved books, she believed in me. She liked my stories. The fact she didn't mind being different from others was a powerful example.

In high school, one of my teachers was a scholar. Mr. Titus held an extra class for three students, a Latin class, because he said we'd need Latin. He was already carrying a full load. He did that because he thought it was important. It was a very small school, but I was lucky. I had many good teachers. There were nineteen in my senior class, the largest in the history of the school.

My father and his seven sisters had grown up on a farm during hard times. I consider them my teachers, vital influences because of the way they laughed and kidded and enjoyed life. Family was the important thing in their lives. The sisters are now in their 70s and 80s, living in Rapid City, South Dakota. I've written about them at their aunt's funeral, or getting together to play canasta, talking about old times.

My parents almost bought the farm where my dad had grown up, but then didn't. They sold the café and went into construction, building homes and farm buildings. They worked side by side for years, putting up wallboard, hanging doors, building fireplaces, sawing rafters. I was the "go-fer" for my father when he spent summer days laying concrete blocks for a foundation or for a hog parlor.

SHELLY: I know your husband has made a difference in your writing life.

MARGE: Don is a tremendous part of my writing. Not only do I write about him (his comment is "Whatever"), but he understands the white space I need in order to be able to write. That alone is fantastic encouragement. I read him my poems, and he comes to my readings. I can't say enough about his influence and support.

SHELLY: What's your writing process?

MARGE: Some poems come "whole-cloth" when I'm writing in the morning, but most of them are carved out of freewrites. Often I write in response to poems I have read. I like to write in cafés with a cup of hot chocolate next to my elbow, nobody else at my table, or maybe a friend also there with her notebook.

Walking is important to my writing process. I take walks around the neighborhood and then write, or I walk on the prairie, or on the hiker/biker trail east of Walton, with my notebook in hand. I don't necessarily write about what I see, but the walking gets me into the mood.

When I wrote the poem "Lost in Seward County," I was freewriting in a cafe with a friend. We had something to eat, took out our notebooks, and decided to write about what had happened since we had last seen one another. I started to write about getting lost driving out to Ted Kooser's place in the country. I was writing as fast as I could, and chuckling. My friend was curious, but she kept writing. I kept writing and laughing. I began to exaggerate, telling a whopper, amusing myself. Later, I revised and revised and read the poem to my husband, who liked it. At my readings, he encouraged me to read the poem. Audiences like it, which surprises me, and people tell me they identify with that feeling of being lost, and of laughing at yourself, and of needing to find a place that feels like home.

In freewriting, I like the phenomenon of "cruise control," as if you feel the accelerator move on its own under your foot, when the writing takes off and you write as fast as you can, following where it leads. Freewriting is about discovery. You don't know what you're going to write, but the poem uncovers itself as it goes along. The freewrite becomes a sled going downhill.

SHELLY: You take part in some writing groups, and you also teach writing groups.

MARGE: In the last few years, I have led a couple of small groups where I give an exercise at each session. We write and then read aloud to each other. It's a type of ear-training. You tend to be a better listener if you don't have a copy in front of you. You listen to get the point, without taking out your red pen and tearing into someone else's work.

I also belong to several critique groups, which I find tremendously valuable. In those groups, we do have the poem on paper in front of us, and we invite criticism. It is extremely valuable to have criticism from readers who want to see what the poem is trying to do.

Like many writers in this state, I got my start when William Kloefkorn came into my classroom as a poet-in-the-school to speak to my students. Then I took his classes and was encouraged to keep writing. He is a fine, fine teacher and poet. Many poets in this state have become part of my community. Their encouragement and example has made all the difference to me.

I also like to attend workshops around the country from time to time. If I can't take a workshop, I try to check out an armload of books, or buy some, by a poet whose work has caught my eye.

Writing is the important thing. Po-biz can get in the way of writing. Anything can and does. I get buried under the po-biz every once in a while. One saying that helps me clear away the impediments is: *Whatever keeps me from doing my work—that's my work.*

Giving readings has a value to me because readings keep me in touch with real people and they help me know how to revise a poem, just by hearing myself read it, without anyone even commenting on it. Revising is very satisfying work. The freewrite comes from a playful part of the brain, spilling out pell-mell. Later, it is as if a different part of the brain takes this rough sculpture and refines it and gets rid of what does not belong. Revising has to do with putting yourself in the place of a reader who has never heard the poem, reading it aloud for the rhythms and also for spots that need clarifying.

When I'm revising, one thing I like to get rid of is explanation. Give the reader credit. I enjoy a poem if it doesn't spell everything out and, conversely, if it doesn't try to be secretive, or exclude me. A balance of clarity and mystery.

How about you, Shelly? When did you first begin to think of yourself as a poet?

SHELLY: Oh, a couple weeks ago. I don't think of myself as a poet; I think of poetry as my passion. Recently when someone was introducing me to her friends, she said, "Shelly's a poet."

I thought, "Me?" It's hard to claim that I am actually a poet. When I finish a poem that I like, then I think of myself that way. Once someone asked me if I make my living writing poetry. (laughter)

My first poem was a get-well card for my fifth grade teacher, Miss Smith. I remember it because my mother saved it. It went something like this:

I'm sorry you have sore toes.
But that's the way it goes.
Soon you'll be on your feet
and back in the teacher's seat.

My mom thought this was a wonderful poem. She was the first person to recognize that I had some kind of writing ability or the desire to do something with language, to work with it. Also there were teachers who encouraged me. I don't remember anyone in elementary school saying, "Oh, you're going to be a writer," but there were ways they recognized my creativity. From early on I was interested in creating things with people. I had opportunity for that at family dinners at my grandparents' throughout my childhood. I have eight first cousins my brother and I played with all those long wonderful Sundays, rambling around the farm.

At Christmas, it would be my idea to do a little play or a musical line-up before we opened our presents. This would irritate my cousins and brother because they wanted to get right to the opening of presents after the meal, but they usually gave in and let me direct the performance, and, of course, have one of the starring roles. We ended up having lots of fun and the parents and grandparents clapped—they loved it. So, I guess that's probably the reason my extended family thought of me as the creative one. Except for my uncle who called me the homely one.

MARGE: Your uncle called you what?

SHELLY: He was always saying, "Oh, you get homelier every day." (laughter) Anyway, the rest of the family, thank goodness, deemed me the creative one.

I was crazy about books. I started out like many people did with Nancy Drew and Perry Mason. I was going to be a detective or lawyer. I read every single Sherlock Holmes I could get my hands on. In high school I got into Steinbeck and Hemingway, Salinger, Ayn Rand and others, and so began this love affair with language and story.

I had some good teachers who loved language—one who had us underlining our verbs, drawing wavy lines under the indirect verbs. This is what we did for four years in grade school, and I thank her for that. So, I had that good base of grammar in those years and then I had these wonderful flower children high school English teachers, fresh out of college in the late 60s, early 70s. It was a wild swing. We read books; we did creative projects. That's when I needed that creativity. Miss Kimble, bless her heart wherever she is, would come into the classroom and plop down into the teacher's desk. She was a large woman in her late twenties. She loved books so much. She would read passages to us, like the passage out of Steinbeck's *Grapes of Wrath* where the truck driver runs over the turtle. I picture myself sitting in that classroom, watching her read that, her eyes welling up, the tears rolling down her cheeks. It was not for effect or for drama; I think most of the time she didn't notice we were there. I was impressed that someone could be so moved by these wonderful passages. She's the one who gave me F. Scott Fitzgerald and Steinbeck and all the greats. She was so moved sometimes I think she didn't even care if we were along for the ride, as long as she could sit there, read literature and get caught up in it.

That's also when I began reading poetry, Sandburg and Frost. I developed a fascination with the life of Carl Sandburg. The life of a poet. The first poem I remember loving was Sandburg's "Chicago." We had to memorize a poem in Miss Kimble's class, and up to that point we had read very little poetry. The poem was in our textbook. I still love that poem so much. *City of the big shoulders.* I think Miss Kimble gave me a B on my presentation. Most of the time, though, the teachers pretty much passed over the poetry sections of the texts and moved on.

MARGE: Which is probably a good thing. It's better than beating a poem to death.

SHELLY: In high school, I wrote essays and research papers and critical analysis, and I wrote drama for the classroom. Once in a while we'd write a poem, and I did get a poem accepted. I thought I had arrived: I'm going to be a poet! The poem was called *The Tie that Binds,* and my mother said, "Of course, we have to buy the book." I realized later they publish everyone, but for me, at that time in my life, it was important for somebody to recognize that poem, somebody beyond Imperial, beyond my teachers. Even if it cost $29.95.

In college, I majored in journalism, but I also took English classes and read like crazy, including Faulkner and Nebraska authors. I read Willa Cather. I took Don Welch's poetry class. He was a wonderful teacher and is a great mentor yet to me today. He was encouraging to all the writers, and we were introduced to great poetry and to workshopping. I loved that.

Then I dropped that whole life. I kept reading poetry, but I was raising my family and working. About ten years later, I took two of my students to a workshop in North Platte featuring Bill Kloefkorn. I didn't know we even had a state poet. I was in western Nebraska and poetry was on another planet. I read about the workshop, thought it sounded like a cool excuse for a field trip, so we drove up there. Like most people, I was taken in by Bill's poetry. He makes it accessible to all of us. That rekindled my interest in poetry, and I thought, "Oh, yeah, I used to love that stuff." I started writing again.

Once or twice a year I would try to do something like that workshop. I met other writers, others like me who have this passion and don't know what to do with it, a kind of craziness for poetry, I suppose like carving ducks or driving racecars is for some people.

I started a creative writing class. I told the school board, "This school needs a creative writing class; I'll be the teacher."

I joined a writers' group. When you are hesitant about your writing, you need somebody who will be your writing friend and mentor. I read a great deal of poetry now; always finding new poets to read and returning again to my favorites: Mary Oliver, Rilke, Milosz, Rumi, Marie Howe, Mark Doty and many more.

Sometimes I think the last thing the world needs is another poet; there are so many good ones out there. Who in the world do I think am? But I've decided the world needs more poets; in fact, everybody should be a poet.

MARGE: You mentioned curiosity as one reason for this project. What do you see as our purpose in doing this book about writers?

SHELLY: I love to capture stories and put them down. Writers have great stories and a wealth of knowledge and experience. We have incredible poets and teachers in this area, not at all stingy with their talent and their time, encouraging others, as I've been encouraged.

Another reason is to get writers' wisdom. They have imperfect lives, like all of us, and have overcome many problems. They did not come out of the crib accomplished writers. I want to hear their stories, and I want other people to hear their stories. When I was a teacher, it was gratifying to have real live writers come in and validate what some of us were doing; to know it's okay if you don't pour red ink all over the students' work. Young writers can be fragile; evaluating a poem is not like grading a math worksheet. For me, it was incredible to be validated. There are other teachers and students out there who will gain from this, who will learn from these writers. I like to work on projects and to create things. Part of doing this book is selfish: I want to interview these people because being with writers is so much fun.

MARGE: I thought maybe it was insanity brought on by the burritos at that last cafe, or that gooseberry pie at the drive-in in Stuart, Iowa.

It's interesting that earlier you mentioned Nancy Drew. My mother evidently asked a friend to give me some Nancy Drew books that she was getting rid of. We didn't have a library in our town, so this woman, Joanne, came into our cafe one Saturday night with a two-foot stack of Nancy Drew books. Remember those green curlicue covers? Joanne had tied white string around the stack, and it was hanging and swinging from her hand. She came into the kitchen of the cafe and gave me this column of books. I cut the string and started to eat them from the top down. I fell so deep into story. My mother would say, "You have to wash the dishes," or "You have to get the mail," and I would swim up from great depths out of the stories to the world where you have to wash the dishes. It's lovely to be deep in a world that someone made with words, with interesting people and interesting events, with clues that you can figure out.

My teacher, like yours, taught us what the sentence is, what the sentence is made of. Mrs. Fischer loved language, and we caught it from her. She had the idea that you might want to know about nouns and verbs and adjectives and adverbs. She taught us to diagram sentences, a skill I find helpful today. I don't draw the diagram, but I know what the subject is, what the verb is, and how the clauses depend on other parts of the sentence, how words hang off other words. I thank her for that. If you love words, you like to know how they work. Scientists probably thank someone for a study of butterflies or of atoms. I thank her for that early study of language.

I was not required to write a great deal, but rather to read. It's better not to write at all than to be mangled by a well-meaning bludgeoner. It's more important that students be required to read than it is to pick apart their writing or even bring a strong light to bear on what they've written.

For reading instruction, Mrs. Fischer tested everybody in her classroom and found their reading level. There were three or four grades there. Then she asked students to forget about what grade they were in, which was a revolutionary idea in my school. She said students would be in a group made of 4th, 5th, and 6th graders, and each group would be reading books at a different reading level. She sold us that, single-handedly. That's no small thing when it's a new idea.

Then she said, "I do not have time in the day to have another group, so Margie and Ruth and LouAnn, here are some books I have for you; you will simply read. These books have questions in them. You will not write the answers, but you will read the questions, and answer them in your mind." We did that. It was great literature.

Just as at home reading the Nancy Drew books, I felt I was in another world, and somewhere out there, miles away, someone was saying, "It's time for math now. You must come out." So we came out and we spelled and we did math, but that time was set aside to go deep into those stories, and nothing could be better. I thank her for that instruction, for that non-instruction. What we can do for children is to give them good things to read, give them time and the expectation to read, and the expectation to spend time outdoors with grass and trees and rivers and birds. Those things do not seem to have anything to do with writing, but mean everything.

SHELLY: Teaching creative writing in junior high, high school, and college is not the same as teaching math or the other courses. We want to be able to test it, to measure how far along students are in their maturation, but with language and creativity that is hard to do. I went in as a teacher the first year with no textbooks, which is probably the best thing that happened to me. There was an old grammar text in the cupboard but it was so horrible, I didn't even take it out, and luckily had a principal who didn't care what I was doing as long as the students were not falling out into the hallways or tying me up in the closet.

Testing has become so important. Administration may not be into poetry or into creative writing, and may not understand how those things work. Creative writing is very personal. Along with the fundamentals of grammar and how to read, there has to be a balance of bringing along the person, the creative person.

Some of the best poems came from kids who loved nothing but math, math, all day long. They'd say, "I hate English," but they would come up with these great poems. There is so much creativity in all the children; some of it goes by the wayside because of rules and testing and time constraints. Don't spend six hours going over someone's writing. I follow the Don Welch method: find the best passage, pass by their desk, tell them what a great line or image it is, and move on. That's what I always wanted when I wrote: to find what was good in it. I'm not saying revision isn't important. There's a place for that. Obviously, there is curriculum, and there are grades. You have to keep students on task, but there are ways to do that without stifling creativity.

The hardest thing was to convince the parents and the administrators that it was valuable to let my students have fifty minutes, one class period a week, to read—just sit in their desks and silently read novels.

MARGE: What feeds your creativity?

SHELLY: Going to readings is important, and conversations with people, and being in the world, being aware of things. At that first workshop with Bill Kloefkorn, I remember him quoting Henry James, I think it was, who said, "I want to be a person upon whom nothing is lost." Those words changed my life. Someone put into words that desire to be a person who participates in life. As you were talking about rivers and nature and people being in the world and not missing life, I thought of Annie Dillard who has a passage in *An American Childhood* where she says as a writer you are different because you are aware of so much and your senses are overcome. She said sometimes acute awareness can be a burden but the alternative is worse. She said she was afraid she would wake up on her deathbed someday and say, "What *was* that?"

My childhood continues to inspire me. Growing up in a small Western Nebraska town, my brother and I, all the kids really, had such freedom and so many unstructured hours, though we might have missed some intellectual stimuli. When the harvest crews came to town, it was the most excitement all year long. The combines rolled in, and strange men poured into the cafes. The drama electrified our town. Ordinarily, kids were allowed to run around, go anywhere at night, play "ditch'em," ride our bikes, go to the park. Our parents would not worry about us, but when the harvesters came to town, I had to be in at sundown. My brother didn't have to be. My dad wouldn't go into the reasons that a young girl shouldn't be around the harvesters. Nothing dangerous ever happened when the harvesters came to town, that I know of, but it was, nevertheless, exciting. Most of my childhood I spent outdoors, and I wouldn't trade it for anything.

The past two years, I've been writing more. I'm not teaching now; I'm still working, but it's a different kind of work. I made a shift in my life. A day with time alone, time to go for a walk, that has fed my writing. Things start coming up when you relax. You don't have the pressures that eat you up.

There are so many great things to do in this world besides write poetry, and it's tempting. Reading takes an incredible amount of time. I've turned off the television. When people refer to some things on television, I feel like I've dropped out of the pop culture. Maybe this is only temporary.

MARGE: What is your writing process?

SHELLY: My process is called chaos. (laughter)

Road Trip

Remember those old movies? Geezers
telling weak jokes on the road to Mandalay,
pipsqueaks making puns while
rolling city to city? Today you and I
follow I-35 from Duluth,

south, as if the great lake had sprung a leak
and carried us toward the cornfields of Iowa.
Our stories spin out in the car:
marriages, a toy bride and groom on a cake,
new, hopeful, flattened.
Our dreams for our daughters
circle the air of the car like desperadoes.

At Des Moines we veer west
and follow a truck. The white line,
like a low wall, keeps us on the superslab.
Humidity sits in the air, a watchdog over mid-America.
We fall silent, ringed with candy wrappers,
Aquafina bottles, a battered box of tissues.

There never was a silence like this
on the road to Mandalay.
Hey, Amigo, take the next exit.
Pull right on in. We'll scout around.
Soon as we locate another vat
of that excuse that passes for coffee,
we've got to start the second reel.

Calling Cardinals

I call cardinals
as my father did,
whistling two notes:
You me. You me.

The cardinal does not answer,
keeping his voice
in a tight red shape in the oak,
in the weight of his body

and line of his tail,
hard orange shell of his beak,
black map around his eye.
The sky above the trees is quiet

as though the voice of the cardinal,
my father's voice,
having left the branches of the oak,
beats its wings out of earshot.

My Old Aunts Play Canasta in a Snowstorm

My Old Aunts Play Canasta in a Snowstorm

I ride along in the backseat; the aunt who can drive
picks up each sister at her door, keeps the Pontiac
chugging in each driveway while one or the other
slips into her overshoes and steps out,
closing her door with a click, the wind

lifting the fringe of her white cotton scarf
as she comes down the sidewalk, still pulling on her
new polyester Christmas-stocking mittens.
We have no business to be out in such a storm,
she says, no business at all.

The wind takes her voice and swirls it
like snow across the windshield.
We're on to the next house, the next aunt,
the heater blowing to beat the band.

At the last house, we play canasta,
the deuces wild even as they were in childhood,
the wind blowing through the empty apple trees,
through the shadows of bumper crops. The cards

line up under my aunts' finger bones; eights and nines and aces
straggle and fall into place like well-behaved children.
My aunts shuffle and meld; they laugh like banshees,
as they did in that other kitchen in the '30s—
that day Margaret draped a dishtowel over her face
to answer the door. We put her up to it, they say,
laughing; we pushed her. The man—whoever he was—
drove off in a huff while they laughed 'til they hiccupped,

laughing still—I'm one of the girls laughing him down the sidewalk
and into his car, we're rascals sure as farmyard dogs,
we're wild card-players. The snow thickens,
the coffee boils and perks, the wind is a red trey
because, as one or the other says,

We are getting up there in the years; we'll
have to quit sometime. But today,
today,
deal, sister, deal.

Marjorie Saiser

The Pelican's Dive Looks Like a Fall

The Pelican's Dive Looks Like a Fall

The pelican's dive looks like a fall,
a mistake. His head goes in OK—
Bingo. But then the tail flips over the fuselage,
and the neck has to compensate. After a while,
the whole thing wobbles upright
with a fish for dinner. Is that OK?
Is content greater than form? Do the spine

and ribs of the fish, its tough curved gills,
the slick skin of its youth and middle-age,
these things which now surely begin to
lose all sheen in the tract of the bird—

do these constitute the greater part?

Or is it grace, is it form—
the way the pelican taxis over the surface of the water,
tilting, correcting,

done for now with awkward flapping,
as if gliding purely on the skin of truth,
as if sliding across the belly of the sea.

William Kloefkorn

William Kloefkorn

WILLIAM KLOEFKORN lives and writes in Lincoln, Nebraska, where he is Professor Emeritus of English at Nebraska Wesleyan. His collections of poetry include *Alvin Turner as Farmer, Dragging Sand Creek for Minnows, Houses and Beyond, Drinking the Tin Cup Dry, Collecting for the Wichita Beacon, Where the Visible Sun Is, Welcome to Carlos, Treehouse: New & Collected Poems, Loup River Psalter, Sergeant Patrick Gass, Chief Carpenter: On the Trail with Lewis & Clark*, and *Covenants*, a book he shares with Utah's poet laureate, David Lee. His books of prose include *A Time to Sink Her Pretty Little Ship, Shadow Boxing, This Death by Drowning*, and his collection of children's Christmas stories, *The Coldest Christmas.*

He initiated the Poets-in-the-Schools program in Nebraska and has read his work and conducted workshops in elementary, junior high, and high schools in Nebraska and across the country. His work has appeared in numerous periodicals and anthologies. His awards include the Lincoln Mayor's Arts Award, the Governor's Arts Award, and the Mari Sandoz Award. He has received two honorary doctorates, one from Nebraska Wesleyan and the other from Midland College in Fremont. In 1982 he was named the Nebraska State Poet by the Nebraska Unicameral. He and his wife, Eloise, have four children and a delightful assortment of grandchildren.

Bill Kloefkorn meets us for coffee at Mo Java, near the Wesleyan campus. This is our first interview, and Bill puts us at ease. He's the master of that.

MARGE: Let's start with your family in Kansas. Tell us about your grandparents.

BILL: My maternal grandmother came from Germany when she was 17 years old. She came here to visit her brother, the only one who was here, Jacob. Grandma came from a large family and I think they were simply shipping the kids out. Jake came over and became a farm laborer. My grandmother was homesick for him, came over to visit, and never went back. She settled in Kansas, after a brief stint in Texas, and Kansas is where she lived until her death in the mid-eighties. I never knew my granddad on my mom's side because he died two years before I was born, so my memory of him comes from what my grandmother said about him and what my mom said about him, which is considerable, as a matter of fact.

On the other side, my granddad's dad came from Germany, so my paternal grandfather was a first generation American, a poor dirt farmer all his life. He had a small family, my dad and two daughters. His wife's parents came from England. That makes me about three-quarters German, I guess, if my percentages aren't skewed. He was pretty much a stubborn German all his life and a poor dirt farmer. That has enormously influenced my work, I think, because I knew him as a kid, so I saw him as a role model, a hero. I loved to visit the farm. He sort of pampered me and my brother, and it was at a time in our lives when that kind of thing was really important. So I still write out of him, from him. *Alvin Turner as Farmer* is based upon him, although the attitudes in that book are all mine.

MARGE: An early interest in language is connected, I believe, somewhat with your grandfather. At least I've heard you tell a story about spelling the word *Chautauqua* for him. Would you credit your grandfather with giving you an early interest in language?

BILL: Yes, right, I think so. I didn't know it at the time. That's what I meant a minute ago when I said I was at a very impressionable age. My grandfather lost his farm in south central Kansas, and bought a piece of really terrible acreage, terrible in terms of farming, in southeastern Kansas near a little town called Cedar Vale. Hilly, rocky, boulders, gumbo soil, so he bought it for a song. He let me go with him in his pickup when he was moving. I went with him as he took a couple of loads. That meant a hundred and twenty miles. Now for me, that was an incredible adventure—to ride those miles with my granddad in his pickup. That was a major excitement, and on one of the trips as we were entering Chautauqua County, he asked me to spell *Chautauqua*. My God, what a word. C-h-a-u-t-a-u-q-u-a. You just memorize it on the spot. It was important, my granddad reacting to that.

He was a member of a group that called itself a literary, where *literary* was used as a noun. He had to memorize little pieces for that literary and as a young man would attend the meetings. Maybe a little bit like our writers' group. I didn't know him when he was attending those meetings. I knew him later, after his creativity had been squelched by the Pentecostal Church, which squelched everything creative and fun. My granddad became a member of that church, probably out of desperation. If you don't have a damn thing, and somebody offers you something, you're inclined to take it, even if it comes only in the form of faith. Faith is something you can hold onto if you don't have anything else to hold onto. That's what faith is for—that's the definition of faith, it seems to me. That church, as much as I despise it, offered him that, and I understand his taking it, and, of course, that meant giving up anything that came close to creativity: amusement.

When I was a little kid and we visited him, we could prevail upon him to recite one or two of those pieces that he had learned and had delivered at his literary. One of them was called "Noah and the Ark." *There was Ham, and there was Shem, and there was Japheth... And they all ran into the Ark.* Wonderfully memorized and delivered. It infuriated my grandmother who was more Pentecostal even than Granddad.

She would excuse herself, go out into the kitchen and rattle pots and pans, make herself obnoxious to show her disfavor. But I and my sister and brother could cajole my granddad into delivering one or two of those speeches, essays, or whatever you want to call them, and, yes, I was impressed by them, I don't know, the language of them, the way he delivered them. The good humor in some of them. One involved a telephone conversation. He stood up and went to the old crank telephone on the wall and had a monologue, actually. It was funny. Of course, in that religion, to deliver a memorized speech that was amusing was even worse than delivering one that was serious. So that really tickled us. There was something about language that at an early age, by way of my grandfather, impressed me.

MARGE: And maybe his losses, too? Loss of the land, loss of the creative?

BILL: Yes, that came later but that was a factor. I didn't understand at the time the losses involved. And I still don't know how he lost the land. I think it had to do with a transaction at the local elevator. This was a small town, about 600 people, and my granddad lived several miles north of town. It could have been that he thought he was not paid for a load of wheat. I don't know what happened, but the farm was foreclosed on and he lost it. The fact, not only that he lost it, but that I don't know how he lost it, is intriguing. You know, your using that word *loss*, Marge, is good, because that's what it is. The loss of his creativity, or the inhibiting of his creativity, the corralling of it, is a distinctive loss.

MARGE: Bill, you know a lot of scripture. How about that language, the King James version? Is that important at all? Was it?

BILL: It was and still is. It's a touchstone. That is to say, it's a language against which I measure all other languages. I grew up in a Protestant church. A couple of notches below the Methodists. It was the United Brethren Church, UB, which became the Evangelical United Brethren Church, which was absorbed into the Methodists when I was about 18 or 20 years old. The churches in town provided all of the social amenities, so if you didn't go to church, you simply didn't have the necessary contacts—the church, the movies, you know, hanging out downtown, hanging out in church. So that's what I did. My parents never went but they always sent us, and insisted that we go, so I went and participated and I was fairly competitive. I would out-memorize my peers and collect my Bible for it, or my New Testament, or whatever the reward was.

The language, some of the King James, is very rich in poetry and a lot of it sort of sticks and becomes those touchstones that I mentioned a minute ago that you use to measure. Now you have to assume that if a touchstone works, it is rich, rich in metaphor. When Job laments his losses and thinks of his early days, he remembers, as he puts it, those days *when my feet*, he says, *were washed in butter.* That's a really rich image and he's remembering that in the midst of all his woes. A line like that resonates, and it works. When you read a line then later, ten years later, twenty years later, it doesn't matter, if that line doesn't have the kind of resonance that the *washed in butter* does, then there's something wrong with it. So you use it as a yardstick for judging the quality of your own writing and the writing of others.

The Old Testament is a deadly, unfortunate history, it seems to me. It leads people to insist that it's holy, which it isn't, that it is the word of God, which it isn't, which leads them to interpret it in their own individual ways and for their own individual purposes, which is unfortunate, because that leads to disputes that lead, sometimes, to bloodshed. But even so, it's still rich—especially Ecclesiastes, Song of Solomon, and some of the Psalms—still rich in language. It's a wonderfully erratic poem and when you spend as much time with it as I spent growing up... I mean, we never had a minister who knew anything about the scriptures. Didn't even appreciate, I think, the sounds in it. Just used it as a jumping off point, usually for his own babble. But when you grow up with that, and spend so much time with it, invest so much time in it, well, it's going to stick to you, whether you want it to or not. It comes frequently, in different ways, into my own writing.

MARGE: Would you talk about the poems you first loved? The books you first loved?

BILL: The first books I loved were comic books. And I really did love them. I liked the looks of them, the color—the splashy color—I liked the drawings, I liked the art work, I liked a lot of the language. I liked the notion that you could say *Shazam* as a boy and become Power. The power of the word. You say *Shazam* and become—what? Billy Batson becomes Captain Marvel. Wow, what a transformation by way of one word. I loved those. I devoured them. I traded. I had stacks and stacks of comic books. If I had them now I wouldn't be talking with you. I would be on the Riviera, you know, drinking Madeira. I'd much rather be here talking with you, as a matter of fact; I never did like Madeira. And France, well... But that really was an important book. And I've already mentioned the reading of the Bible verses that we had. Innumerable.

Another book that influenced me greatly was the catalogue, the Sears catalogue, and Montgomery Ward. Again, the color, the layout, the type style, the whole drama, the whole format of the catalogue, just overwhelmed me. And the fact that it contains all those things that I can't have makes it even better. Well, I can't have the things in the comic book either. I mean, I can say *Shazam* but I'm not going to turn into Captain Marvel, but I can read about somebody doing that. And I can't have that cowboy outfit in the catalogue, but I can read about it and imagine that somebody has that outfit. I can imagine that I have that outfit. You could afford a catalogue. I think catalogues were given away then or mailed, or whatever. But we always had a catalogue. Those were absolutely major.

I didn't read much in school through 18 years. Very very little. I don't remember reading much of anything in elementary school, junior high school. But we were *read to* from time to time. I had a couple of teachers who read to us to open the classes, fifteen or twenty minutes. I had a teacher in the fifth grade who did that. Did you do that, Marge? If I taught elementary school today, I can't imagine not doing that.

One of the teachers, this is in one of my poems somewhere, read a James Fenimore Cooper novel—it took a whole year to do it—read *The Last of the Mohicans*, and I got hooked on that, couldn't wait to hear the next installment. It takes a year to read that at twenty-minute swatches, but I fell in love with it, the whole thing. It was not only the book, the chase, the capture, the release, all that sort of thing—it was the teacher. Watching her read it. Because she obviously liked it, and as I recall, read it well. I don't know whether I was more in love with the story or the teacher. They sort of mixed, kind of a combination, but see, I remember these because they were so few.

I remember reading a little story in grade school called *Cow Pasture Backfield*. This little kids' football team lived in a rural area and practiced out in the cow pasture. *Cow Pasture Backfield.* Then they came in and whipped the city kids—the town kids. I remember that and, again, I think I remember it because it's only one of two or three that I read. Or had read to me.

In high school, practically nothing. A friend of mine picked up a novel by P.G. Wodehouse called *Leave it to Psmith.* Psmith spelled, of course, P-s-m-i-t-h, and he gave me a copy of that book after he finished it and said, "I think you'll like this." Well, I'd never had anybody give me a book and say "I think you'll like this." It wasn't a comic book; it wasn't a catalogue. So I read it.

During my senior year I actually read two or three P.G. Wodehouse novels; I thought they were really great. That was a happenstance thing. That was outside the classroom. I just don't remember us reading very much. We surely read some things, but not very many, so I was in college before I started any serious reading.

MARGE: Why should anybody write?

BILL: Well, it's one of many ways to make some order out of chaos. Or out of confusion. Or out of anything. And it doesn't have to be confusion or chaos, it could be a record of happiness. If something happens to you that's fortunate, to have a record of that good fortune is, seems to me, a healthy thing. You can go back to it and be reinforced by it. It's possible that you could go back to it twenty years later, and learn what you were twenty years earlier.

Let's say you write a poem when you are 27 years old and you're full of vinegar and you are feeling good, and it's a poem of great exuberance, good spirit. Let's say that twenty-five years later you've become a kind of curmudgeon, if not a downright cynic. Let's say your cynicism gets serious. Let's say you go back and read that poem that you wrote some years earlier and you discover, maybe, that you haven't always been a sonofabitch, you know, that you had at one time in your life a good heart. That can be a good thing to know. Actually, it can be a good thing for other people to know.

I think writing is mostly a way of ordering things. What we want, as much as anything else, is order. We want social order, we want political order, we want religious order. And we will do whatever is necessary to maintain our own sense of order in all these and other categories. When the towers fell, one of the first things we did, after a lot of people prayed, was to do something that would restore, or begin to restore, some sense of order. Some sense of order. And it may be a long haul, but the effort to restore order is always there. We cannot exist without a sense of order. We cannot live in the midst of anarchy and live fulfilled lives.

There are many ways to achieve that order, many ways, of course, and to some extent we narrow when we say, well, prayer can offer the hope. If we can't have the order, we can pray for order, true enough, true enough, but I think writing can be a form of prayer. Sometimes we narrow a definition of prayer. People helping each other—that's a form of prayer. And usually they're trying to do it to maintain order or to find some sense of order.

Even if the subject of the poem is chaos, the poem itself, on the page, is ordered. It's thought through, the words are carefully chosen, the writer wants the words to say—to suggest—what the writer honestly feels and thinks, so he's putting into a shape, into an order, something that, in terms of subject matter, may be highly disordered.

Young people now are writing poems about the tragedy. And that's exactly what I think they are doing—they are trying to find, on the page, some sense of order. Anybody who scorns that should scorn prayer, because our writing is a form of prayer, it seems to me.

There are a lot of other reasons, I suppose, for writing. Writing is a record. It's a record of not only what we did but what we thought while we were doing it. It's a record of attitudes, of values, and that's important to posterity, I believe. It's important for us to know what the Greeks were thinking 800 years BC because when we know that, when we discover that, we also learn that sometimes we're thinking the same things, and that makes a connection between us and the Greeks. The writing there spans 2,800 years. It humbles us and it unites us. We think, oh, those people had their miseries too. They were thinking along the same lines that we are thinking. We are, then, a community of sorts. Writing makes a record of that—not simply what happened, who, what, where, when, but the *why*. Attitudes, then, and feelings, become a part of that record.

MARGE: I know that you've helped a lot of people in this state to find and foster their creativity. How do you nurture your own? What do you do to feed your creativity?

BILL: One thing I do is read. I find myself going back to things I've read before, frequently. A poem of yours that I liked twenty years ago pleases me today. Why not go back to it? I do like to read new things. So, reading.

I don't read enough. And I don't read variously enough. I read one newspaper. Once in a while a student will bring in the editorial page from the *Wall Street Journal,* for instance, and say, "Here's an editorial I think you'll like." I'll read it and I'll think, Gee, I would have missed that if you hadn't brought that in. That reminds me how narrow my reading is in terms of newspapers.

The same thing is true of periodicals. There are so many periodicals and I read only a small percentage of those. And a small percentage of what's inside the small percentage. But it feeds.

I don't have any tricks in the sense of any place that I say, well, if I go there I'm going to write a poem. I don't have any places to go to do that. I like a variety of stuff. I'm kind of lazy. I mean, I even like to watch baseball. What a terrible thing to say, terrible in the sense that there are so many things about baseball that irk me. But I still like to watch almost anything that's competitive, and one reason, in addition to the competition, is the admiration one can have for what the human form can do, physically and mentally, when it's at its apex. Just the incredible things it can do. How somebody can swing a round bat and hit a round ball 480 feet. That's an amazing accomplishment. So I like that kind of thing. Things that might seem mundane that I get a kick out of. I get a kick out of grandkids. Very common things.

SHELLY: You are going to leave here in just a little bit to go to your class. Tell us about what you do in your classes. What's your structure?

BILL: Right now I am teaching one class. It's a poetry writing class and we do not begin with elements of poetry or with elements of prosody. I begin by having them write a poem, putting something down on the page, and very fundamental questions sometimes arise, like "How long should the poem be?"

And I say, "Well, make it as long as you like."

"How long should the lines be?"

"Make them as long as you like."

"What should the subject be?"

"Let it be what you like."

I get a sample of their interests from the word go. I want them to feel they can write about anything in any way they prefer. With that stuff in hand, we can talk then about matters of form, we can talk about matters of prosody, but always with their poem in front of us, so that we are not talking abstractly about some aspect of poetry.

I like to give some direction without that direction being dogmatic. For example, after the towers fell, my class met that afternoon, Tuesday, September 11, 2001, only several hours after the Pentagon and the twin towers were hit, and I didn't know what to expect. The campus was subdued, as many places were—either frantic or subdued or some kind of combination. They were all there. And I read them two poems from my memory of World War II: one, the poem that came from the bombing of Pearl Harbor, and the second one about the day that the bomb was dropped on Hiroshima, August the sixth, 1945, and three days later on the ninth on Nagasaki, a poem that I wrote coming out of that. I was delivering the paper, the *Wichita Beacon,* at that time and I was in the seventh grade.

We talked a little bit about that and a little bit about the towers and so on and then I asked them to write down some things, some reactions to the falling of the towers and the Pentagon, and I encouraged them to be specific. Where were you, specifically? Were you with anybody? Who was that person you were with, or persons? What were their names? What were you wearing? What were they wearing? What was the time of day? What was around you? What was the weather like? What was underfoot? What was overhead? What kind of day was it? What were the colors of the clouds? Were there any clouds? And so on.

I encouraged them to write specifics and I did that with great reservation. I had no idea what would come of that. Well, right now we are looking at those poems and they're quite impressive. I think they are doing what I mentioned to Marge a minute ago, they're trying to put down on paper, in an ordered way, something that is quite vexing, but again, we have something on the page to work from.

There are so many ways to approach the teaching of writing. I've heard teachers say, and I'm sure that they are sincere, and I'm sure that they teach their classes well, that they start with matters of prosody, they want the students to know the types of rhyme, they want them to know the types of meter, they want them to know this, that, and so on. *These,* they say, *are nomenclature.* Before you put the gun together, the weapon together, you should know the nomenclature. And that might work very, very well.

Usually those teachers say if students are going to be really good poets, they've got to know that. Okay, now that's where I take a little bit of umbrage. I'm not sure that all my students aspire to be really great poets. I think they want to write well, most of them, I think they are a little curious about what all this involves, but I don't think they're egomaniacs in terms of the writing of poetry, and besides they can learn those things later. I don't want those elements to get in the way of their early writing, so we start with the whole poem and we go from there.

We look at those poems throughout the semester. I may tell them what I want their next poem to focus on. In fact, the next assignment is a poem that focuses upon a person, zeroes in on a person, and we talk about that in some detail. If you deal with a person in your poem, you want to focus on the distinctive features of the person. You don't want to say, well, Aunt Lizzie had two eyes. A lot of Aunt Lizzies have two eyes. That doesn't distinguish, that doesn't describe Aunt Lizzie, it begins to define her as a member of a group. What I want to know is what's distinctive about the member of the group.

When you get down to that distinctive element, then, *then*, you're beginning to describe. So we talk about that in some detail, and that can be involved and *extremely* interesting because it might not be a physical thing at all.

The person might have a gesture that defines her. The lifting, for example, of the left hand to the mouth to indicate embarrassment, whether the embarrassment is the individual's fault or whether it's somebody else's fault. The automatic movement of a hand here, there, or yonder can tell us a lot about that person.

So I ask them to write the poem with a person in it. You may admire the person, you may despise the person, you may have feelings of both admiration and hate for the person. Whatever. That's a direction. Then you can write about that person however you like. You can use whatever form you like, and we'll see how it works. So it's a kind of loose direction. I don't want them to just go off in eight directions at the same time but, on the other hand, I don't want them to write from a formula.

We do a lot of looking at what we've written. I think that's what the students want to do. They want to look closely at what they've written and they want to get their peers' reactions and they need to learn which reactions are sensible and which aren't. Of course, the writer has to decide that, and sometimes that's a tough thing to decide, but over a period of time I think the students can take their peers' comments, together with the instructor's comments, assimilate them, and should be able to come up with some kind of revision that's better than the first draft.

SHELLY: In the workshop situation, the kind of thing you are talking about, do your students move along towards trust in each other? How do they handle criticism?

BILL: Very early they have to trust each other and know that they're not there to be picked on, that what they write about is far less important than how they write about it so nobody's going to say, "What a stupid poem that is, you're writing about a merry-go-round." Well, that's not stupid. The merry-go-round might have been written poorly about, but a merry-go-round can be a significant part of one's life. Someone in class the other day was on a merry-go-round, she said—this was right in the middle of a poem where a couple of lines come in to say that she was on a merry-go-round when she heard of the death of her friend. Somebody came running across the play yard, stopped the merry-go-round, and told them about the death of one of their classmates. That was in the middle of the poem and then she went on. It just jumps out at you. There's a merry-go-round. What a place to be to hear of the death of a classmate, so the merry-go-round becomes significant, it becomes a part of that experience,. That can be *far* more important than writing about sitting in church listening to a sermon.

SHELLY: I know you have gone out into many high schools in the last twenty years or so. There's a lot of emphasis right now on testing and also on getting the kids to write. So let's say you are talking to writing teachers who are going to go back into their classrooms, there's no administrator anywhere in sight, and you say, "If you really want to teach these kids to write…" What are you going to tell them?

BILL: If you really want to teach them to write, have them write. Have them write. And hope that you have few enough students so that you can give each of them some attention. The demands on public school teachers are almost out of sight. To learn how to write, you write. And then you have to have some responsible reaction to the writing. And that includes not only the teacher but the peers, and you can't do that in a mob. You have to have a group small enough so that you can spend a little time with the writing.

You can't test that, you can't judge that as you judge someone's knowledge of the Civil War. You just can't do that. The testing can become a murky and complex thing.

I would tell them they must write. The teacher says, "Well, I have them keep a journal every day."

"Do you look at the journals?"

"No, but I just have them keep a journal every day."

My guess is it's not a bad thing to have a journal. You keep journals and out of these journals you get some really good stuff, some poems and stories, and you have people in whom you have confidence read these and talk about them. We're dealing with language and in order to do that well, you have to have people who know how to handle and manipulate language. It's not a magic thing. It's not a thing that you wait around to be inspired about. Good writing is a result of writing and responsible reaction to the writing. It's really as simple as that.

SHELLY: Do you remember a teacher who somewhere along the way made a difference for you, steering you towards the writing life? When did you know you wanted to be a writer?

BILL: I first had an inkling that I liked writing when I was a senior in high school. I had a teacher who was a first-year teacher (teachers in my school tended not to stay very long—it wasn't a great high school). This young woman was very good. I was audacious and I went up to her the first day after class, and told her that I had not been enjoying English and wanted to know if I could spend some time in study hall instead of in her class. Now that's a terrible thing to say, and as I say it here, it embarrasses me, but I did that. She looked me in the eye and said, "Come back and we'll talk about it after football." That worried me because she had given me "the old eye." She said, "Come back and we'll talk about it." She should have hit me over the head with a branding iron.

Well, I was nervous; I dropped a couple of passes in practice. I went to see her after practice; she was staying late just to talk with me and she said, "Why do you feel that way?"

I said, "Well, I've had—my English classes have been extremely boring." This is terrible for a guy to say to a teacher that he hasn't given a chance. "And we haven't done anything, we haven't read anything, and I would just like to spend some time in study hall."

She said, "You spend your time in study hall. You go ahead, you go to study hall but on Friday, I want you to bring something in to me that you've written. You have to write something and bring it in to me." Boy, was I nonplused. I really was. Well, I did that. I went to study hall and I sat there and the first couple of days, I just looked around. And I didn't know whether I was on vacation or incarcerated. I really didn't.

Finally, about Wednesday or Thursday, I thought I better get something to take to her, so I started writing a story. I didn't know where to go, how to do anything, but I started writing a story, and I wrote about two pages.

On Friday we didn't have football practice; that was the day that we played the game, so I took it in to her on Friday. She would sit there about thirty minutes. Twenty-thirty minutes is all, and read.

She read that, and she said, " I kind of like the start of this story. I want you to keep writing on it." So I went back the next week, and did that for about four weeks, and I finished my story.

I thought it was incredibly long; I think it was twenty-two pages after it was typed up. She had been reading it all along and commenting on it, and I got interested in it. I actually started working on the story. I also found her really interesting. Finally, after we'd talked about that story, it was finished. The name of the story was "Like Father, Like Son." You can imagine how bad that story was, but for all its badness, she had a lot of things to say about it that I thought were interesting.

When she finished critiquing that story, I asked if I could just come back into class. She won. She knew what she was doing, exactly what she was doing. I went into class and I loved the class. Absolutely loved it. From time to time I wrote little things for her. Extra credit things for her.

My best buddy in class, Ray Asper, couldn't write anything. She had us write a couple of little papers. I wrote one for him and he signed his name to it and handed it in. Everything just went beautifully. Yes, so that was my first encounter until I got to college. Thirty years later, I had a call when my first book came out. I was at Wesleyan, sitting at Old Main. Room 119, Old Main. I had a call, and it was Wilma Stevens. Of course when she identified herself I said, "Oh, my God. Are you still teaching English?"

"Yes, as a matter of fact I am, but I'm not in Kansas."

I said, "Well, where are you?"

She said, "Grand Island High School. And I want to know if you'll come out and read to my class and talk with my class." So we arranged that, and I spent a day with Wilma's students and had a great day. As I was leaving, she said, "Oh, I've got something for you," and went back to the desk. And you know what she had for me. She had Ray Asper's paper. She said, "I've been meaning to give this back to you, and I knew you'd show up some time." That's the kind of teacher she was, the first really major influence on my writing.

William Kloefkorn

from Alvin Turner As Farmer

from Alvin Turner As Farmer

I am a dirt farmer
Who dreams of poetry.
Is that so strange? Is anything?
I have bent myself thankfully
Over the heat of cowchips.
When the lespedeza flowers
I breathe its blooms.
The calf I winch to birth
Grows legs like oaks to graze on,
And stuck hogs bleed for breakfasts.
This morning at milking
I kissed the cow's warm flank
And she kicked the milk to froth beneath my knees.
I forgave her,
Then cried with the cats.
Now the manure is in bloom,
Thistles defend the driveway,
And corncobs gird the mud beneath my boots.
Plotting harvests,
I roam my acreage like a sweet spy.

Easter Sunday

At the upright piano
Ernestine Trotter
sits in close and
heavy combat
with the choir: she
will play louder
than the choir
can sing, or
die trying.

*   *   *

The minister speaks
of that force
strong enough to overcome the
immovable object.
He leans into the
pulpit, tipping it
forward until
somebody ohs.
When the juice is
passed I help my-
self to a double
portion.

*   *   *

Mother says that
for every container
there is the right
lid out there
somewhere. Yet
Ernestine I am told
will never know a
man. I watch her
pound the upright
in the general
direction of
oblivion, with each
stroke watch its
keyboard rise
as if the savior
we are singing about
again.

* * *

When I shake the
minister's hand
I shake limp
skin, take the
long steps down-
ward three at a
time. In my father's
house are only four
small rooms. I can-
not wait to shed
these unnatural
clothes, cannot wait
to go outside to
breathe where the
visible sun is.

Last of the Mohicans

-for Robert Hepburn

Last of the Mohicans

Each morning to start things off
Miss Yoder read to us
from a book so thick
I could not stop watching it,
read to us a story of capture,
and of flight and then of capture,
each morning her voice
going suddenly silent
at a moment when something awful
or maybe something terribly sweet
was about to happen,

and that's the way I have come
to live the other parts of my life,
my eyes on a book whose thickness
almost imperceptibly lessens,
she had read the story *praise be!* and *alas!*
so many times before,

and when one morning she wasn't there,
and thereafter never was,
how I expected her substitute to carry on,
though she never did,
that unfinished book
gone forever with Miss Yoder, herself a mystery
unfinished,
though day by day I have come
to realize the romantic extremities
of capture and of flight and then of capture,
of taking up what someone else

began, however incidental or deliberate,
however thick the volume we must alone conclude,
however thin.

William Kloefkorn

Epiphany

It happens not so much on schedule
as at those moments when
something with something else
beautifully collides,

Nelson taking the ball from Mitchell
on a fast break, for example,
then stopping suddenly short
to break the school record from twenty feet,
the ball at the height of its high soft arc
like a full moon fully risen,

or the student in Composition
reading aloud the surprising words
of her essay,
weeping at the new loss
of something lost a long time ago,
the eyes of the boy on the back row
saying I must have been blind–
she's wonderful,

the ball descending then
to flounce the net
like a rayon skirt,

the young man on the back row
studying his hands
as if learning
for the first time ever
what they might be holding.

My Love for All Things Warm and Breathing

My Love for All Things Warm and Breathing

I have seldom loved more than one thing at a time,
yet this morning I feel myself expanding, each
part of me soft and glandular, and under my skin
is room enough now for the loving of many things,
and all of them at once, these students especially,
not only the girl in the yellow sweater, whose
name, Laura Buxton, is somehow the girl herself,
Laura for the coy green mellowing eyes, Buxton
for all the rest, but also the simple girl in blue
on the back row, her mouth sad beyond all reasonable
inducements, and the boy with the weight problem,
his teeth at work even now on his lower lip, and
the grand profusion of hair and nails and hands and
legs and tongues and thighs and fingertips and
wrists and throats, yes, of throats especially,
throats through which passes the breath that joins
the air that enters through these ancient windows,
that exits, that takes with it my own breath, inside
this room just now my love for all things warm and
breathing, that lifts it high to scatter it fine and
enormous into the trees and grass, into the heat
beneath the earth beneath the stone, into the
boundless lust of all things bound but gathering.

William Kloefkorn

Love Song at Midnight

If there is magic on this planet, it is contained in water.
—Loren Eiseley, *The Immense Journey*

Love Song at Midnight

At midnight
I awaken to the sound

of moving water,
voodoo water, water

with its hocus-pocus never
ending, water that compels

whatever else is chiefly water
to acknowledge change that water

never ending must unendingly
promote,

I awake now in the silent tent
aware of change, this body

chiefly water changing,
voodoo body, body

with its hocus-pocus never
ending, body that arising

moves outside
beneath a yellow moon

to listen more distinctly
to water

moving, water
in me and beneath me

on this shoreline
changing, water

that will take me until it
having done so

further takes me.

Don Welch

Don Welch

DON WELCH is a Nebraska native and the author of many collections of poetry, including *Deadhorse Table, Handwork, The Rarer Game, The Keeper of Miniature Deer, The Marginalist, In the Field's Hands, Fire's Tongue in the Candle's End, Every Mouth of Autumn Says Goodbye,* and *The Breeder of Archangels.* His most recent book is *Inklings: Poems Old and New* (Sandhills Press, 2001). In 1980 Welch won the Pablo Neruda Prize for Poetry, judged by William Stafford. He holds a BA from Kearney State, an MA from the University of Northern Colorado, and a PhD from the University of Nebraska — Lincoln. He served as a consultant and participant in the ETV documentary, "Last of the One-Room Schools," televised in September of 1995, and worked for ten years in the Poets-in-the-Schools program in Nebraska. He retired as Reynolds Professor of Poetry at the University of Nebraska — Kearney. Welch, a long-time racer of homing pigeons, lives in Kearney with his wife, Marcia.

The Welch family farmhouse sits in town. Its sunny white porch looks out on the streets of Kearney. Don and Marcia make us at home in the living room, complete with doughnuts and tea on the coffee table. They know us well. Shelly and I are only two of the many who have been made to feel at home in this room.

SHELLY: You lived in Columbus, Nebraska, when you were growing up. Tell us a story about yourself as a child.

DON: In Columbus all the professional people, the bankers and the lawyers, lived on the north side of town, like almost any railroad town, and the poorer people lived on the south side. It was among the poorer people that you found all the pigeon raisers, so I would get on my bike and ride over the tracks and spend all day Saturday with these old Czechs and Poles and Bohemian guys. That's where I learned to drink wine because one of them, Anton Warloski, only had homemade bread and homemade wine, that was lunch, and I would eat with him. I was about eight or nine years old. I would eat and drink with him and then I'd go home. My mother was a WCT-er. She'd say, "Don, what's that I smell?"

I would always say, "Mom, that's pigeons."

In the winter I would go down to Anton Warloski's and hook my fingers in the chicken wire and stand there and watch his pigeons for hours. He would come out and say, "You dumb kid, get home. I watched your knees shaking; you can't even control your knees, you're so cold, get on home!"

I'd say, "Well, just a minute," and I'd stay another hour and watch those pigeons. Everybody, I think, has got some quirky thing like that in his or her life that you get started with when you're a kid and just never give up. The two big *P's* in my life are *pigeons* and *poetry*.

This morning, over a half a century later, the garbage man pulls up in his big truck in the alley behind our house where I have my pigeons, and he says, "Hey, you raise pigeons?"

I say, "Yes, I do."

He says, "I've raised pigeons all my life. I got started when I was a kid. You get started when you were a kid?"

So here we were talking while Marcia was trying to get out of the garage. His truck was blocking the alley and the two of us probably could have gone on an hour talking about pigeons.

SHELLY: What was there about your family that

may have influenced your writing?

DON: My father gave me a rite of passage into the world of hunting and fishing and athletics and hands-on physical things. My mother's side of the family were musical, bookish people. I was an indoors and an outdoors kid and I remember liking both worlds.

When we're kids we have no idea what's influencing us. Later I got to know my mother's brother, who had loved chickens and pigeons when he was a kid and also loved to read, so I think I resemble him in a lot of ways. We always had a good time when we got together. There was a certain affinity that he had for me and I for him, probably because of similar temperament.

SHELLY: When did you start writing?

DON: The first poems were when I was 35, 36, something like that.

MARCIA: I have some earlier poems than that. (laughter)

DON: Yes, you do. They are very bad poems, but they're heartfelt.

SHELLY: In high school, did you have the notion that you would be interested in the literary field?

DON: No. There was nothing in high school and not much as an undergraduate in college, but I think the temperament was always there. In those summers when I spent time with my grandmother on the farm by Broken Bow, she and I were the only ones there, and I had the whole world of the farm to myself. To a great degree who I was and what I did at that time is in Dylan Thomas's "Fern Hill." I awoke to the same kind of morning and I *sang in my chains,* you know, *green and golden.*

It was a wonderful world to be in and I never had any difficulty filling up silence, which probably should have been one of the first clues that I had things going on in my head that would eventually find themselves on paper. When I was in high school, I was an athlete and I thought that all poets were sissies, because that came out of the macho athletic world, but unconsciously I didn't believe that. I never believed it, and it's that deep down stuff that usually is the truer stuff.

SHELLY: How did it happen that you started writing?

DON: The first poem I wrote that I was happy with was "Funeral at Ansley," and I can't say for sure what it was that made me sit down and write that poem. I wrote it about fifteen years after my grandmother died, and three years later, I asked my dad when we were hunting if we could go to the Ansley cemetery because I wanted to check out some things. He was a little mystified by this, but we went up there, and although it was later in the fall and the kingbirds and catbirds had already migrated, all the rest of the things that are in the poem gave evidence that they had been there.

I wanted to go back to the cemetery because I wanted to see whether I'd made up the imagery in the poem or whether the imagery was a part of the scene. It was, and that gave me an indication that everybody has a "hidden head." These things go down into our hidden heads and stay there for years and years. When we begin to write, they come up again.

When I was a Poet-in-Residence for the Nebraska Arts Council, many kids dramatically illustrated that their heads are full of stuff they are absolutely unaware of until they begin to write. That convinced me that not only does everybody have a hidden head, but probably everybody has one good poem in him or her. All you have to do is write enough and it will come out.

MARGE: I would like to ask both you and Marcia: how have you found your way to balance the writing and the family?

DON: Marcia can tell you that for many years when I was teaching and writing she took care of the kids and the house, and paid the bills, and did everything, which freed me up to do things I liked to do. Without her I couldn't have done them. I just really could not have done them.

MARCIA: I taught for a couple of years and then I was able to stay home and do what I loved to do best, which was keep the house and take care of the kids. So, for us, it worked out well.

DON: My writing world came over into her world when I would read her my poems. She has an absolutely indelible, alchemical sense that she puts on a poem, and she knows *Bam* just like that, whether that sucker's any good or not. I gave her a bunch of poems the other day and she whips through them and puts them into groups, good and no good. She's never wrong, so whatever that mechanism is, it operates a lot faster than my mechanism does.

SHELLY: Do you have favorite poets you read?

DON: Seamus Heaney has been a favorite of mine for a long time. When I first began to read Seamus Heaney, I discovered that he had what I call that intertwining of influences; he is an amazingly learned man but he also comes from a farm in Northern Ireland and much of what he writes is out of that physical farming world.

When we were in Ireland three years ago, we got within twenty miles of where Heaney grew up, close enough to see that Heaney's part of the world is like the world around Broken Bow.

Before I retired I had an opportunity—in fact, I demanded the opportunity—to teach a graduate class in World Literature. I chose four poets: Pablo Neruda, Derek Walcott, a French-Canadian woman whose name is Anne Hebert, and Seamus Heaney. After I had chosen, I thought I want Tomas Transtromer in there, too, so I added him. They are all strong poets. On the one hand, they're very physically rich in the imagery and the tones that they write. On the other hand, they're not afraid to push thought into good, truthful, and beautiful dimensions.

Those are things that American poetry has sorely lacked in the last forty years.

American poets kind of folded up. I was talking with Dana Gioia briefly about this when he was here, and he said that the institutional or university poem has become flat and lifeless. This is why he has never wanted to become a part of any university. I don't want to put words in his mouth, but the impression I got was that if he stayed out of it, he could have a more vigorous poetry. I think he's pretty close to the truth. The contemporary American poets that I like right now are people who have strong tones in their poems and aren't afraid to push their poems into strong emotions and deeper convictions.

MARGE: Would you talk about what makes a good teacher of writing? What would you like to see for the young writers in this state?

DON: Writers write because they have to. That's the only reason that anybody writes. You just don't feel good unless you're writing. When you first begin, you have the usual expectations: if you write, you're going to write something profound. Well, most of the time you don't. If you write, you are going to be famous. No, sorry, that's not true either.

You never say this to yourself, but this is the intent: if you write, it is a benign way to be an egotist. I mean, you won't find somebody blatantly saying, "I'm really good," but you will find poets saying, "Would you read this poem?" Then after you get all those things worked out of your system (because reality comes in and crushes them or filters them out), you say to yourself, I have to write because I have to.

For beginning writers, the best thing that teachers of writing can do is: (A) Be enthusiastic. If they want to write, that's great, that is really great. (B) Be a good reader; be a responsive reader. (C) Don't take beginning writers' work too seriously. I mean by that, don't tear up a beginning writer's work, feeling that if you do it today, the beginning writer is going to write something tomorrow which is shoot-the-moon stuff, and it will be the direct result of what he or she learned yesterday.

Writing is a long, long process. Writers don't know what their voice is for years, until they get enough written. Then when it starts to come, I get out of the way. I run like hell in the opposite direction because I don't want to do anything to prevent that voice from maturing and flowering.

In graduate work we talk about what may be irrelevant material in a poem or where certain passages have developed a rhythm. I ask, "Do you think this is the dominant rhythm of the poem?"

Both in the undergraduate and in graduate classes, I always try to read poems from the inside out. I talk with people who teach and who read poems from the outside in. They come to poems with some kind of predetermined, preconceived notion of what a poem should be. They think the poem would be better if this preconceived notion could be seen by the student. I never want to do that.

Students almost always write free verse, and the way to read a free verse poem is to read it from the inside out. If you can find out what's in-forming the poem, then you can see whether the poem is doing what the impulse of the poem says it should do.

To carry that over into life, that's the way people should live. Try to find out who the person is before you say I don't agree with you or I agree with you wholeheartedly. I've tried to tell students that there isn't any difference between reading a poem that way and reading people.

There are few people who want to talk about what informs a poem, what the impulse of the poem is. It's great to come across people who look at a poem and say: right here is a rhythm, and this rhythm is the very thing which gives the poem the infrastructure that it needs in order to give it a pulse, the impulse that fuses emotion and thought throughout the whole thing.

For a long time, because form has meant virtually nothing in American poetry, the only thing that we have been able to talk about is what a poem says, which is a contradiction to the whole idea of what a poem is.

I recently read some poems in a journal whose title I'm not going to mention. There was nothing poetic about the poems, other than the fact that they were shaped to look like poems, so they would have been far better as prose because prose is so much more invitational. Prose says to you, "Come in, relax, take your time, see what is happening in my house."

But a poem, because of its narrowness, requires you to squint, draw your attention down, be ready to focus right now. When you come to a poem that is really prose, but looks like a poem, those two things don't go together. You think you're going to date a poem, but you end up dating prose, and it's a real let-down.

SHELLY: Why is poetry important to the world? What is poetry's place in the world, especially at this time?

DON: Poetry is the closest thing that anybody can get to prayer. It works in the same way prayer does. To use an old figure, if you fall on your knees and pray, you go down to go up, and the same thing is true in reading a poem. You read down in order to go up. That's why when a poet keeps writing down, and then makes a discovery near the end of the poem, an emotional and intellectual epiphany or revelation, that is the moment in which the whole poem transcends itself.

I don't think you can get a better moment, a better experience than that. It can happen as you are walking and thinking, but because the poem is concentrated into the best words in the best places, the poem has a more valuable shape than anything that we can get when we're simply walking and thinking. It's that kind of concentrated, beautiful, good, and truthful experience that comes together in that particular moment that makes the poem valuable.

SHELLY: You've taught a number of years as a Poet-in-Residence. You've taught in grade schools and high schools throughout Nebraska. Why do children love poetry?

DON: Kids like poetry because it is part and parcel of being human. When I was doing residencies, I'd go from a second grade to a sixth grade to a ninth grade to a twelfth grade in one day and see how enthusiastic the little kids are for poetry, and then how that begins to fade out. Kids begin to hear other kids say things about poetry and most of them aren't true. Some of the best poems written for me in public schools were written by kids who said they didn't like poetry. They just knew they didn't like it, and then they hauled off and wrote great poems. Good sounds, good rhythms, truthfully good stuff are all parts of kids' lives, and they like to have them come out. And they come out in surprising ways.

The other day one of the guys at coffee asked me, "Isn't it hard to ask a kid in school to write a poem?"

I said, "I never ask kids in school just to write a poem."

He said, "Well, how do you get them started?"

I said, "I get them started in the same way we got water out of the pump on the farm. You have to prime them. You know, put a little down, and get a lot up."

He said, "What do you do, tell them how to write?"

I said, "No, what you have to do is give them a start."

He said, "Like what?"

I said, "Well, like a Japanese haiku: *The temple bells stopped, but the sound kept coming out of the flowers.*"

What I love to do is take that into second, third, and fourth grades because it's a simple little thing and short enough for them to listen to. I would write it on the board: *The temple bells stopped, but the sound kept coming out of the flowers.* I would ask them, "What's this mean?"

They knew what it meant, and we'd talk about it, then I'd say, "Okay, we're going to write a poem similar to this. Get out your paper and your pencils," and they'd get out their paper and pencils. I would go to the board and erase *temple bell.* The ___________ stopped, but __________." I'd leave the blanks there. Then I'd say, "Can you think of something in your life that stopped but it kept going on? It really didn't stop." I remember a little girl who wrote: "Their marriage stopped, but their love kept coming out of the blue." Wow. Third grader.

I always had some kind of primer to use with kids and that was usually enough to get them going, for instance a little warm up: *I am inside a ______, it is ______ in here. It is very _____ in here. I am being _____ in here.* I used that at Eddyville and a fourth grader whose name was Patrick said, "I am inside a poem, I'm inside the P, it is noisy in here, I am inside the O, it is quiet in here, I am inside the E, there's not a thing going on in here, I'm inside the M, I feel good in here."

Isn't that something? He's the kid who came up to me at the end of the week and said, "Don't tell anybody, Dr. Welch, but I like poetry."

SHELLY: What do you think is difficult for teachers in trying to teach writing?

DON: The thing that is difficult for elementary teachers is that they are being asked to do so much and they have so little time to do it. I just got off the school board where I tried for the last two years to get elementary teachers more planning time. Couldn't do it. Businessmen have this mentality that if you're not teaching, you're not working.

If teachers had more planning time they could get not only more writing out of their students, but they could get more writing looked at. I voted for block scheduling at the high school. They went to ninety-minute periods because it simplified the teachers' day and gave them four big classes and time within the classes as opposed to seven periods, 45 to 50 minutes long, in which they are flying from one thing to another. Even the teachers who didn't like block scheduling at the beginning now understand that it's better.

I would hope that every school system would let kids write creatively. One teacher said to me in a summer workshop, how do you grade it? I said, you don't. You don't grade it in a traditional way. You lean over and look at something a student has written, and when you find a good phrase or line you put your finger on it and you say, "Wow. Way to go." Then you move on.

SHELLY: Do you think teachers are doing more of that? You think that process is happening?

DON: I would think that less of it's going on and probably even less will go on. We've become so test-oriented that public school teachers, for their own sakes, are going to have to do more drill, more memorization—which is not all bad, it's just that, like most revolutions, this one will go to an extreme. It will go to the extreme where teachers spend every moment in the classroom preparing kids for tests that the state says you must pass and pass well, because we're going to put the results in the paper and we're going to show you, Kearney, how you match up against Grand Island. I don't know of any teacher who wouldn't say, hey, I don't want to be left hanging out there.

MARGE: You've walked a great deal around Kearney and written poems. Many of us are looking forward to reading the Alley Poems. How did you get started on them?

DON: The real start is that I used to be a runner, then I had a heart attack, and I couldn't run anymore, so I turned into a walker. Walking, after running, was— gee— it wasn't even like kissing your cousin. Then I discovered that I could take a notebook with me and write. If you get something going in your head, you can get three or four lines, and you're saying to yourself, I can't risk not remembering this. If you don't have a piece of paper or tape recorder, you'll forget what you've done. I put a little notebook in my pocket, I started walking, and a lot of things came together.

As I told Marcia, I walked the southeast part of Kearney, because it took me all the way back to my pigeon world in Columbus when I was a kid. In some ways it has changed the least over the years. People don't have the money down there to buy the things that they do in this part of town. I feel at home when I walk alleys in the poorer sections of town, despite the fact that all kinds of dogs don't like me. Oh man, they've got more dogs down there, and some of those suckers are so big I cross my fingers and hope the chains aren't rusted. I have a poem about walking around the edge of a garage right into the faces of three rottweilers in the back of a pickup. I think that poem's going to be a pretty good one.

Another thing that came together was that the notebook was small so I couldn't write a long poem, and I really can't write long poems anymore. I'm at that point in my life where the poems have to be short and pithy and have to have some kind of emotional impact, and if they can have all three of those things, they can be an alley poem. A lot of rhyme came back into those poems. Almost all of those poems end with rhyme.

MARGE: After September 11, maybe all of us have to deal with more fear. What do you see as a way for poetry to help us?

DON: Poetry has something to do with tragedies like this or any other tragedy, but not in a direct immediate sense. I would prefer that what kids do with their poetry is to write in a sensitive way. If you keep them writing in a sensitive way throughout their public school lives, you couldn't ask for better kids, sensitive not only to what they feel but what other kids feel. This, consequently, might make them more human.

If you can take them all the way from kindergarten through grade 12, and have some kind of sequential movement from one world of poetry to another world of poetry, the kids are going to be more sensitive. Now, of course, people in the education department would say, "Could we have a test for that?" The test is to talk to the students and read what they've written when they're seniors and see whether it's all added up.

SHELLY: You've touched many lives. I speak from experience because you have encouraged me early on and through the years. In 2001 you were honored at the literature festival along with Bill Kloefkorn. How did you feel when you were told that you were getting this recognition, as well as the statue at UN-K?

DON: When that came down the pike, and I got that "bronze me" that's standing over there on the campus, I was absolutely shocked and grateful and humbled. I didn't know what to say. I walked around for days like Gary Cooper. He used to say *Yep* and *Nope,* and that's about the only thing I could get out, monosyllables, like *thanks*.

I was very pleased and very humbled, especially to be honored at the lit fest with Bill, who's been a life-long friend. Our lives have not only been parallel, but they've intersected at good moments and that has been great, too. Bill comes out of the same small town midwestern life that I came out of.

SHELLY: Marcia, what do you think of the accolades and honors and the influence Don has had on students through the years?

MARCIA: Over the years students have called, they've emailed, they've stopped in on vacations. When he was still teaching, they'd drop in at the office. About twenty-five years ago, in a class that was very inattentive, Don was paying a nickel to anybody who would answer a question. Everybody just sat there. Finally this one kid answered a question and Don flipped him a nickel. Several weeks ago, that student came back for Homecoming and gave Don a card with the nickel and also a roll of nickels. He said this was the interest it had accumulated.

DON: Teaching kids and reading a book are the same thing, because when you read a book, what you do is co-create meaning. You bring to it whatever you think, your attitude, temperament, education. You create something out of it. Teaching students is the same way. You read kids in the same way you read books, and you co-create something in a class which is one part them, one part you, and the third part is education.

I feel privileged to have been able to do that kind of thing. Teaching is a lot like writing a poem: you don't know where you're going, you don't want to know where you are going until you get to the end, and you hope you make some significant statement which is going to be pleasing not only to you, but someone else.

I could have gone into the automobile business with my dad and made a hell of a lot of money. When I said, "I'm going to graduate school," he looked at me like Wow, why would you do that? But maybe he had an inkling, I don't know. He got out of coaching and teaching when he was making $2,400 a year. He could not raise a family on that and went into the automobile business. He made money but he always regretted not being a coach and teacher. I stumbled into something that I liked for the rest of my teaching life.

MARCIA: I think you have to be willing to make sacrifices.

DON: I don't know whether I would have survived as a public school teacher. I was fortunate that I was able to get a job at UN-K when I was 27 years old. We taught a far heavier load than teachers do now, but still it gave me time between classes to prepare and grade papers, and, ultimately, that's why I think I became a poet rather than a prose writer. I'd get a poem started in between classes, then run off and teach and come back and take a look at it and revise it, but a sustained narrative, I had no time to do anything like that.

I've tried to keep in touch with teachers, former students that I've had. I can't tell you how much I admire those people. They are my heroes. Public school teaching takes place in an incredibly high energy atmosphere. If you don't have a great love for teaching and a power pack, as both of you know, you're going to burn out, *boom*, just like that. I regret that there are so many people in public life who have no idea what public school teaching is like.

MARCIA: All the years when Don was teaching eighteen semester hours, he would bring 170 term papers home over Christmas vacation to check. Every vacation other than Christmas, he was out among the schools. After twenty some years I said, "You either quit doing this vacation thing or I am going to leave you and all the kids and the cats and the pigeons and the whole kaboodle."

SHELLY: And she'll take those love letters with her. (laughter)

MARCIA: The college and the high schools didn't have the same vacation, so when the kids were on vacation, he wasn't. When he didn't have to teach quite so many hours, things worked out much better.

SHELLY: When we think of Don Welch, we think of a great poet and a great teacher, but we also think of a great love story. It's not like you two are holding hands all the time, but there's this teamwork thing. One of the great moments on the bronze dedication video for me was when Don asked you to come up to the podium.

MARCIA: Me, too.

SHELLY: It's magical. It's amazing. How many years have you been married?

DON: Let's see. We were married in '53 so we are two short of fifty. Forty-eight.

SHELLY: How is it that we can watch a video or sit in your living room and know there's this great love story?

DON: Well, I don't know. We've occasionally talked about that. We're at the point in our lives where we don't have to say anything out loud. We know what the other's thinking. We both feel that we've been extremely fortunate. It's just one of those things where I cut through an auditorium of an administration building one time, and I heard somebody playing a drum. Marcia had come off a full summer of being a lifeguard at the Gothenburg pool. I looked at her and I said *Wow*.

MARCIA: I was much thinner and much tanner then. (laughter)

DON: She was about the color of that bronze statue out there and absolutely blonde. So, anyway, we feel very fortunate that we've had forty-eight years.

MARCIA: I think the turning point was about 1960. Don had a chance to become a vice president at a college in Minnesota. He had gone there for an interview, and I was excited because his salary would be three times as much. I was packing, almost. He called and said, "I can't do it. I just can't do it."

I said, "What?"

He said, "I can't be an administrator. I have to stay in the classroom." So I unpacked everything. That was a good move for us. Not moving was a good move. Kearney was a wonderful place to raise a family, small enough that the kids had a lot of freedom.

SHELLY: And they all know how lucky they are?

MARCIA: I think so.

DON: One of the regrets I have is seeing so many small schools in Nebraska forced to close because of the economics. Those of us who write poetry know: small is beautiful. In every small school that I have visited, I could give to students the time that I wanted to give. There was the chance for greater education to happen.

I would like to see small schools stay open but they're going down the tubes.

Burr Oak School on the South Loup, they tell me, is closed. Huntley, Ragan, Edison, Bloomington, Naponee, Riverton, all those schools are just buildings. The kids are being bussed 20, 30, 40 miles to a big school.

MARCIA: These schools all closed a year after Don was there, but I don't suppose that had anything to do with it. (laughter)

DON: But at least kids have had the opportunity to begin there. If they began in the small places, that's never going to get out of their systems, and it's going to be there if they want to go back and draw upon it as some kind of resource.

MARCIA: Tell them about the lunchroom that had the flying saucers.

DON: That was the school with Patrick, the student who wrote the poem, "I am inside the P." At lunchtime, I was eating my first flying saucer; a flying saucer was a piece of minced ham bologna and then a blob of potatoes on top of that and a dollop of cheese. The cooks were supposed to heat it, and this bologna was supposed to curl up like a flying saucer. Well, mine was just limp and oily. So when Patrick came over to me and said, "Don't tell anybody, but I like poetry," I saw my chance. I said, "Patrick, I won't tell anybody if you'll do one thing for me."

He said, "What's that?"

I said, "Eat my flying saucer."

Don Welch

Funeral at Ansley

I write of a cemetery,
of the perpetual care of buffalo grass,
of kingbirds and catbirds
and cottonwoods;

of wild roses around headstones,
with their high thin stems
and their tight tines
and their blooms pursed
in the morning.

I write of old faces,
of cotton hose and flowered dresses
and mouths which have grown up
on the weather.

And I write of one woman
who lies a last time in the long sun
of August, uncramped by the wind
which autumns each one of us

under catbirds and kingbirds
and cottonwoods, and the gray-green
leaves of the buffalo grass.

June

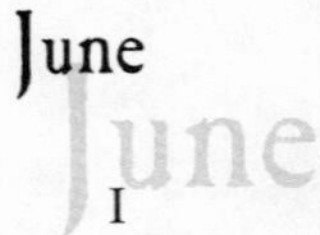

I

All day in the field's hands.
The easy is what we dream of,
the hard is what defines us.

II

Evening.
Beside a lamp
being courted by mayflies,

I take off
my wedding ring
and set it on the table.

In the dusk
the worn gold fills
with light well above the level.

III

In the dark
light is the only authentic,
love is touch at its zenith,

and a long marriage
is a conviction
which does its time well.

IV

By luck, by love, by work.

In the turning of the seasons
there is the music of these bells.

Don Welch

Poet in Residence at a Country School

The school greets me like a series
of sentence fragments sent out to recess.
Before I hit the front door
I'm into a game of baseball soccer.
My first kick's a foul; my second sails
over the heads of the outfielders;
rounding the third base, I suck in my stomach
and dodge the throw of a small blue-eyed boy.
I enter the school, sucking apples of wind.
In the fifth-grade section of the room
I stand in the center of an old rug and ask,
Where would you go where no one could find you,
a secret place where you'd be invisible
to everyone except yourselves;
what would you do there; what would you say?
I ask them to imagine they're there,
and writing a poem. As I walk around the room,
I look at the wrists of the kids,
green and alive, careful with silence.
They are writing themselves into fallen elms,
corners of barns, washouts, and alkali flats.
I watch until a tiny boy approaches,
who says he can't think of a place,
who wonders today, at least, if
he just couldn't sit on my lap.
Tomorrow, he says, he'll write.

And so the two of us sit under a clock,
beside a gaudy picture of a butterfly,
and a sweet poem of Christina Rosetti's.
And in all that silence, neither of us
can imagine where he'd rather be.

Letter to Aanya, Two Months Old

Throughout the world,
wishes shrivel on cold stones

or dry and crack
like disembodied blood.

Fanatics, especially those
with sectarian tones,

will never love you
the way that universal well,

the source of love,
can love you. Know then,

Aanya, there are those
who bring this love

like water up, who drink
and are made whole.

This is a love
which asks you to walk

naked through the world
with nakedness your shield;

and long before
you understand the heart

of its great mystery
it will crucify you.

If those who know nothing
of its inner strength

believe you weak,
show them how love bends

iron to its gracious will,
or throws itself at storms

which might unbone it.
In the fury of this world

there is no stronger verb
than love. It is the root

which lives through drought.
Aanya, my small noun,
may it find you out.

Don Welch

About Your Classrooms

for Laura Rotunno

About Your Classrooms

The unimaginative believe there are no rooms
which remember those who absent them,

that absence vacuums everything
in its sleep.

No so. For years what moves
in a classroom are its vital ghosts.

Oh, it's true, those who hated these rooms
or suffered them impassively are gone.

But not you. The good memory of yourself
is what you've earned to.

For you these classrooms have been
like the ivory of a narwhale's tusk,

and you our scrimshaw artist
intricate at work.

You have honored us
by taking such remarkable care.

Few shape absence into memorable air.

Note to a Young Writer

—while looking over her shoulder

Note to a Young Writer
—while looking over her shoulder

If you're one of the ones
for whom the best sounds
are like conch shells
held to your ear,
swirl out of yourself
the hard whorl of words.

And think of it this way,
your journey over,
your poem's just begun,
listen to what laps out of silence
and comes ashore at the edge
of the word.

Brent Spencer

Brent Spencer

BRENT SPENCER, novelist and short-story writer, is the author of *The Lost Son* (Arcade Publishing) and teaches creative writing at Creighton University in Omaha, where he is co-director of the graduate program in English. Among his awards are the Wallace Stegner Fellowship from Stanford, where he was a Jones Lecturer in Creative Writing, and the James Michener Award at the Iowa Writers' Workshop, where he earned an MFA. He has been awarded fellowships from Yaddo, The MacDowell Colony, and The Millay Colony. His fiction and poetry have appeared in *The Atlantic Monthly, The American Literary Review, Epoch, The Missouri Review, GQ,* and elsewhere. His most recent book, a collection of stories chosen as one of the best books of 1996 by *The Village Voice,* is *Are We Not Men?* (Arcade Publishing, 1996).

MARGE: Let's start with your growing up years. What kind of a kid were you?

It's noisy and crowded in The Mill at this hour, so we take a table way in the back. We keep Brent Spencer supplied with coffee. We place his chair facing the wall for the sake of our tape recording, trying to keep other sounds to a minimum.

BRENT: I guess I was a bookish kid. My mother had to persuade me to stop reading and go outside and play. She thought you lose your eyesight if you read too much. The only reading material in the house was *Reader's Digest* and *TV Guide.* That was it. Very working class. Actually, working class when we had work. We were really a very poor family. A single parent home. My father had had some college, and after my parents divorced my mother thought anything to do with education was too much like him. There was so much bad blood between them that she didn't want anything like that around. So you had to sort of read *Moby Dick* like it was pornography, under the sheets at night.

She'd say "Are you reading under there?"

"No, no, no."

Then years later, when I was about thirteen, I found—God knows why I was in there—but in her closet I found a stack of Civil War books, a good fifty or so. At the time I thought it was just very odd. Then a few years ago I mentioned to her some Civil War book that had just come out. She started talking about the Civil War clearly as someone who had read about it for many, many years and knew a great deal. I realized then that she was this closet reader, too.

My step-father is a person who is very proud that the only book report he ever handed in was of *The Virginian.* He handed it in a dozen times and even then he never read the book. So it was not a bookish household and if it was, you had to get away with it in secret.

MARGE: A stack of fifty is quite a stack.

BRENT: Yes, there were books I'd later learn about and recognize. It's interesting to me; my mother reads a lot but you never see a book out anywhere. *TV Guide,* that's it.

SHELLY: How about school? Is there a teacher you remember?

BRENT: I had a lot of good teachers. I had a good English teacher in high school. I wrote poetry on the side, though I wouldn't tell anyone that. I belonged to several community theater groups so I was up until midnight every day rehearsing a play or doing the lights. My first period teacher would let me doze in the back of the room based on the fact that I was learning about Shakespeare from the plays. I was very grateful to her. She would talk to me later about the literature. I felt I learned a lot even if I wasn't quite awake in class.

The next important teacher to me was Phil Rizzo, who was an unpublished but brilliant writer and teacher of writing. He was a loud, brash, Italian-American from Philadelphia who had a cackle and a bitterness about the world that was just what I wanted as a sophomore in college. I got to like him. He would invite me to his house and we would talk. He'd unload about the latest crime against humanity by the city council.

I did learn about writing from him, little things and big things, learned to appreciate the *Iliad*. He had such enthusiasm that you could not not like something when he started talking about it. I ended up typing his manuscripts. He would dictate his novel on tape and then I would type it, sentences taking shape under my hands, like I was writing a novel with training wheels. He never did get published. The last I heard, he's written a dozen novels, all of them fascinating in one way or another. He was a big influence. He made it okay to talk about writing and to do it in a more public way.

SHELLY: Is this when you started thinking of yourself as a writer?

BRENT: I don't think I've ever thought that. Every day I think I don't know how to do this, but I'm here at the desk so I might as well try it again. In the theater days I never thought of myself as an actor. I just thought I'm having fun doing this. Same thing with writing.

The more I wrote, the more painful it was, and the fun was harder and harder to find. No, it was easy to find, but you become aware of how far you are from how good you want it to be, and that gets painful sometimes.

There were other teachers. There was a chemistry teacher who seemed very creative, whose words I think of sometimes when I write, even though he had no interest in writing. There were other college English teachers, a very close-knit smart group in a small college, pushing us to the limit. For two years I stopped writing because I realized how little I knew and that I should learn about literature before I pretended I could do it myself. That was a good lesson to learn, stop for a while, and soak up as much as I could.

MARGE: You memorized plays, and you were *in* the stories on stage, moving about.

BRENT: That taught me a lot. Being in, for instance, *The Taming of the Shrew,* knowing one part completely, and by the time you finished rehearsing knowing every part—that was an education for a writer. You knew a whole play word for word, and to have all of a Shakespearean play or a Shaw play in your head at once was great. I still remember huge chunks or bits and pieces of those plays. It's like seeing an old friend when it comes to mind.

At the time I didn't think of much connection between the poems I was writing and the plays I was in. I thought they were two different things I did. I didn't realize that poems and stories were actually written by human beings. For all I knew, the plays sprang like trees from the ground.

MARGE: I understand you do your writing in a writing shack.

BRENT: It's about 10 feet by 10 feet, white siding, probably sixty years old, with a little peaked roof. It used to be a gardening shed but I replaced the windows and put bookshelves in. I have a desk and a sofa, a couple of end tables, a filing cabinet. I told myself that I can only do writing in there; I can't do school work.

It's on the site of the original house for the farm, one of the first farms in Nebraska. When I step outside my writing shack, I can see what's left of the foundation from the original stretching out from the door. The owner of the farm was a man named Teddy Blue, who drove cattle up from Texas to the railhead. The farm is right next to the tracks so he had a great spot there. Teddy once rode his horse into Lincoln and shot out all the brand new streetlights for fun. He was 86'd from Lincoln for life because of that. Among his drovers was Sam Bass, the outlaw, who at the time was just a cowhand working with the herds.

But what's great is, in his old age, Teddy Blue sat down with a historian from the University of Oklahoma and dictated his life story. She published it word for word as he spoke it. I was able to find a copy; it's called *They Pointed Them North*, all about raising cattle. I feel the history of this place when I walk around.

SHELLY: We hear people talk about the "writing life." What's your definition of the writing life?

BRENT: I used to think it was a life where you pretty much wrote all the time, but I think more and more that you're not really writing well unless you're living well, and that means being connected to people and land and activities outside the writing. These things feed the writing. Sometimes I wish for more privacy or some long chunk of time for myself to write, but in the end it's not good for me. I have to be out in the world. It's like going back to a well. The writing life is a matter of being able to write every day and talk with people about writing.

I spent a lot of years working at basic factory jobs where nobody cared about writing or books, where I didn't know anybody who had read a book, let alone tried to write one, so it was hard to figure out how to keep going. I ended up at universities so I could be around people who liked books and talked about them.

The ideal writing life is where you don't have to apologize for writing. A lot of people have to apologize, like I did as a kid. They have to hide it, do it in the dark in order not to seem strange. That's not everyone's experience, but I came from a working-class family where everything you did was supposed to lead in a straight line to a weekly paycheck. You could not say, "Well, I want to be a writer." Maybe that's another reason I never thought of myself as a writer. If I ever said that as a kid, I would be laughed at absolutely with the deepest scorn. It would be like saying "I want to be a prince or king of my own country." (laughter)

MARGE: Could there be any advantage to growing up in that kind of family?

BRENT: In a way, yes, because writers mostly are outsiders. I think if you were too much of an insider, you'd be too content in your life. Writers, to some degree, are discontented people who are trying to make sense of things, and when you're an insider, everything makes sense.

MARGE: How do you manage to balance your time and energy?

BRENT: I always think of Paul Newman in *Cool Hand Luke*. When the prisoners in that place were working, they always had to announce to the boss what they were doing, so they'd say, "Going for a pick now, Boss. Shoveling the dirt now, Boss." I have to be accountable to my writing boss. So if I'm not writing I have to say "Getting dressed now, Boss. Heading out to the writing shack now, Boss." (laughter)

It's very easy for me to get distracted as far as work goes, especially at the farm, where there's a whole lot of stuff to do. I have to have very strong boundaries. Every morning from 7:00 to 11:00, I have to write or at least sit there. That's why I made the shack so I can't do anything else but write. You can't connect to the internet from there so I have to focus on the work. Otherwise the boss gets mad.

SHELLY: Is this a different schedule than you've had before?

BRENT: In some setting or another, I've always had those hours and I've tried to write every day, though I've broken that rule. If I mess up for a couple days running, I get very anxious with the rest of my day. I get nervous and feel like I've done something wrong. And I have. You lose your chops, the way jazz musicians will say, "Unless I'm playing every day I'm not as good as I can be."

Especially with novels, if you're away for a while, you have to reconstruct that whole thing in your head all over again. It's very difficult to hold all of that in your head at one time. Whether it's working at the kitchen table, or in a bedroom, or in a coffee place, or at school, I've had to say, "Well, I don't do anything else between 7:00 and 11:00 today." And if I can work later, then that's great, too.

Recently I was at Yaddo, the artists' colony, where there was nothing to do but write. It was strange to get up at 7:00 AM and go in and write until 11:00 PM and feel exhausted but know there's nothing else to do there. I could go for a walk but that'd be over in an hour. I found myself sleeping for an hour and then I'd get up and write for two more hours. Then I'd sleep for twenty minutes and I'd write for another hour or two, around the clock. It was a weird schedule, but it seemed to work well. It made me realize that this must be what it's like to be Stephen King or someone who can do this on their schedule instead of squeezing it into the empty corners of the day.

MARGE: Are there things you do to keep yourself energized while writing in your writing shack?

BRENT: I listen to music sometimes. It has to be instrumental music. If I hear words, it gets into my head too much. Lately I've listened to a lot of jazz, some classical. I have some books out there, but I'm worried about that. I'm worried about just reading for four hours. I dip into a book now and then; I'll read a couple of pages. Sometimes I'll write a letter as a way of warming up.

I try to do the Hemingway trick of finishing the day in the middle of something where I know pretty well what's going to happen next, so I can go back to it.

SHELLY: Why is writing so important?

BRENT: I'm the kind of person who has to stare and think a long time to understand some things. When I write, I seem to understand things better. Even if it's completely different from reality, at least I feel like I'm getting a chance to sort of meditate. It's a form of meditation.

SHELLY: Do you think your characters come out of your life?

BRENT: Bits and pieces. Not a full-scale character, but some incident or physical feature, a line of dialogue or something. Nothing fully formed. The characters don't walk out of life and into the fiction, I hope. That would be too weird to fully bring somebody straight in from life. I know people who do that, and I admire their work. I just don't know that I can do that.

I don't have any interest in disguising my life and calling it fiction. Even if there are elements of my life in the fiction, they're only minor elements. I'm just trying to look for material and I think, "Oh, there's that thing that happened to me; I'll put that in there."

I think in some ways I was saved by the right words in my life. I'm not sure I can point to which words they were, whether they were spoken to me or I read them, but in some sense early on I got the impression that words saved me, and I keep thinking I can find words that will save other people if I work hard enough and don't settle for the words that first come to mind.

I never look at a full story and say, "Oh, what a wonderful story." I look and I say that little part there, there's something that makes sense to me in some important way, and I'm glad I was able to get to that. If it has taken the whole story to get to that point, then that's fine. It's this desire to find the right words that will save a life, and it may be my life again. I've been working for the Jesuits too long maybe, but there is that sort of salvific feature to writing that is important.

I don't think of it as comforting, necessarily. Not necessarily that 'come unto me' kind of feeling. Sometimes the hard truth is a way of saving a life, too. I keep thinking if you work hard enough you can get little glimmerings of that, and that could be enough to make your life happy.

SHELLY: How do you work the humor into your writing?

BRENT: It's not working it in, it's trying to keep it out. I have such a tendency toward the bad joke, the cheap joke, that a lot of my effort as a writer is saying, "Oh, got to cut that joke out" or "That's not funny, I thought it was, but it's not." So when a story comes out with any humor at all, it's really one-tenth of what was in there originally.

I see the humor in the depressing thing or the tragedy and I can't always disentangle those two. Pretty much that's the way life is, where there are these funny ironies. Even when there's a terrible thing that's happened, there's some sort of weirdly comic feature to it.

Neither of the extremes is the only truth by itself. It has to be put together in some way. I guess I think if there is a God, he has a great sense of humor and maybe a cruel sense of humor. I sort of want to echo that sometimes.

In *Prince of Tides* somewhere Pat Conroy says he's interested in the "dark wit of the luckless." If somebody said that about me, I'd be very pleased. I am interested in characters who are luckless, characters who are not just outsiders but losers in some way, yet are redeemed in terms that don't make them winners but mitigate the losing, making it less terrible.

SHELLY: How do you know when a story is good?

BRENT: I still don't know. I never know. I work on something a long time until I can't work on it any longer and send it away thinking nothing will come of it. And if it gets published, I'm just stunned. I'm always stunned. I'll think they've made a terrible mistake but it's all right with me. (laughter)

So I'm very good with editors. Editors like me a lot because they say "Well, we have these suggestions for change" and I'm completely open. I don't understand the writers that say "No, no, this is my vision and it's perfect the way it is." It strikes me that that's nuts; there are many people better informed about the writer's work than the writer.

In one case, I sent a story to my agent who sent it out, and a few weeks later it was accepted at *GQ*. First I didn't know they printed fiction and then I thought they'd made a mistake and then I thought, "Am I going to be around all these sweater ads?" (laughter) They had a wonderful editor there who had some great suggestions, and I thought, "She's so right." My book was in production at the time and I asked if they could stop so that I could replace the draft of the story they had with the one she had suggested changes in.

SHELLY: I thought "The Last of the Nice" was a terrific story, and the audience at the lit fest loved it. Did you have a reason you chose that story for the reading?

BRENT: I thought the audience would like it. There are some funny things in it and it has local geographical references that I thought would be interesting. There were serious elements to it, too, so I hoped it wouldn't be just funny or just serious. I had read it once or twice before at places and people had seemed to like it so I thought, "Maybe I can fool these people, too."

MARGE: What makes good teaching? What do you think of when you think of good teaching?

BRENT: I think of energy. I think of enthusiasm. My favorite teachers, whether they were writing teachers or chemistry teachers, were those people who had this sort of passion for what they did. They never gave you room to think "I don't like this." They were just too excited.

I was watching Animal Planet last night, watching these young guys who pick up the snakes. Before I always thought, "This is disgusting and dangerous." But the other thing I hadn't realized is how knocked out they are by what they do. "You've got to see this beautiful, beautiful creature." It's some man-eating thing; they're so excited, and I wish I could capture that note in the classroom. That's the goal, always to do that, but sometimes I'm focused too much on the people in the room who don't want to be there, so then it's hard to be excited.

I think of Theodore Roethke, whose work I studied in graduate school. *Energy* was the word he used to characterize good teaching. The stories of his teaching are all characterized by high energy enthusiasm for the work. He said that's the only thing you can teach: energy.

You can't teach someone how to write well, but you can convey this spirit toward them and if they get it, they'll write better. On my best days after class, I come away thinking I hit this mark. On the worst days, I am nervous and unfocused and tired, and that conveys. Like cats and dogs, your students reflect your feelings intuitively. If I go in there depressed, they are going to end up depressed.

I go in sometimes with a story I've read and liked a lot, and I'll say "Look at this wonderful story, and here's why it's so wonderful." I can tell that some people in the room want to go sit down and read that writer's work. They've been infected. I keep trying to teach concepts, strategies, tricks, and I continue to do that, but the real thing is energy.

I also like to teach creative self-doubt. Sometimes a student comes to me in my office, saying, "I've got this story I'm working on but it's crap. I don't know what to do with it." Then when I read it, the story turns out to be good in some really interesting way. It may not be polished, but it's got something that no other story has.

But when a student comes in saying, "I know I've written probably the best story you've ever read," it is always utter crap. You have to find a way to get them to improve the story and they're not going to. They say, "It's done, it's perfect, it's just the way it needs to be." I don't know what to do with that exactly except to keep working, keep tapping away at some soft spot until they come around.

But I love those nervous ones who come in and think I'm just trying to make them feel good. One said, "This isn't even a story; these are just different paragraphs about the bad boyfriends I've had in my life and there's no plot."

I started reading these devastating portraits, one after another, and I told her, "This is a story just as it is." She pretty much left it that way, except for a couple of thematic references that she threaded through to hold the whole thing together. It won an award in the English department. If you have a certain level of dissatisfaction or self-doubt, and energy, you can produce something good, but if you have too much satisfaction and too much confidence, you're not going to see what needs improving.

So energy and self-doubt. I love the Sufi parable that Robert Bly tells. There was this classroom of little kids being taught to count. They each cover a piece of paper with the number 1. The teacher tells them to fill another page with the number 2. They all go on except one little boy who continues writing 1. He's got ten pages of the number 1. The teacher says, "You're behind, you can't do this, you've got to catch up, we're all the way to 10."

He finishes another page of 1's, and he says, "I think I've got it now." He goes up to the blackboard and he draws a 1. The wall cracks in half along the spine of that 1, and two halves of the wall fall away. (laughter)

That kind of doggedness and attention and staying with it is important. I keep going back to Flannery O'Conner and the notion that a writer has "a certain grain of stupidity," and that's what I want to cultivate, the sense of "not getting it." I have to stare harder than other people to understand things that seem to make sense very quickly to a lot of people. I think if I do that I can maybe see deeper into that thing than they can. That's what I mean by self-doubt: I think I get it but I'm not sure. I'll stay here a while longer and think about it some more. I think this passage does justice to what I'm trying to write about, but what if I try a few other ways?

I once put a story into the mail. As soon as it fell into the box, I knew exactly which three and a half pages should have been cut. I had worked for nine months on that story, through fourteen or fifteen drafts, so you'd think I'd have gotten it by then, but no. If writing were easy, it'd be less interesting.

SHELLY: Have you always taught on the university level?

BRENT: I do a high school thing here or there but not as a regular job. I taught at a couple of prisons. Everything from community colleges to Stanford, from creative writing courses to business writing, technical writing, all kinds of things, but mostly universities. Since I was about 24 or 25, in some form or other.

SHELLY: What is the essence of Nebraska for someone who hasn't lived here all his life?

BRENT: I can think of landscape answers. The Sandhills are unlike anything else in the world. That I find fascinating. I've lived in California, Texas, and all around, but I'm very fond of Nebraska's landscape and I bristle like a native Nebraskan if people outside the state say "Oh, yeah, that flat place." I say "No it isn't."

There's also that double nature of Nebraskans. There's an absolute friendliness that you don't see elsewhere and maybe also a hidden criticism that goes with that. There's an openness as well as a secret judgmental side, which is probably true everywhere, but it seems like the friendliness is so out there that it surprises me when I find the hidden reserve and judgment. I may be wrong, but I've been here about nine years and I seem to see this. It's not absolute friendliness and openness. There's something hidden; there's some locked room in the heart of every Nebraskan.

SHELLY: Teachers talk about finding one's voice. How do you describe your voice as different from others?

BRENT: I don't know exactly because I can't step aside from it. I look at my work and think, oh, there's a variety of different voices, but I think it's probably true that there is a kind of voice print that's true for every writer. The stories that I enjoy writing the most are the ones like "The Last of the Nice" that have a manic narrator, that have an element of comedy in them and an element of pathos. They're hard in a lot of ways because you have to keep your energy high in the writing. It's relatively easy to write an opening paragraph that can be very exciting. But then the danger is that everything is going to fall off and I have to devise other ways to keep the energy high. It's like a symphony that starts with a crescendo. Where do you go after that?

I'm interested in the subject of working class people who are not privileged. I get tired of reading stories where the character never seems to have a job; they're always on vacation. I want to make sure the main character has a job. In most cases, it's a job I've actually had, so I know something about it. It's kind of fun to say, "Well, do I still have jobs in my history that I can draw on for this story? Some jobs I've held for only twenty-four hours, but that counts. (laughter)

I like all kinds of stories with all kinds of voices. I just got the new Alice Munro book. There's a thoughtful quiet voice she has and I'm fascinated by that. I've got a couple stories that try to be like that, but that's something I just can't touch at all. I still love it. I read some experimental fiction and I think this is so great, it must be fun to write, but it's not my voice.

SHELLY: Who are some writers who inspire you?

BRENT: I'm always excited when I pick up new stories and read them. John Updike I like a lot and John Cheever. I've already talked about Alice Munro. I love Lorrie Moore who I think is so funny and so touching at the same time. She's a model in some ways.

I can't get enough Shakespeare. Thomas Hardy I love. Dickens. A whole pile of things. I love a good detective novel, too. I keep reading everything, like some magpie picking up anything I can use and storing it away. I like Amy Hempel, Larry Brown, Lee K. Abbot, Mary Gaitskill, Joy Williams, Jorge Luis Borges, Grace Paley, Tim Gatreaux, Barry Hannah, Raymond Carver, Tobias Wolff, John L'Heureux, Amy Bloom—a whole host of people. And I'm lucky enough to be married to one of my favorite writers, Jonis Agee.

SHELLY: Do you remember times when you got news from a publisher and felt that your hard work had paid off?

BRENT: I don't think I've had those moments. I've had a lot of good news over the years, but I'm afraid I'm too neurotic to appreciate it. I had dinner with one of my literary idols recently and found that she's just as neurotic as the other writers I know. (laughter)

I had a story in *The Atlantic* some years ago, and when the editor called to tell me they were taking the story I think I said "I already subscribe to *The Atlantic.* Thank you very much." He had to tell me again that they were taking the story; I was very pleased and I told him so. But the minute I hung up I thought this has to be a mistake. Even if it's not a mistake he can change his mind, I bet, so I'd better not count on this. I waited for weeks and weeks without telling people because I thought it was not going to come true.

It's how I was raised. My neighborhood was Polish and Lithuanian most of my childhood. One day I saw this woman with a baby, and when another woman said "What a beautiful baby," I watched as the mother spit on her baby's forehead and started criticizing the other woman saying, "Don't curse my baby that way. You compliment somebody that way it's not a compliment, it's a curse and will bring bad luck." I was influenced by that sort of thinking. Don't take too much pride or joy in these things because it might make it go away. I'll think, "Well, I had that good luck yesterday but now I've lost whatever I had and I'm just no good at this. I should quit right now. I should get a factory job because I do know how to do that."

SHELLY: Where was your neighborhood?

BRENT: In northeastern Pennsylvania outside Wilkes-Barre, a little town called Kingston. My parents still live near there. It's very Polish, Lithuanian, Czech. When I was a kid I knew some Polish, because that's what people spoke. Mostly curse words; the Polish equivalent of "Get out of my yard," things like that. It's still that way when I go back, very poor.

SHELLY: What does your family think of what you've written?

BRENT: I think they're pleased, but you know they've never read a word I've written. When I bring a new book, I give it to them and they look at it. I know my mother has read some things because every once in a while she'll say "Well, I noticed you used that thing that Uncle Henry did in that story." But that's all she'll say. My step-father, who has never read anything, will say "I love it, this is great." And he'll immediately go to the china cupboard and put the book up there next to the teacups. It's an object to look at, it's not something to read, and since there are some bits and pieces in it he might be embarrassed by, I'm kind of glad about that. They're pleased, but it's a very low-key household. They'll brag to their friends but they won't tell me they're pleased. My step-father still says "What do you do exactly? I don't understand."

I know a writer who's got a couple well-regarded books out under a pseudonym because she says her family would be very critical. I have said for myself that if I were to write about family things, I would do it no matter what, and take the consequences later. But I haven't had to really. I haven't had to pay that piper.

SHELLY: What projects do you have down the road?

BRENT: I have two books that I've been working on for a few years. One is a novel that I've written, rewritten, and am now rewriting again. It's very frustrating. I finished the fourth draft and sent it to my publisher, who said, "This is fine, you could make money with this, but it doesn't quite have the edge to it the other books have." So he gave me some good advice and sent me home, rewriting it pretty much from the ground up so now it's like a whole new book.

Then there's a non-fiction book about my birth father. The last ten years of his life he lived in a camper driving often along the U.S./Mexico border. He ended up drowning in the Gulf of Mexico. I found his papers and retraced his routes along the border and have written this book about his travels, so it's about Mexico, and about my father, and about fathers and sons. I'm trying to finish both of those things and write the odd story here and there.

MARGE: Do you start with a blank screen with that novel you're rewriting?

BRENT: I had the characters, certain features of their personalities, and actions in mind, but I've just rewritten it. Every once in a while I'll bump into something and think "Oh, yeah, this is like that part" and I'll pull in a piece from the older draft though I don't know if it will stay. It's not as hard as writing it fresh because I do have a lot in mind, but so far all the events have been completely new. I'm used to working and reworking the text that I have, but Jonis has been saying "You might want to try just turning the old manuscript face down and starting fresh." It's been interesting and it feels like a better piece of writing.

MARGE: What's it like to have two fiction writers in the same household?

BRENT: Wall to wall neuroses. No, it's good, it's invigorating to have somebody right at hand, being each other's coach and agent. Jonis will say, "You know, Brent, that factory job is looking better and better for you." (laughter)

Save or Turn to Stone

Save or Turn to Stone

"You should have visited last weekend," she says as we stare at the icy sludge lying in the center of the green, all that's left of Winter Carnival. "The theme this year was 'Camelot Frozen in Time.'" Slushy castle walls drip in the February sun. Knights on horseback collapse onto stiff gray grass. Nearby, a man is chanting, "Change, change, change, change." I can't tell if he's a beggar or an evangelist.

It's Friday and happy hour in this New England college town. Anne's taking me for a drink to get a feel for the place, a method we've used on other towns.

The bars are filled with lacquered wood, beveled mirrors, and men in suits. It's been six months since she started teaching here, since we've seen each other. We talk about my job interview at a prep school in Massachusetts.

"It went well, I think."

"So what are you worried about?"

"I don't know. The cabdriver who took me to the interview said, 'I hope you like snotty little rich kids.' And besides teaching, I'd have to live in a dorm. I'd also have to coach a sport called Survival 101."

"You're kidding."

"No," I say. "You take kids into the woods and try to live off the land for days at a time."

"You?" she says. "You couldn't find your way out of a well-lit closet."

She's right and I laugh. I remember being lost along the Lehigh River. I was thirteen, a Scout at Camp Acahela. For hours I thrashed around in the woods. I thought the night would come and I would die, but then I saw a tent through the trees. Mine. I limped into the clearing, exhausted, covered with scratches, my ankle swollen and blue from a fall. At camp, everything was normal. My friends were swimming, carving wood, tying intricate knots in pieces of cord. I don't know what I expected. Search parties, I guess, helicopter reconnaissance. But no one noticed I was missing. No one knew that, purely by chance, I was still alive. I went to my tent and wept because I was lost in the woods and no one cared, and because I was too ashamed to tell anyone.

"You'll be fine," Anne says. "You'll get the job. I don't see what you're worried about."

"I'm worried I'll get the job."

We finish the night at a place called The Inn, where the waitress grudgingly brings another round after last call. And still we're able to get out before the bar lights go up.

In the street Anne says, "Well, we didn't find it." She means we didn't find the Truth, the epiphany that proves the world is worth the trouble.

"Don't despair."

"Despair I can handle," she says. "It's hope that kills."

***

Saturday we hold our heads in our hands and make sorrowful noises. We lie quietly on the rug for hours, thinking, listening to music—Kristofferson, Bach, it doesn't matter.

We lie in each other's arms and say, "We can't do this anymore." We mean drinking. Later we'll walk into town and browse the shops, eat dinner, and get an early start on another night of drinking.

She's tall and thin, an ex-athlete, ex-cheerleader, and there are parts of her life she no longer understands. Another person seems to have lived that life. Now she teaches philosophy. She's against shoddy thinking. "That's just bad philosophy," she'll say when she disagrees with me.

Her son, Tbor, is the Grandfather of Assassins. All he wants to talk about is the on-line game he plays with people he's never met. His cell leader, Mawa the Unmerciful, has it in for him.

"He was trying to get me killed by giving all these powers to Aldebaran—psionics, flame hurling, stuff like that." He's sprawled on a brown recliner, his voice quiet and careful.

"In the end, I had to die, but Mawa let me choose my death, so I turned into a ring of binding and made myself a gift to Aldebaran. When he put the ring on his finger, he got trapped in eternity. So in a way I guess I won." Anne and I laugh. We have both been married and divorced. We know about the ring of binding.

Tbor has been shuttling between parents for years. For the last two or three months he's lived with Anne.

"It must be hard to be moving all the time," I say.

"I'm used to it," he says quietly, the same careful tone he uses to tell his gaming adventures.

On Saturday afternoon, Anne and I go for a walk, leaving Tbor to his game. We call out goodbye, but the only answer is the sound of the keyboard's chatter and jab.

"I like him," she says, clapping her hands and cocking her head. "Isn't that amazing?"

The day is warmer than we thought, so we leave our gloves and scarves in a bookstore locker downtown. The streets are full of parents and children. Every shop is a wood-frame house with shutters, varnished floors, and hanging plants. Only the hardware store suggests that people need more to live their lives than homemade ice cream, running shoes, and two-for-one margaritas.

"What are we doing here?" she says with mock misery. She means why aren't we somewhere with real people and good bars and Okie music. She means how have our lives come down to this. I don't tell her that I envy her job and would trade places in a minute. But she knows.

"You buy all this, don't you," she says, gesturing at the crowded street.

"No," I say.

"Yeah?"

"A little." She has an office with enough bookshelves, an easy chair, and a window overlooking the green. I buy all of it.

"They're the same snotty kids you're so worried about teaching, only older, with more attitude. Were we ever like that?"

Lately, she says, she's been having strong flashbacks to her childhood. What it felt like walking to school. Practicing the piano for hours. Other times, too. Sitting beside a pool, drunk on rum and California sunshine.

I think I know what she means. The trouble is, too many things keep happening. Especially in memory, where everything happens at once. You're walking to grade school in Indiana, the tarred road sticking to your feet. All at once, you're at a woman's door, proposing marriage, signing divorce papers, giving a fifth of Scotch to the new husband, who's on his way out the door with a cocktail waitress. The past keeps piling up. There isn't enough room for it all.

Anne wants the world to work. Her second choice is to understand why it almost never does. She wants to know why she got married, why she got divorced. Why my reaction to the world is always so much milder than hers.

"Things don't seem to bother you," she says. "I wonder if that's true or if you're just not saying."

"I don't know," I say.

"You know," she says. "You're too nice to people. Underneath, you might be Mr. Ego. You're probably completely indifferent to everybody around you."

"Could be true," I say, "except who cares what you think?"

We laugh, but then she says, "That's what I mean. You turn it into a joke. I want to know." She's chewing the corner of her mouth, something she does when she's thinking or worried.

"People just don't bother me," I say.

"Of course they do," she says, "and you owe it to them to get pissed off."

We're having our afternoon drink at a bar called Ned's Gator or something. When the bartender comes to our table he leans on his elbows and stares at Anne with big watery eyes, smiling. When he goes away, she says, "What's his problem? I don't like this. Now everything's ruined."

I say, "Maybe he's high."

"Ruined."

"Or maybe he's in love."

She slaps the table and laughs her big throaty laugh. People turn and stare. "What's the matter? They never heard somebody laugh before?"

Anne's metaphor for a world that works is the Good Bar. A place where they know you well enough to bring your drink before you ask, but not so well that they kid you about how often you're there. Not too crowded. Not too empty. The light's just right and the music is old. A place where you can meet somebody who won't turn out to be an ax murderer. This is not too much to expect from the world.

When I first met her, I thought she was moody and overcritical. Nothing pleased her. Later I understood her better. She wants a kind of purity not found in nature.

"My ideal," she says, "is to live in one room with nothing but a rug, a chair, and a lamp."

Her real problem is that she can see the dark side of so much that seems good. This is why she suspects the motives for my indiscriminate kindness. She writes about what she calls "deadly virtues"—integrity, honesty, loyalty. Maybe even kindness. She wonders if I tolerate people I don't like as a subtle way of ignoring them. I wonder, too.

I see her standing in the doorway between two rooms—one has a rug, a chair, and a lamp; the other is full of people. Sometimes the empty room is lonely. Sometimes the people stare when she laughs. To choose one room means losing whatever is good about the other. As philosophy, the dilemma is unattractive, an ugly duckling. It lacks irony. It's not as intricate as the Escher prints on her walls, not as elegant as the Wittgenstein she likes to quote, not as raw as the Hank Williams she punches up on the jukebox. But it's true.

Her territory is the threshold between choices. If she were lost in the woods and saw her own tent through the trees, what would she think? Would she be relieved that she had found her way home? Or disappointed that her courage had not carried her away? Probably both.

At dinner, Tbor keeps making cryptic references to the game. "Explain it or shut up," she says, and laughs.

"It's simple," he says, his voice solemn, "Characters can have different ethical alignments. Neutral evil, lawful evil, chaotic evil. Neutral, lawful, and chaotic good. Even neutral, lawful, and chaotic neutral." His look becomes sly. "Most of the time, I'm lawful good. But not always." I'm wondering if I'm chaotic neutral or just neutral neutral.

Somehow Aldebaran shook off his paralysis and lured Tbor into a room with moving walls of flame. But Tbor, who's now Ossian the Ungood, trapped Aldebaran with an enchanted gaze, giving him only two choices: save himself by becoming Ossian's slave, or let Ossian's gaze turn him to stone. Aldebaran chose stone. I can tell from his voice that Tbor is disappointed and a little amazed at his friend's choice. We always are, I suppose.

The job I interviewed for is a good one but would keep me busy all the time. When I'm not lost in the woods with my survival class, I'd be prowling the dorm, sniffing for marijuana. If don't get the job, I don't know what I'll do. If do get it, the same. Either choice is the wrong one. Or the right one. I'm neutral neutral about it.

What's my ethical alignment regarding Anne? Chaotic neutral or just neutral neutral? And which is better? If you don't react when the bartender stares at the woman you're with, does it mean you're secure or indifferent? In the end, ethical alignment, like luck, probably doesn't come in flavors.

Save or Turn to Stone

Sunday morning is lazy. A week of false spring has ended, bringing back the cold and snow. We get a fire going in the fireplace and sit on the floor in front of it to read. I drink cider and Anne smokes. We don't say much, but we're both thinking the same thing—we didn't find it. No epiphany, no dark cloud crackling with light; the scales have not fallen from our eyes. In the morning, when we wake up, we'll be the same people. How sad to be no wiser than we are. To walk into the wilderness of the new day and lose our way again.

Later she drives me to the bus station, giving me a thumbs-up when I wave to her from the window. And then the bus pulls out and she's gone in a blur of gray-green hills and trees. I'm sorry to leave this shabby landscape behind—the fields lying like abandoned rugs, the sudden rivers and small streams edged with ice. I'm sorry to feel our weekend slipping away, becoming a memory that someday will seem strange and not at all like us. What will we think when we look back? Will we shake our heads at how we were so close to home and still so lost? We love each other. What question does that answer? Which fate do we fear most? Save or turn to stone? In the seat ahead of me sits a blind woman. Over and over, she sweeps her hand across the window, as though she can read the landscape through the cold glass.

Jonis Agee

Jonis Agee

JONIS AGEE is the author of nine books, including a book of poetry, *Houses,* four novels: *Sweet Eyes, Strange Angels, South of Resurrection,* and *The Weight of Dreams*; and four collections of short fiction: *Pretend We've Never Met, Bend This Heart, A .38 Special and a Broken Heart,* and *Taking the Wall.* A Nebraska native (born in Omaha), she was educated at The University of Iowa (BA) and The State University of New York at Binghamton (MA, PhD). She is Professor of English and Creative Writing at The University of Nebraska-Lincoln. Among her many awards are an NEA grant in fiction, a Loft-McNight Award, and a Loft-McNight Award of Distinction. Three of her books—*Strange Angels, Bend This Heart,* and *Sweet Eyes*—were named "Notable Books of the Year" by *The New York Times.* Her newest books are a collection of short stories called *Taking the Wall* (Coffeehouse) and the novel *The Weight of Dreams,* which won the Nebraska Book Award for 2000. *Acts of Love on Indigo Road: New and Selected Stories* was published in February, 2003, by Coffeehouse Press. She owns twenty pairs of cowboy boots, some of them works of art, loves the open road, and believes that ecstasy and hard work are the basic ingredients of life and writing.

MARGE: Jonis, as a child, you are said to have ridden your horse on the streets of Omaha. I've come to expect just about anything, but that's an unusual image. Did you actually ride horseback in Omaha?

JONIS: Yes, it's true, I'd ride my horse into Omaha when I was a kid.

MARGE: Sounds ideal. Did you have an ideal childhood?

JONIS: No, it was difficult. My parents were difficult people and we had a big family; I had a weird childhood. It was wonderful when we lived in the country outside of Omaha. We lived in the middle of big fields; that made it perfect, that stamped me. Then my father went to work abroad and we moved. We would spend summers with my mother's mother down in Missouri. When we moved back, we moved into Omaha. It just broke my heart to lose the land and all the animals and the crazy stuff we did. But at about that time my grandfather bought a farm outside of Omaha, and I got a horse.

MARGE: So that's how you came to ride in Omaha?

JONIS: I would ride around the countryside, too, and meet other kids, you know, strangers on horseback. You could do that kind of thing then. It was very pleasant. When I stayed with my grandparents, my grandmother wanted help with the dishes or had little chores, but they left me alone so I could be gone for four or five hours. It was a great pleasure going out into world and finding your way, and I think that was a lot of luck, a lot of luck for me.

MARGE: Really important, this time alone?

JONIS: To write you really have to be able to spend time alone. If you can't stand to spend time alone, you're not going to make it as a writer. I didn't even know I was learning to be contemplative. And I also

Jonis's office in Andrews Hall is large and comfy, with a western feel. Jonis gets up from her computer and welcomes us. We know this is a busy time of year for her, and that she gives much time to her many students. We feel lucky to be seated on her couch with an hour ahead of us to talk. Jonis has us laughing from the get-go.

did learn to meet people. I'd go visit neighboring farms and get people to give me food and stuff. (laughter)

MARGE: And you haven't quit.

JONIS: We all have a landscape that imprints us, and I was imprinted with this landscape, its spaciousness. I tried to live on either coast and could not stand it. Upstate New York was the closest I came, but it was gray about 300 days out of the year. It was pretty horrible. Then I went to LA and I couldn't stand the ocean. Isn't that weird? I don't mind the wind blowing because you know it's going to stop, but the ocean—I felt pushed upon, like listening to highway traffic.

Pioneer women described the wind, and when I've gone out to the Sandhills to research the novels and talk to the people, that's one of the things people mention offhand, that the wind never stops blowing. They'll say, "If it doesn't stop soon, I'm going to go crazy." I've experienced that. Once when I was out there, it had been blowing the whole time. I pulled off the road, there was nobody there, and I got out into the wind. There was something about it. It was in your ears; you couldn't think.

MARGE: When did you begin to go to the Sandhills?

JONIS: Well, I started my trips out there in about '90 or '91, I think it was, so it's been a recent love affair. I had wanted to move out there. My sister and I had land together for a while there but sold it. I didn't have the heart to put anything on it. I didn't want to be the one to civilize the Niobrara River. It's really beautiful land.

SHELLY: When you were growing up, who did you feel closest to, identify with the most?

JONIS: Not my siblings. I had an older sister and an older brother, and we had a lot of sibling rivalry going on. My little brother and I played together a lot. We had an odd family because first there were three of us, then my younger brother and a baby, and then my mother had another baby when I was sixteen. It was sort of a glued together group, and the last two were another family.

The people in my family that meant the most were probably my grandfather and my step-grandmother. They gave me refuge on the farm. My grandfather started a business college in Omaha, and my father went into business with him, and they both taught there. Both of them were great readers. Everyone in my family is a reader and I think that made a big difference in my education. There was never any question about going to college; you had to do it. It would have been like saying you weren't going to high school (laughter) and then you were supposed to go out and do something with yourself. It was my grandparents who gave me a place to go away and hide out when I would have trouble at home. They were very supportive. Feeling you were liked and you didn't have to perform for them—I liked that. I've read studies about how kids succeed. Just one mentor makes a huge difference.

MARGE: What do you remember about school?

JONIS: Well, you remember the teachers who didn't like you. (laughter)

I remember trying to get this fourth grade teacher to like me. I could not figure out what the heck was wrong. I seemed to like myself a lot. Maybe that was the problem. (laughter)

There were librarians who let me work in the library. Grade school and junior high libraries are nice places—they were for me. I always loved books and I liked being there. I thought about being a librarian for a while, but I'm kind of a noisy person when I get around other people so that probably wouldn't have worked out. But I loved reading; what writer doesn't? I love people who say they want to write, but then they say "I don't really like to read." Well, then, writing will be an interesting experience for you. You have no idea what anything sounds like. (laughter)

In Central High School, I had some great teachers. There was one man in the English department who always told me I was going to be a writer, based on my compositions. I kind of felt like I was going to do that, too. He wanted me to go to Sarah Lawrence. He was on the board of directors at Sarah Lawrence and he said he would get me in. My parents wouldn't even let me apply because it was too far east. Besides they wanted me to get a teaching degree and Sarah Lawrence didn't offer a teaching degree. I wondered for years what that would have been like, to go to a really good school, but probably I needed to find my own way. I did go to college, obviously, but I did not take a teaching degree. (laughter)

MARGE: You've said you're noisy when you're around people. When you're writing, are you quiet? I think of you laughing sometimes as you're writing.

JONIS: Well, I do sometimes laugh when I write. Sure, if I think it's funny, I'll giggle. I react to my work. You know what that's like, you go into a kind of zone, you're not thinking: "Here I am doing writing." When it's really working well, you're just writing. If I have a scene and I think it's funny, I'll laugh because it's almost as if I'm watching it on screen. I'm reading it myself for the first time. Parts of it make me cry, sometimes, if I write something very sad that moves me, you know.

Do you find that with your work, you can move yourself? It sounds kind of egocentric but I think it's quite the opposite. It is that point at which you have suspended yourself so utterly that you are encountering the work in this other place and if it's moving, it's moving. I have work—and I'm sure you do, too—that when you read it in public there are some scenes or poems where you have to fight your emotions constantly to not break down and weep. You can tell it's moving the audience, too, so that happens, but not all the time. Certainly one's work doesn't go up and down between weeping and laughing. There's a lot of middle ground where you're just working.

SHELLY: Can you talk about the writing zone? Do you have habits that help you get to that place? Routines?

JONIS: I discovered years ago that I'm not a morning person, but to write I had to become one. I hate it when people say "Oh, you're a morning person." I'm not. I never teach in the morning. I'm not good for about the first five hours. I don't need to see any human beings. It's a good time to write. I'm not in a bad mood. I just don't want to hang out with people at that hour of the morning; I like a private space. That might be something that comes from my family. I remember my father getting up hours before he had to go to work and sitting in the dark and drinking cups of coffee and smoking cigarettes, as if he had to prepare himself, and my grandfather would do the same thing. I don't know whether it's the genetic old farmer stock or what, just something we all have.

When I was in college I stayed up half the night and that was good because I was writing poetry. You can write poetry in the middle of the night. To write fiction, you have to get up when you're fresh and have some energy and go to work. When I'm working on a novel, I do try to write every day, because otherwise you're starting over, over and over. With teaching I've discovered that my students do best if I can get them to write every day for a couple of weeks in the beginning of the semester.

I have an assignment where I ask them to write a story every day. It can be as short as you like, it can be a long as you want, but you have to finish it that day. Then you start a new one the next day. By the end of the week they're really writing. By the end of two weeks, you've got some respectable things going. It's that sitting down for the first time after you've been off for a while that is hard. I think the same would work with poetry. Just say, "I'm going to write a poem a day." They can be lousy. Give yourself permission to practice and to be lousy until you get to the good stuff.

MARGE: I've heard you say that when something in the day catches your attention, when some image stays with you, that image must be used in the writing. Would you talk about that idea?

JONIS: It's what I call paying attention to what you're paying attention to. That developed for me out of the research I was doing on my second novel, *Strange Angels.* I first started going to the Sandhills having very particular ideas about what I wanted. I'd get frustrated when the event I was looking for or the piece of information I wanted and felt I needed for the book wasn't forthcoming and I couldn't find it. After a while I began to realize that the things that were happening instead were things that I needed.

I take a writer's notebook as I drive. You don't have to look at the notebook when you write. (laughter) There are things my unconscious mind selects. The attention writers have is a giant sieve, and we put all experience through it. The things that catch in that screen are the things for your writing because the rest of it just leaves. What is there that you are seeing on that given day is yours. It's your message. That's for you.

When I write that way it's very effective for me, rather than feeling I have to work so hard to manufacture it. I've begun to respect the fact that I am constantly working. I don't think writers ever go off duty. I'm constantly paying attention. I can take notes all day long, just look around and see where my eye is going to land.

You look at a particular thing and you suddenly see something in it. That's what you need, rather than discounting it. I always discounted that material before, thinking, "Where's the special thing? Where's the unique thing?" rather than knowing you have to individualize that, you have to put that in your story now.

It may be a form of meditation; it's certainly a form of attention. It's a way of going into yourself and trusting yourself. That's something that older writers understand after a while. It's hard for younger writers to understand that you have an infinite amount of material inside you and more is gathering all the time. It's like going to the bookstore and seeing all the new books all the time; you feel like you'll never catch up. Sometimes I feel we should call a moratorium on publishing for two years (laughter), so the rest of us can read and catch up.

There's so much material; there's so much coming into us all the time that we can use. A lot of the training I like to do with newer writers, newer to the game, is how to pay attention, how to begin to find your own material or you own voice, how to pay attention to what you notice and to value it.

I wanted to go to the Badlands because I felt my second novel needed a trip to the Badlands. I kept thinking, "It'll really be a good novel if I get the Badlands in there." I went out one particular weekend and spent Friday night in Valentine. I thought, "Okay, Saturday I'm driving to the Badlands, this is it, and then the novel will be fabulous because I'll have all that experience of driving through the reservation." So I get up, ready to go to breakfast, I park my car, I come out, and the keys are locked in the car. I spend all day with some locksmith from the local hardware store, meeting all these town citizens who are giving me terrible advice on how to get the keys out of my Subaru Legacy. We went on and on. We even took a lunch break. The deputy came by, everybody came by, cowboys, they all had advice. They would slow their trucks down and look to see what we were doing.

About three o'clock in the afternoon I was ready to throw a rock through the window. Finally I said to the man helping me, "I'm going across the street and fax the car number to the Subaru dealer and see if they can fax back a key picture." That's when the guy popped the lock. But the day was ruined for me, because I knew I had to go home on Sunday and that was it, no Badlands.

I was just so furious. I thought, "It's ruined my life because now when am I going to have time to go back and do the Badlands and make this a brilliant novel? These characters could have come to something in the Badlands." I got into the car. There were huge thunderclouds coming in from the south and west. In the Sandhills they can roll over you, these big purple monsters. I ignored it. I drove straight into the hills. "Well, they'll have to give me something. I'm so furious. Something will be out there. I'll make the world cough up its genius for me; it's just going to have to produce an event," I said.

The biggest honking storm came over those hills. I watched it stepping from one hill to the next to the next, such a driving rain that a bird actually stalled in front of my windshield—flap, flap, flap, as hard as he could in the wind and the rain. Cattle trucks were pulling over. I pulled over once, being beaten to death by this rain. I still hadn't gotten the message. Finally, the rain abated and I started back. As I came up toward Valentine, there was a huge double rainbow against the black sky. It was beautiful, earth-shattering. I figured it out: "Oh, this is what you are supposed to see, not the Badlands, you idiot. It was this that was waiting for you all the time."

It taught me a huge lesson. I did go to the Badlands eventually and I didn't use them. There wasn't anything in the Badlands for me. It was that double rainbow; I did use that. I used the storm. It taught me about myself and all the manufacturing of events I was still trying to do, rather than finding what's organic to the place and the people. They didn't live in the Badlands; they lived in the hills. That was for me a big changing moment in researching and attention. I have an essay where I talk about this day and that whole event, what it did for me as a writer.

I look for what's around me and I feed it in. I also read newspapers and a lot of magazines. Any piece of print, anything that catches my eye I cut out and save and use: things that happen to people, odd stories, and pieces of information. I love pieces of information. Doctor's offices, pamphlets, they're great sources of information. Lots of language, that's the thing we have to look for as writers, new language. We need to be constantly researching that language.

SHELLY: You talk about paying attention. Does it ever irritate you that you can't get out of that, that you always are the writer, always observing, always taking notes?

JONIS: There are two times when it's troublesome. One is when I'm intensely writing and I have to go do something else, go teach, or go socialize. You know I love to teach. But I'm still in that other world, and I can't be fully myself.

The other time is when I'm tired. "Well, there's another thing to notice, there's another thing to notice" and you want to say "Shut up!" but you're afraid to say it because you don't really want it to shut up, you just want a break.

Sometimes I read mysteries because I don't have to pay that much attention. It's an escape for me to go to movies, too, except for slasher films which I can't stomach much of, and I don't do cartoons, but everything else. Is that what you're talking about?

SHELLY: Yes, escape of some sort from being the writer and always observing, and wanting to write that down instead of just living.

JONIS: People who aren't writers and newer writers aren't aware of the fact that it is a double life. We pay for the act of being a writer and it's probably the same thing other artists have to pay for. Writing is good and it intensifies our lives, but it also removes us from our lives. We're sometimes more the onlookers than we would be if we were another kind of person with another kind of job. We sometimes don't enjoy fully because we are also using it as raw material.

My last husband said, "You never go on vacation!" He hated it because I'd bring my work with me. He wanted to go traveling without that kind of business going on so that we would have a joint experience, but I was always experiencing it in that other way. If there are dues to be paid, that's one of them.

It's a double life. I don't think it's particularly great to be raised by a writer if you're a child because you're constantly being analyzed as a character and parts of your life might show up in print. Your mom or dad is often missing in action because they're looking at you with that particular glazed look on their face. In their mind they're writing. Sentences are coming across the screen. I feel sorry for my daughter.

MARGE: You have a lot of energy, but I wonder what you do if you don't have it. How do you keep that energy or renew it, if you ever get down?

JONIS: When you teach, there are periods when you're not going to be able to write. That's what teachers always complain about. I spend a great deal of time on other people's imaginations and other people's work and often there's nothing left over. The good part of the job of teaching and working with other people's imaginations is that when it's good, it gives you a lot of energy; it's like sparks, an electrical connection.

There are times when I think "I'm going to go home and write." There are other times when it's exhausting. It's depressing to not have time for your own work, but most people who are writers do not earn their living as writers, so we're all doing something else, your "day job." The only answer to this question is to write. Writing is always the answer to every question about writing.

Sometimes you're starting to get depressed and negative about the world and you hate all your friends because they're not being nice enough to you, nobody understands, they're all consumed with their own lives, and you feel like you don't have enough money and you've wasted your life and you're no good as a writer, everybody else is better. When I reach the last drop of water in the well, I think either I can die down here or I suppose I could go and write a sentence. It's almost a way of stripping away the world and all the distractions.

It's like that Medieval play where Everyman goes to his grave by himself and he keeps saying to his family and his friends and his coworkers, "Will you go instead? Will you go?"

They all say "No, no, no." Nobody will go for him. For me it's digging into a psychic place of aloneness. Not that I'm necessarily depressed when I write because when I'm really writing, I'm not anything, I'm just writing. But I feel like I have to shed the world. I don't say, "Now I have to shed the world," but I feel myself pulling away and that's always depressing, to pull away from the world, to convince yourself to do it. It's as if I'm exhausted and worn out in one way, but in another way there's a whole reservoir of energy waiting, a different kind of energy, not a social energy, a private energy, the energy of the imagination. Once I release that into the work, then it's energizing, although I'm quite exhausted after I write each time, aren't you?

MARGE: It's like a workout.

JONIS: It's taken me a while to figure out that it's a process. Write, write, write, and then there's no more, there's nothing there, you sound stale to yourself, you're bored, it feels as if you're worn out. I've learned I have to take a break and let the well refill itself.

I used to think that I could make it all come out at once and that's not true. I used to think also that I had to be careful not to take too much at once, as if in life there's only a certain amount of water. Now I realize it's the Ogallala Aquifer. If we're in a drought or there's a lot of demand on the water, we're going to get brown water. That's when you need to take a break, when the brown water shows up.

I met an older writer years ago who said, "I've reached a stage in my life where it's all right not to be working on something at every given moment." He's the one that really taught me about those rest periods. You come back much fresher.

Writers go into a self-hypnotic state through those little mantra activities, sharpening twenty-five pencils, that kind of thing. Graham Greene would have to go downstairs every day before he started work and find in the street, as cars passed by, a certain combination of letters and numbers. When he did that he knew he could go upstairs and write. All of us have these little devices, the triggers to go into your writing state. I set up my little ritual. Do you guys have that?

MARGE: Often walking is part of my writing routine. Also writing in cafes.

JONIS: I've got to have my cup of tea, and things have got to be in a certain place. Set that up, and then we're off to the races.

SHELLY: You've mentioned loving to teach. Could you talk about working with young writers, with newer writers? How do you approach that?

JONIS: That's such a huge question. The most important thing to accomplish in a beginning course is to teach them the basics of a form in a way they can understand. I take them step by step in both poetry and fiction through the mechanics: "OK, here's how we do characters, here's how we do lines of poetry, here's image, here's metaphor, here's plot, here's dialogue."

At the same time I work on putting them in touch with the sources for their own writing and alerting them to when they get material that is original. You can always tell because that's where the best writing is, the moment when their voice becomes alive. Usually there are a few students who are already in voice, they already have material, they're raring to go. They write a couple of things and discover they can really write. That doesn't happen for most people. For them, it's a longer, slower process.

The writing teacher doesn't want to be a psychoanalyst, but you do have to dismantle some of the barriers that people have established in their imagination, the barriers to expression of self. I can usually tell when somebody's stopped up, when there's material they are afraid to approach. I work with that person individually, not that I want their work to be confessional, but it's writing down whatever it is there at the top like a big cork, writing it down even if they never show that writing to anyone.

I spent a long time working with young Catholic women, middle-aged Catholic women, midwestern women, very concerned with being appropriate, not offending people, so I had to develop some techniques because you can't be a good writer if your goal is to please people. You have to be able to take some risks. I'm not saying they have to write about their relatives or expose family secrets, but they have to be willing to tell the truth and tell the truth in a way that is the contract between them and the page. That's what I work on, the two-pronged approach, the form and the personal material.

SHELLY: Could you give an example of that?

JONIS: I have two examples. I had a student who kept taking creative writing, but there wasn't any life in any of her work. She learned how to do the form in her poems and her stories. You felt there might be something there, way deep, but she was clearly using language as a disguise for a lot of things. I do this exercise where I say, "What is it that you're not supposed to write about? Don't tell me. I want you to write down what will happen if you write those things. Who are you going to freak out? Who's going to be furious with you? What will happen? Don't tell me, I don't even have to see this, but I want you to take one of those subjects and write it." She did, and lo and behold!

I said, "You don't even have to show me what you write, just begin to realize the real relationship is between you and the page. You don't ever have to show your work to any other human being, but if you can't trust the page, you're never going to be a writer."

After a while you learn how to submerge the direct transcription of experience and break it up and make it satisfy you. I give my students the example of Dickens. Dickens was obsessed with being impoverished and orphaned because of disruptions in the family as a child. All of his work has impoverished orphans in it. Obviously that's answering some need for him, but he doesn't have to address his own life, directly.

The other case was a young student who was working on first person. I was having them do the collected works of someone not themselves. It needed to be a real or historical person. This woman had been in a previous creative writing class and the work was, again, very abstract, just words on a page. I was teaching them about dreams and conscious dreaming. She had been one who held up her hand and said she never dreamed. Now that's an interesting thing to ask a class, because the person who never dreams usually has some things going on. We explored all the different dream theories that exist, all the various studies. I said, "I want you to set your alarm for two or three hours after you've gone to sleep. You will be dreaming when the alarm goes off and I want you to immediately wake up and write that down."

I also wanted them to use their dreams in their writing. I wanted them to figure out how to dream the dreams of the people they were writing about. My student woke up in the morning and there beside the bed, in her own handwriting, was something she had no recognition of. She didn't remember waking up in the night. It totally freaked her out because it was a first person, a woman's voice: "I'm here, we're all here, we need to get out, I have story to tell you" and it was going on and on. She thought she'd had a schizophrenic breakdown. She was in nursing, an occupational therapist, and finally one of her friends said "No, no, it's good" and convinced her to come and talk to me.

I said, "This is great. These are the voices of characters, of people who want to come out. They're saying we're in here, we're just stuck." Her father was a doctor, she was an only child, her parents so loved her, this wonderful young woman from northern Minnesota. I met her parents, great people who knew she had been unhappy. She wanted to please them by going into nursing and occupational therapy, but what she really was was a creative person. I said, "Write what these voices are telling you." This great writing started coming out.

It was as if that other person and that boring dead writing died, and for the next year she was producing a couple of poems a week, chapters of a novel she was giving me every week, and a short story every week, a huge unclogging of material. She was a great writer. I wanted her to go to grad school, but she still had that impulse to serve. She went down south; she's done a lot for impoverished people, and is working on her second novel.

That was the most dramatic thing I've seen in my life. It might have happened to her anyway, eventually, but it confirmed for me that when I see that stopped-up writing, you know the kind I'm talking about, there is something stopping it and if you can work with the person, something will unstop it. I did the exercise, the one I described earlier concerning a list of what you can't write about, but it wasn't that anything bad had happened to her in her life. She had a wonderful childhood, but she had gotten onto this thing of wanting to please her parents so much. They didn't want that. They were happy that she switched to English and writing because they had always said she was creative and had this other potential.

MARGE: That's a great story.

JONIS: It was pretty astonishing. Most of the changes you see in writers aren't that dramatic.

SHELLY: What about the flip side in teaching, the frustrating part, the part that weighs you down until you think you don't want to do this anymore?

JONIS: I've got forty-four fiction students this semester. I'm completely exhausted reading stories from forty-four people. I've got some very, very good writers, a couple of people ready to publish, but it's the volume. I like to teach literature on and off because it's a relief to read polished work. It's harder to get back to the level of publishable writing when you've exhausted yourself teaching people how to do the most elementary things. I imagine it's like being a concert musician, having to teach beginning piano or violin. It dulls you in a sense, not that the students won't rise up and become great writers. Some of them will. It's the sheer volume.

SHELLY: Do you work on each manuscript with them and give them advice?

JONIS: I've got to, that's my job, I've got to read everything. When the writer suddenly gets it, that's what I'm looking for, that "I get it" moment. It happens every semester. Waiting for that moment is like holding your breath for sixteen weeks. People develop in writing at such an individual rate. There's no way to predict it.

I had a student years ago, an Australian, who wasn't a very interesting writer. She was mechanically fine but the stories had very little life to them. She went away in January to a cabin in the north woods and came back with the most astonishing story. I think she needed to be away, and from then on she was a writer. She gave me faith again that people develop at different rates. When her genius showed up, it just showed up. We wait for that moment and that's what keeps me going. I have to believe that every single person can do that. There's no predicting how and when they will bloom.

In his book, *The Triggering Town,* Richard Hugo has the best defense of why creative writing should be taught. He believes, and I believe this, too, that every single person is capable of writing a poem or story that tells some form of truth and does it in a good enough way that they can be proud that they did that for the rest of their lives, something original, fresh, genuine. He said most students aren't going to be writers but that the experience strengthens them.

I was questioned about creative writing while teaching at a Catholic women's college. One of the nuns said, "You'll only produce a publishing writer every eight or ten years. That's a waste." I tried to point out that it was strengthening the students. They were using the imagination to construct something that didn't exist before. I think that translates, transforms, transfers itself into their lives in other ways.

You're working with the psyche and the person in a different way than almost any other course. It's not a body of knowledge you acquire; it's a way of using yourself and your knowledge and making a whole out of something. The artistic process is so important. A lot of bravery is involved in a good writing class. If you've been brave and put the truth of experience and the truth of your observation into a group of people and have been successful at it, that's an incredible learning tool. It's not like having a test where you get an A. That's all well and good, but it's not the same as creating something. Once you've done that, you can do that in other fields. It gives you courage to raise children and have relationships because you've been successful and it's something wholly out of yourself.

SHELLY: If you notice what students save, it's the creative that they value. Do they save the old biology papers? No, but they come back and ask, "Do you still have that poem I wrote in ninth grade?"

JONIS: That's a very good point. This is the one thing that you did that you can hang onto. You were true right there. The same is true if you paint a picture. I've got all my awful little art projects. I wanted to be an artist all through high school and college but I wasn't any good. I couldn't draw, I didn't have it, language was where it was going to be.

I teach adults at the Iowa Summer Writing Festival now. In every walk of life, every profession, to write novels has been the secret desire of so many people, it's scary. When you teach adult workshops, you realize everyone wants to do this. The novelists sometimes get derailed by thinking about money, but the poets have no illusions about that. I debunk the money business for novelists so they face reality pretty quickly, but writing is the thing; to make it in a form and give it to somebody, that's the urge.

SHELLY: What are you writing now?

JONIS: I've got a collection of stories to go through and revise and maybe write one or two more. I've got a novel I've got to sit down and redraft again. I keep redrafting it. I'll turn it face down and rewrite it and see what happens.

SHELLY: We told your husband, Brent Spencer, we would ask you what it is like to be married to a writer.

JONIS: Brent is a very good reader for my work. He's tough, and I'm tough on him. Even before I fell in love with Brent, I fell in love with Brent's work. I thought he was hilarious and smart. I think it's good his writing place is out of the house. When he's in the basement and I'm upstairs, we can hear each other if one of us goes up or down stairs, and we kind of meet in the kitchen. (laughter)

Earl

Earl figured it was a chicken and egg thing—who drove who crazy first. Fact was, both of them were about out of the roost. Reeva believed the Bible from cover to cover, and she believed the cover too. It didn't help that the old preacher had brought on his nephew, who was really that bastard kid of his from down in Greenville. His mama Dorcas worked at the Warren County Public Works, flagging on the highway crews that tarred and graded roads all summer long, and driving a salt truck in the winter. The preacher had his hands on Dorcas long before she got saved by God and the county, and now her kid was the preacher-in-training, since Reeva's church was so far into Christ's belly, there wasn't a seminary good enough for them.

And he was young and Earl's wife wasn't so old. That was a fact. Not as old as he was, so Earl had decided to have a talk with somebody. That's where the crazy part came. First he packed a lunch, two ears of sweet corn from last night's supper, a chunk of steak, a slab of American cheese, a burrito smothered in pale green sauce from breakfast—now that Reeva had taken to embracing new cultures they were having all kinds of weird stuff first thing in the morning when he could barely look a cup of coffee in the eye, let alone green slime—and five crescent walnut cookies the old Czech lady on the next farm over had made. She always paid him pie or cookies for mowing her lane with the wide sickle bar on the back of his tractor.

Well, he put the food in a plastic bag from the Sun Mart. They had about five hundred now that Reeva was recycling to show she loved all God's creatures too. He just wanted to cycle them all right down to the burn barrel, throw some brush on top and have a nice fire, but a man learns after fifteen years of a new wife to let a lot of it go. Or do it where she can't see it. He'd gotten rid of so much of her recycling so far the gully that was getting out of hand by the creek was almost full of bottles, cans, newspapers, cardboard, rags, paint and oil cans, machine parts, pieces of the hog shed he would have burnt in earlier years. Maybe she was right—it was taking care of the erosion, although she thought he was dumping the stuff in the bins off Highway 2 or driving it all the way into town to the Catholic Mission Store. Good thing she avoided Catholics.

After packing his lunch, he carefully scraped all the crumbs off the counter into his hand and dumped them in the sink, waited for the ants to swarm, then turned on the water and rinsed the whole lot down the drain. There. He couldn't kill anything when she was around and the house was wriggling with flies and ants and spiders. He looked around, and caught his reflection in the window to the barnyard. He had to admit it—he was probably too old for what he was about to do. If she were home, she'd stop him.

Reeva was in town having her hair done again. Second time this month. She was a good looking woman, that big mass of red hair brightened from the bottle, freckled skin that about drove him crazy, orangey brown eyes the color of fox fur. That little scar from her lips to her chin hardly showed at all—even though she said it made her look like a pirate and she'd have it fixed in a moment if he'd give her the money.

Earl wasn't cheap. That wasn't it. He just thought she looked as pretty as a woman needed to look—plenty pretty enough for him. He didn't even like her to wear make-up, and he was secretly pleased when Merle the old preacher said a word or two about it. Now that Merle Jr. was praising her natural beauty, though, it made him regret his stand. Maybe he should encourage make-up and drive her up to the medical school in Omaha to see a surgeon. A man shouldn't take such a hard line he gets knocked over it when the wind shifts on him. That reminded him—even though the heat index was 107 this afternoon, things could change. He'd take a suit jacket and wear his best straw cowboy hat. He wasn't above trying to impress the preacher or his kid, regardless of what the little bastard's birth certificate said. He'd pressed his suit pants too, and polished the toes of his brown cowboy boots so he wouldn't show up looking like an old farmer hunting for his young wife.

On his way back through the living room, he picked up the photo album sitting on the desk by the front door they never used. He was closing the door to the basement when he saw the .12-gauge leaning in the corner of the landing. It was loaded for rabbits and weasels, his current customers at the vegetable garden they figured he planted every year so they could enjoy their summers without having to work too hard for food. He juggled the album, lunch, and jacket and tucked the shotgun in the crook of his arm. It prickled his scalp to walk out the door this way, but he headed directly for the pickup.

The last of the chickens were pecking around the pole beans he'd strung up next to the garage, but most of the crop was finished or had gotten too old and hard. Years ago, with the first wife, he would've picked those and boiled them down to softness with some fatback and onion. Reeva didn't can or freeze or cook from scratch either if she could help it. But Earl kept the custom of the garden and the beans, picking and preparing them in a poor imitation of Opaline's recipes which those darn sisters of hers came and took when he married Reeva. Took the card box, the cook books, the department store dress box full of clippings of things she was going to cook. He was too embarrassed now to buy his own book, wouldn't know where to start, so he pretended to cook. And ate it, no matter what it tasted like. Fortunately, the vegetables turned out hard or mushy, bland either way. He knew enough not to burn things, though he couldn't get the lumps out of mashed potatoes to save his soul, and he secretly loved the ready-mades with chicken gravy Reeva bought at the Sun Mart when she picked up a whole broiled chicken at the end of her shift. Meanwhile, their chickens were dying of old age and raccoons.

He settled in the truck, the album of their Las Vegas wedding pictures snug against his leg, took a last look around his farm, and thought about the business at hand. He was driving out the lane when he spotted the riding mower with the flat tire, tilted next to the tree line. He should be taking that tire off and getting it in to Ham's Tire for repair. The grass was going to seed around the mower. Nights he dreamed about mowing, that's how much it had taken ahold of his life. When they woke up in the morning, Reeva would relate these complicated dreams about traveling to foreign countries, knowing other languages, being chased by serial killers, and he'd just have the mowing troubles to report. No wonder she was turning her attention to Jesus and other men.

In his current craziness, Earl had begun to think of the deity as another man. He knew it was wrong to be so suspicious, and as he pulled up beside the mail box, facing the wrong direction on the dirt road, praying the rednecks from a mile on didn't come roaring over the hill and put him in the ditch with their latest twelve-pack of empties he was forever retrieving from the deep weeds, he thought maybe he should turn around and leave it all alone. Then in the mail came the weekly church bulletin with the attached envelope for donations and the father and son picture of Merle and Merle Jr. looking like a skinny-ass Santa and a whippy young elf the way they were smiling, all teeth, hungry for Reeva's paycheck which she was now slipping whole, her signature confirming the donation, into the envelope every week. It was her money, he kept repeating to himself, but it did no good. A man and a woman had to agree on major purchases, they promised each other the first year, and he was not purchasing this particular form of salvation for Reeva. Not even God could make him do that. He threw the bills and bulletin on the shotgun and they slid off onto the floor along with the Sun Mart weekly flier whose loss leader was always some kind of beef. They must slaughter half the cattle in Nebraska, Earl figured, but he had mastered the barbeque grill and nothing was better than those t-bones unless Reeva was on her kick about meat, eyeing the steak like a dead baby as he flopped it over and grease sputtered and sparked on the coals. All winter he'd just savor that smell and taste, hauling the grill out as soon as the lawn showed any sign of green at all. So that was another thing.

He made it up the gravel road onto the blacktop with no mishap, turning toward Greenville. It wasn't until he hit the outskirts ten minutes later that he began to have doubts about what he was doing, and when he saw Highway 2 heading south and east, he tugged the steering wheel and coasted smoothly onto its four lanes. Nebraska City, it said, 39 miles, and he thought he'd just go along a little further and then pull off while he figured this thing out.

But the longer he drove, the less he knew. Another sign of his craziness he figured, and when he saw the sign for Saxon's Farm Fresh on 91st, he pulled off the highway toward Cheney. He'd never been this way. Then he turned into the parking lot and got out. What he needed was something he hadn't grown himself—he didn't know what. He looked at the Royal Red Apricots big as tennis balls, felt their soft blushing skins, passed up the smaller strains of apricots, the sweating peaches and plums the tiny fruit flies were busily swarming, and went inside the small pole barn where a young girl, so young her breasts were barely suggestions under the tight blue striped tank top, was heaving on a big butcher knife embedded in a huge, long watermelon. When it broke open, the juices ran pink, he could just tell they were cold and sweet, and the meat shown that red ripe it got just before it turned mealy. He watched her wrap a half carefully in plastic, then heft it in both hands and carry it over to an open cooler to sit on top of the whole melons, all of which were impossible in their size, large enough for entire families of parents and kids, cousins and grandparents, uncles, aunts, in-laws, these were picnic and party and family reunion melons—all much too large.

She wrapped the other half, then suddenly looked up at him. She was a very young girl, just on the verge of sullenness and lipstick, already unwilling to smile at any adult. Just as suddenly he wanted to please her—Is that for sale, he asked stupidly, grateful when she simply nodded.

You want it? she asked, cradling it like a baby in her arms, unmindful of the wet against her shirt.

Yes, he said and followed her to the make-shift checkout counter.

Can you put it in something so it doesn't drip all over? He paid the two dollars and watched as she hauled out a recycled Sun Mart bag and slid the melon half in. He could have sworn it wouldn't fit, but it did when she lifted and held the two flimsy handles out to him. He'd never trust a plastic bag, so he took the melon into his own arms, cradling it as she had, feeling the deep cold seep into his shirt, calming the heat that had been waiting there all afternoon.

In the truck, he made sure the safety was on the shotgun, and tipped it so the butt rested on the floor and the barrel was wedged against the door, pointing out the back window. He shoved the photo album over so the watermelon could sit beside him, pressing its cold nose against his leg like his dog used to, as he turned around and headed back the way he'd come. He kept seeing himself delivering the melon, so rich and cold, the sweet flesh filling their mouths until they laughed. They'd have it for dinner—they'd eat the whole thing in one sitting, just the two of them, and not once, not once would she glance out the porch window toward the tall rows of corn pressing against the yard fence, her face filled with a kind of longing that hurt to look at. He'd tell her then that gods are just dreams with deadlines, and that he was never going to leave her. And although he knew this wasn't going to work, he had to try because they were both crazy in this heat and the lunch was going rancid and the gun was bouncing dangerously beside him and a man, no, a person, had to feel like they weren't going to be put aside just because they hadn't suffered enough.

Barbara Schmitz

Barbara Schmitz

BARBARA SCHMITZ grew up in Plattsmouth, Nebraska, where the Platte and Missouri Rivers meet. Except for two years in Garden Grove, California, she has lived on the plains and traveled to exotic, wonderful places including Naxos, Greece; Ladekh and Kashmir, India; Konya, Turkey (to the tomb of the mystical poet, Rumi); Bali, and, most recently, Jerusalem and other parts of Israel. She has degrees from Wayne State College, and UNO, and has studied writing at Naropa Institute where she was Allen Ginsberg's apprentice. Other writing teachers included John Neihardt, William Stafford, and Kathleen Spivack. It was from Ginsberg (and Stafford) that she learned to engage in the writing process, allowing 'something to occur.' Other influences are her family, Jungian psychology, Sufism, and her students at Northeast College (where she taught writing and literature for 30 years) who wanted to read accessible poems.

Her full-length poetry book, *How to Get Out of the Body,* was published by Sandhills Press in November 1999. She has a second book of poems forthcoming from Backwaters Press. Her chapbooks are *Making Tracks* (Suburban Wilderness Press), *The Lives of the Saints* (Main-Travelled Roads), and *The Upside Down Heart* (Sandhills Press, 2003). Other recent publications have been in *The Logan House Anthology of 20th Century American Poetry, Times of Sorrow/Times of Grace, The Nebraska Poet's Calendar,* and *Escaping the Yellow Wallpaper: Women's Encounters with the Mental Health Establishment.*

MARGE: What was your childhood like, and what was there that may have pointed you toward writing?

BARBARA: I grew up in Plattsmouth and went to Catholic school. I had two older brothers who finally admitted about two years ago that they were mean to me. (laughter) I was the only girl in the neighborhood so I was the one they always tied to the pole and stuck with the plastic knives. I learned to scream and my mom would come running out of the house with her dish towel, saying, "You leave her alone! You leave her alone!"

They'd say, "Oh, we didn't do anything to her. She's just yelling." My middle brother had to give me a ride to school on his bicycle. He always pushed me off about a half block from school.

My dad worked for the city water department so we would walk there at noon and he'd give us a ride home, because we had an hour for lunch. We had our big meal at noon and then walked back to school with plenty of time to diddle around. My brothers always ditched me. That was probably the beginning of being a writer because I walked by myself and looked at everything. They didn't want me, their ugly sister, tagging along. They built a shock machine with their erector set, put two batteries in, and would turn the crank and shock me. They'd get me to hold the handle because they gave me attention. All their friends would come over, and I'd sit there and get shocked. (laughter)

At Catholic school with the nuns, I was a good little kid, but I was still intimidated, so it made me very quiet, I think, and watching my P's and Q's, not wanting to do anything wrong because I didn't want to be humiliated.

MARGE: I believe you have a story about not being allowed to sing in the choir.

BARBARA: It think it was about third or fourth grade when I had to stand up in front of everybody and sing while Sister played the piano. I didn't know what to sing because we never sang at home. I can't remember what I decided to sing, but when I got done, she turned around and said, "It's no use, Barbara, you will never be able to carry a tune. Go

We drive up to Barbara's two-story house in Norfolk. She welcomes us and brings us through the back door into the gracious home she has made for her family. We admire the art and antiques and the photographs Bob has taken of Barbara and their son Eli. We are soon seated at Barbara's round oak table before a window filled with ferns, blooms, and foliage.

sit down."

I was the only kid in the whole school who didn't get to sing in the choir. I had to stay in the room and do my math assignment when they all went to choir practice. For years, I could hear Sister saying,"You'll never be able to carry a tune." When people sang Christmas carols, I wouldn't even try to sing. But in the poem in my book, I lock Sister in and stick her head in the piano. (laughter)

MARGE: Your schooling must be quite a source of material.

BARBARA: Those poems keep popping up. They're not quite all done yet.

MARGE: And you've written about your mother and father.

BARBARA: Quite a lot. My new book, soon to be published, has a whole mother section.

I think had my mother been born in a different time, she would have been a feminist and maybe a grade school principal or had a day care center or something. She was very good at playing with kids. When she played with our son Eli, she'd be having as much fun as he did. Just entered the space and played. Eli would cry for a long time when his grandma would leave, because she was his best playmate.

The Depression had an effect on my parents. They were engaged for five years and didn't have any money. My dad was breaking rock at the rock quarry in Louisville and giving the money to his parents so they could save the family farm. He wanted to be a farmer but my mother said, "No, I cannot be a farmer's wife." She got him a job at the city water department where she was a bookkeeper. They moved to town and he did that his whole life.

My mother canned thousands of jars of green beans and apricots and cherries and pickles. My parents had one whole city lot for the garden. They fed us through our childhood from the garden and the fruit trees. We would have enough potatoes, carrots, and onions to last all winter.

SHELLY: How do you think you are like your mother?

BARBARA: At her ninetieth birthday, I thanked her for the gift of stubbornness and persistence, which is what you need to be a writer. I thought I wasn't like her at all because I didn't want a domestic life, and I didn't want to spend time taking care of a garden. I wanted to get as far away from that as possible. But in values and ways of approaching life, and in conserving, we are the same even though our lifestyles were different. She was a very devout Catholic. That was our big battle, because she couldn't understand why I would reject this gift they had given me. I didn't reject it. It's all in me. It formed my character; it simply has a different form now. She struggled with that; she thought I was going to hell because I didn't go to Mass anymore, and *she* was probably going to hell because I didn't go to Mass anymore. Finally, about a month before she died, she said, "Are you right with God?"

I said, "Yes, absolutely."

She said, "Well, then it's okay." She was able to let go of that. She was strong and took on death like nobody I've ever seen. On the way to the nursing home she gave instructions: take my coats down to the Senior Citizens' Center this winter, and I want my wedding dress to go to the youngest granddaughter. If there's anything in the house you want, go get it. And then one day she sat up in bed and said, "Oh, what have I done with my life?"

I said, "You want me to tell you what you've done with your life?"

"Yes, what have I done?"

So I went through all the canning she'd done, and all the fruit and the vegetables, and the jars, and her kids she had raised and all the roses she had pruned. And she said, "Well, then it's okay." She took death on like an incredible warrior.

SHELLY: How are you like your father?

BARBARA: Hmmm. That's a little harder. My dad and I were always struggling for something we could find in common to talk about and we never did find it. He would continually tell me about football teams and I wouldn't know what he was talking about, but he couldn't think of anything else to tell me. (laughter) He was creative and hardworking. He carved all of the names of his children and his grandchildren out of wood, and did other creative projects in his workshop. I think actually he was more creative than my mom.

MARGE: Do you remember a time when somebody regarded you as a writer or made you think you wanted to be a writer? How soon did that happen and what form did that take?

BARBARA: Allen Ginsberg told me I should take myself seriously as a writer. He said, "You should be reading."

I said, "Oh, I'm reading a lot," and I named all the books I was reading.

He said "No, you should be *giving* readings." He went through my notebook. His eyes kind of popped, and he said, "Did you write all this?"

I said "Yes. Is that a lot? "

He said, "That's a lot." He asked me questions about how I wrote. He really took me seriously.

MARGE: Was there a teacher or relative before Ginsberg?

BARBARA: No, I would say I was discouraged rather than encouraged. When I was a kid, I would make little books, but nobody paid any attention, so I didn't pay much attention. I won a DAR essay contest in high school, and I took a creative writing class in college, but I can't remember that I was particularly encouraged.

SHELLY: How did you get to Allen Ginsberg? What took you that route?

BARBARA: A friend of ours, actually. We went to visit him at Naropa. I was about thirty, and I thought, "If I'm going to be a writer, I guess I better do something about it."

MARGE: Ginsberg asked you how you wrote. What was your process like at first and what is it like now?

BARBARA: When I studied with Ginsberg, he gave assignments such as to write for an hour without stopping, and talk into a tape recorder for an hour and a half without stopping, to see what happens when you hear your voice making sounds all that time. I would write several times a week, just open my notebook and not be too concerned with product, just doing the process. It's like that now when I'm writing poetry. If I haven't written for a while, maybe there's nothing that's too interesting, but if I'm doing it regularly, there's a poem almost every day.

Filling the blank page is like a psychic process; things start flowing through you. But when writing a novel, you've got to plan it and use your intellect . You have to figure out how this thing is going to tie together, and it has to have a plot. I find that harder because I'm more in my head. Most of my writing that's good doesn't come from my head, it comes from some place else in my body. I don't know the form as well for the novel, and I don't have the form crafted so I can forget about it and just write. With poetry, since I've written so long, I'm not worrying about form. Poems are not so much an intellectual thinking process.

I try to walk if I'm working on something. Lots of times I get a first line when I'm walking and that comes out of the rhythm of the walk.

I am interested in how body work affects writing. Both Natalie Goldberg and Julia Cameron talk about writing coming from the body. I would sometimes have my students walk for five or six minutes and then write. Some of them just didn't get it. I said, "Wear warm coats and scarves and gloves because I want you to walk outside. You can't talk to somebody; this is a meditation. You're clearing out the day, you're setting a rhythm, and then you're going to write." Afterward, everybody that wanted to would read aloud what they had written. That's how I started class the last two or three years, and suggested that, if they were stuck at home during their writing time, they should use part of the time to walk, and see if that made a difference.

One of my students was *so* in his head and I kept saying, "I wish you'd get out of your head, into your body."

He said, "I don't know what you mean."

Another student in the class was studying yoga, so I asked, "Could you do some yoga for us in class next time?" Of course, the one that needed it wasn't there, (laughter) but we all wore comfortable clothes, we did yoga, and then we wrote.

That's when I wrote the poem called "Yoga," about being pregnant with Eli. In the poem, I'm standing on the step doing a yoga posture. The poem was written twenty years after Eli was born, but it came right out of doing the yoga postures.

SHELLY: Has your teaching style changed over the years?

BARBARA: I turned to having students do much more writing in class. Read and write, read and write. I didn't do so much of that in the beginning; it was more assignments to do at home. Later, I was using the group energy more. I'd say, "It isn't a big deal; we're just writing and reading, and writing and reading. Sometimes it will be good and sometimes not so good; sometimes you don't even know, and it doesn't make any difference." As the class went on, they got much more relaxed and almost everybody wanted to read.

MARGE: How did your friendship with Natalie Goldberg figure in your writing and in your creative process?

BARBARA: I liked what she read in the Naropa workshop, and so I went up and started talking to her, but she kind of ignored me. I talked to her another time and then she said, "Well, do you want to meet in the cemetery and read poems to each other?" (laughter) So we met in the cemetery.

The second time she took me to the New York Deli and told me she was going to buy me some chocolate cookies. I'm not real interested in sugar or chocolate, and as we walked up the hill to the townhouses in Boulder, she ate the whole sack of cookies. (laughter) So that was the beginning.

I brought her here to Northeast Community College to be my first visiting writer. She had a lot of energy and the students liked her. That was before she was famous; she was just a person who was writing. It got a little strange because she became famous and I was nobody. She was getting books published and I didn't have anything published.

In her last book, she has a whole chapter on how I learned to write. She came to finish out my visiting writers series before I retired, and she remarked then that we were able to really be together and go deep, while a lot people she knew in the beginning had quit writing and it was sometimes hard to be with them, because they were envious and not writing anymore.

Natalie was a checkpoint. Every once in a while she'd get a packet of poems from me. After our last reading she said, "Well, do you want me to talk about the poems you read?"

I said, "Oh, they're out in the car."

She said, "Well, if you want to go get them, we can talk about them."

I said, "No, I know they're good. You don't have to put your stamp on them."

SHELLY: Are there some things that would have further nurtured and encouraged your writing at any point?

BARBARA: There was a dark time when some discouraged my writing as much as possible and excluded me from readings. That was painful. But then one year Marge heard me read at the Nebraska Literature Festival and invited me to write with her, which we did for a couple of years. She introduced me to the Prairie Trout group, and all of a sudden I felt I had a community that was supporting me. That was a turning point. I had felt I was alone, writing, and nobody was seeing it, nobody was appreciating it. I was busy raising Eli, so I didn't get poems sent out in the mail. That was a time when I would have liked some friend close by to talk to and get encouragement from. Where I will choose to live in my retirement will have to have a writing community. I have a writing group now; three of my former students, and then Lisa Sandlin comes sometimes, and so that's very supportive.

MARGE: Do you have any advice about forming groups?

BARBARA: I think you need at least one writing friend. At least one and maybe two that you can show work to and get feedback from. I suppose you could do that in the mail if you had somebody that corresponded with you.

MARGE: I know that your husband has been very supportive of your writing.

BARBARA: Yes. I was working on my novel Sunday and thinking, "Oh, this is no good. Spending all these years on this, and this is no good." So I asked Bob, "Can I read you a little bit of this?" He was very enthusiastic about it. He's always been there, coming to my readings or taking care of Eli so I could go to writing events.

MARGE: Has traveling to India been important to your writing?

BARBARA: I think not just India, but Turkey and Bali, seeing those cultures and perspectives and different states of consciousness. We traveled with my spiritual teacher, Shahabuddin David Less, so that's been a huge influence.

MARGE: Your spiritual teacher has been a huge influence?

BARBARA: Yes, right. During the recent seminar with him, he took my book and read my poems to everybody. He read about six or seven poems and did some teaching and then at the end of the session, he read a couple more and said, "These are Barbara's poems, this is her book, and it's for sale." I sold all my books except one and he asked, "What's my commission?" (laughter)

I said, "Well, here's the last book; you can have it."

I don't know if people understand my poems because some of them are about spiritual experiences, but my spiritual teacher always gets them. I figure at least there's one person out there that experiences them deeply. It's very interesting to hear this male read my poems; he reads them very well. It's a different experience having the poem come back to me that way. He's a kind, smart, funny person who is a model for how I want to be in my life.

SHELLY: Is your teacher here in this area?

BARBARA: He lives in Sarasota, Florida. Bob and I have traveled with him. He likes to take people to exotic, sacred places. We went to Bali and to India and to Rumi's tomb in Turkey. It's a spiritual teaching to travel with a group of people and have to put up with what you have to put up with. It forces you either to break or learn to be flexible and grow.

SHELLY: That's an interesting perspective because usually I want a vacation to be perfect.

BARBARA: The places he takes you, let me tell you, it ain't perfect. (laughter) Usually nothing works.

SHELLY: Can you tell us a couple of moments where it was very powerful, and maybe later did enter some of your writing?

BARBARA: I have a long poem, "After India" (published in *Times of Sorrow/Times of Grace)*. That experience was like flash after flash after flash. One of the most powerful moments was when we stayed in a resort in the Himalayas. Some of us rode horses and some walked to the top of the mountain. It was during the war with Pakistan. We were in Kashmir, where the US government had advised us not to go, but we climbed to the top of the mountain and danced and prayed for peace. More than forty of us were gathered around a rock, which for us was representing the conflict. We were all touching it and praying. The Kashmir horsemen asked, "What are they doing?" The translators told them we were praying for peace, and the horsemen began to cry, saying, "But it isn't even their country. They came all this way to pray for peace?"

MARGE: I've heard you talk about the all-night chanting and the dancing when Eli was a baby.

BARBARA: The Kundalini Yoga people, who are Sikhs, believe if you say this chant on the summer solstice two and a half hours before sunrise, and if you chant continuously, you will be enlightened. A group of us went to a farm near Winside the night before the solstice and camped out. We got up at 3:30 in the morning and climbed to the top of the hill and started chanting over and over. I had Eli in a baby carrier on the front of my body. Right before daylight, the music just shot through me and I started dancing the chant. I grabbed people's hands and danced about the last half hour with Eli bouncing on my chest. Then as we were going back to the house, we kept looking for the sun but couldn't see it. We thought maybe it was going to be a cloudy day. Somebody in the house popped a champagne cork, and just then the huge orange disc of the sun was visible.

We've done this chanting ritual lots of places. One time when Eli was little, Bob and I were on the roof for the chanting, and Eli woke up. I got him and took him out on the roof. I told him what the chant was and he said, "I can't say that." I told him I would say it for him. Then he chanted a little bit, and an owl hooted. Eli's animal has always been the owl, so I said, "Ah, Eli, it's working."

SHELLY: It seems an amazing journey from a very Catholic upbringing to this spiritual dimension in your life. What are some of the difficulties of that, living in Nebraska, a very conservative place?

BARBARA: My neighbor was saying, "Oh, I get so sick of people thinking I'm weird because I'm a Democrat."

I said, "Hey, Bud, how would you feel being a Democrat and also having some sort of strange religion here in the Bible Belt?" (laughter) We just kind of do what we do.

To my spiritual teacher I said, "I get tired of feeling like the town weirdo."

He said, "Well, let me tell you something."

I said, "What?"

He said, "You *are* the town weirdo." (laughter) Somebody has to do it.

SHELLY: When did you become interested in this religion?

BARBARA: Sufism (The Sufi Order of the West) technically isn't a religion. It's a mystical teaching, strictly noncompulsory, based on experience, being polite, opening your heart, seeing the Divine in everything and everyone.

I stopped going to the Catholic Church because it didn't seem to have any meaning for me. Shortly after we moved to Norfolk, the Transcendental Meditation people came to town and gave a class on TM. We were interested in that, and we let them use our house. We started doing TM probably about 1970. We got interested in Buddhism. You can blame it on the Beatles. (laughter) It was George Harrison who took all the Beatles to India and they met the Maharishi.

SHELLY: Why is writing so important to you? Why is it important to write?

BARBARA: It's lots of things for me. I see my own mind and I see how my mind is working. Writing is great for your memory. I remember minute details from years and years ago, because I am noticing always and writing it down. I embrace my life.

When you write, your life becomes precious because you're witnessing it and embracing it and writing it all down. Writing makes your life so rich.

I wrote for a long time without publishing a book, but that didn't matter because there were lots of other wonderful benefits. For me it was a kind of meditation. If you do a writing practice, you're spewing out all the junk, which is quite akin to meditation. Writing was the one thing that really centered my life, that was always there, that was constant, that I did no matter what.

SHELLY: As a teacher, was it difficult for you to get students to understand why poetry is important, or why the writing life is rewarding?

BARBARA: For the comp students who don't have a deep abiding interest in writing or literature, it was difficult. I got frustrated trying to explain why literature would be important. When I retired I said, "Well, now I don't have to tell people why it's important to read anymore!" (laughter)

It was such a struggle because there's so much media stuff and I was trying to tell them why their lives would be better with reading, and what's lacking without it. Some who found their way into the writing classes seem to have that need, already, to write. There was something pushing them in that direction. While maybe they were not as ambitious as I would have liked, they still thought it was important for them for some reason.

SHELLY: Do you miss teaching?

BARBARA: Because I'm so engrossed in writing the novel, I haven't thought about teaching. There are wonderful moments in teaching where everything clicks. Somebody asks a question and you come up with something to say that you hadn't ever thought before. There's all this exciting energy. That was the wonderful part of it, but I used a lot of my creativity just to motivate students. I would spend time thinking about what to do to get them interested. I was burned out. Coming home, I didn't have as much to bring to my work as I wanted to. I had a couple of night classes besides the day classes, and I ran a visiting writers series which was the equivalent of another whole class and which I got no release time for, so it was a big job. But I imagine that I will teach again somehow, somewhere.

MARGE: What was the first poem you fell in love with?

BARBARA: Probably something in grade school. The nuns made us memorize poems like "The Owl and the Pussycat." I liked that stuff. I thought, "Gee, these are neat:

Elbows and knees
are mysteries
of which I become aware,
dwindled at night
to half my height,
and folded up in prayer.

Where do they go?
I do not know,
when on my bed I've laid me,
but crooked or straight
may I give great
glory to God that made me.

I learned that in second or third grade.

MARGE: What makes good teaching?

BARBARA: Somebody who's really alive and vital. I think teachers teach themselves. The material is just an excuse to talk about things. One of the best teachers I've experienced was a Sikh Bob and I met when we went to visit friends at the University of Santa Cruz. Our friend took us to class, which was taught by this little Sikh, who said, "Oh, these things are just excuses for us to get together and exchange some love." While we were in class Bob and I could see a small heart painted on his face about where his third eye was, but when we went up and looked at him he didn't have any heart painted there. There was a rosy aura around him. We were just some friends of one of his students, but he sat down and spent a couple of hours with us as if we were his long lost friends. A year later we came back. He was sitting on the same bench. We walked up and he said, "Oh, it seems as if just yesterday we were speaking." That guy was a great teacher. He was full of love and light and knowledge and he sat down and shared it with you.

SHELLY: Are there things to try to avoid when you have students who are just beginning, whether it be in high school or college?

BARBARA: What Allen Ginsberg did was to pick out what he liked. He'd say, "Why waste time talking about what you don't like?" I try to find something good that we can emphasize and say, "Do more; try to do some more like that." People have tender egos, and those taking little baby steps are so vulnerable, especially in a first writing class. If somebody jumps on you and says, "That's wrong," some will never write again.

In San Francisco recently, I took an advanced fiction workshop. The two teachers did not have grace in the way they talked about another's writing. I got helpful information, but the day they critiqued my work, Bob had to sort of pick me up and put me back together. The instructors told one man to throw his away and start over, and he left. He said he had a family emergency and had to leave, and then before he walked out he said to the teachers, "I don't know why you thought you had to be so rude to me." After he walked out, one of the teachers whispered to the other one, "Should we address that?" The other said, "No, let's go on." He never addressed it.

I had a private conference with him at the end of the week and he was encouraging. He said, "I know I was real hard on you."

I said, "Yes, you were."

He said, "But I'm rooting for you to pull this together." Those two didn't know a whole lot about teaching writing. They could use some lessons in how to talk about what people could do to improve their work without making them feel so pulverized. The class cost a lot of money, too—a lot of money to get beat up! (laughter). The man who was told to throw his away was the most needy person. He was some kind of CEO and was trying this book out. I've been writing for thirty years and have received a lot of rejections slips, so I thought, "Oh, I'm going to be all right." But if Bob hadn't been there, I don't know if I would have been all right or not.

MARGE: What poets do you think young writers should read? What novels?

BARBARA: I've just been reading James Salter, who is wonderful. His work is so poetic and intense and beautiful. I think for anybody who wants to write fiction, he would be great. I love Susan Minot for fiction; she has a new book called *Evening*. I'm reading some Somerset Maugham. I think for fiction, writers should read a whole lot to see who they feel affinity for. You start by reading. There is so much out there. It's just exploding.

For poets, I think people like e.e. cummings and some of those wonderful old experimenters are great. Young people should not limit themselves only to contemporary writers.

Another important thing is to go to readings. I didn't understand poetry until I went to the nightly readings at Naropa. Words just started washing over me, and I understood about sound and, for a while, didn't even listen to meaning. That was a wonderful experience. I recommend students go to live readings, and also watch those Bill Moyers tapes of poetry readings and interviews.

I also think writers should read people in their own region. There are tons of wonderful Nebraska poets. Read local people for sure. And get excited about some one you have an affinity for. I taught Sharon Olds for years because I felt she was addressing things that were relevant to the students.

SHELLY: Your work in progress now is the novel. Do you want to say anything about that yet?

BARBARA: It's very hard. (laughter) I don't know if I'd advise somebody to do that without going to school and studying how to do it because I've been working on it for ten years. I could only work in the summers because I couldn't work at fiction when I was teaching. There was so much I didn't know and I finally learned how to do a plot and tie all that together but there was so much more I needed. What I do want to say is I think if you start something as a writer you really need to finish it. People say, "Well, if it's so much trouble, why don't you just walk away from it.?"

And I say, "I can't do that! I've started this, I've committed so much of myself to it, I have to finish it the best I can, make it as good as I can make it." It would be really bad for me, I think, to walk away from it. So I'm learning how. I didn't like revising when I first started writing. I just hated it. And Ginsberg always taught, "First thought, best thought." That's nice, because you don't have to do anything over. (laughter) It was hard for me to revise. Now I'm enjoying it because when I sit down there's already something on the page. I don't have to pull it out of myself every day as you do when you write a poem or do your writing practice. There's already something there.

Some people are more naturally poets or more naturally storytellers; I'm not a person who is a big storyteller. Bob loves to tell stories; he'll start way back at the very beginning and go on and on and on. (laughter) I don't do that; I want to get to the point and say it and get out. Writing fiction is counter to my way of writing generally. I had to learn how to sit for long periods of time.

Now I don't have a clock and I don't have a watch. When I came back from India, all my watches either broke or fell off or disappeared or the band broke or they quit. I went through about four or five watches and finally I said, "Okay, I get it. I'm not supposed to wear a watch."

I go into my writing room and I work and I don't even know what time it is. When I was a young writer I was always looking at the clock, wondering, "How long do we have to sit here?" I've learned it's going to take as long as it takes.

I've also learned to develop things in more detail. Some of my poems now are longer than they used to be. I used to complain to Allen Ginsberg, "My poems are so short."

He said, "Well, what's wrong with short poems? William Carlos Williams wrote nice little short poems."

Short poems were all I could manage in the beginning. Now I have some poems that are two or three pages. That's probably an influence of the fiction.

SHELLY: Are you still writing poetry as you are working on the novel?

BARBARA: I haven't very much. Mostly I'm working on the novel. Also I'm trying to send poems out and trying to find places to send my poetry manuscript.

SHELLY: Is there anything you really want to do, down the road, whether it's travel or other goals?

BARBARA: I want to travel some more. Bob and I are going to Sarasota in January to take a month-long seminar with our teacher.

I have a file with some essays in it. I would be interested in doing some essays, but I have to finish the novel first.

My mother gave me all the letters my father wrote to her when he lived in Weeping Water and she lived in Plattsmouth in the thirties. He came to see her only when his brother came in with his Model T. A couple of years before she died she said, "I've read all these letters, and there's nothing in them that I care if you see. Would you like to have them?"

I read some aloud at our family Christmases when she was still alive. I said, "I'm going to read you a couple of letters that Dad wrote to Mom." So she heard me read them to the family. I wouldn't mind doing something with them. Maybe that could be some kind of historical novel where they could be the characters. I could use that time period, the Depression. I think probably I'll have to have a project or I'll have a panic attack. (laughter)

SHELLY: You told us some great stories about you and your brothers. Can you go back again, to a story about you as a child that foreshadowed who you were to become?

BARBARA: Well, my mother always wanted to buy me dolls because she loved dolls. She was so happy when she finally got a little girl after she had those two boys. I had no interest in dolls. I didn't understand what they were for, what we were supposed to do with them. One Christmas she asked me what I wanted and I said, "I want a book and prayer book."

She said, "That's what you want for Christmas? Don't you want a doll?"

I said "No." So I got a doll and a book and a prayer book. My mother was totally astonished that this kid just wanted a book and a prayer book. I always had the interest in reading.

When I was about twelve, I'd read all the Hardy Boys and all the Nancy Drews and all the nurse Pat and the kids' stuff. I had read everything in the library, so I said to the librarian, "I can't find anything to read. I've read all this and this and this."

She looked at me and said, "My dear, you can read anything you want in the library."

I said, "You mean I can go into the adult section?"

She said, "Anything." So she gave me the whole library when I was twelve years old.

Gift

My husband says
I must forgive her,
Sister Anita, who made me
audition for choir standing
in front of the whole 4th, 5th,
and 6th grade classes.
She plucking the piano
like an unforgiven chicken
and me standing staring
at the rough wooden floorboards,
my heart not yet learned
its songs to sing.

He says I must forgive her
even though she said,
"It's no use," and branded me
with the permanent stain of "never."
"Never," she repeated
"be able to carry a tune."
He says I must forgive
even that I was the only one
forced to remain behind
doing my math assignment
while every other child
joined the angel army
trooping off to practice
sweet carols for Midnight Mass.

And I must forgive
that I couldn't be there
even pretending I was singing
for the Baby Jesus when
the Christmas Eve star faded
into morning light.
I must, he says, think
of something good to say
about her: big stony woman
in dragging black robe
and steel-rimmed glasses.

She's probably stuck somewhere
in the ether, he says,
head locked inside a piano
having to hear disembodied
squeaky voices for all eternity.

I CAN'T THINK OF ANYTHING

Then I remember her explanation
of eternity changing me
from carefee child to weathered
philosopher,
chin on my hand, staring
into summer evening.
The hummingbird flicking his tail
on the earth-sized ball
of hardest imaginable metal
only once every 100 years.
How long it would take
to wear it away, she said,
was only an instant of eternity.
My spirit nearly left my body
speeding heavenward visualizing
that bird, that ball, that endless
flowing ribbon of time, time, time.

I Kiss You

I kiss you, Mother, in eternity.
Where are you flying
this hot July day?
You didn't want to clean.
You'd done enough on earth.
One room a day,
floor always scrubbed.

You can come visit.
See earth's sparkle
through my eyes.
Would you like India?
the heat, the hot spices,
stinky, strong smells?

You'd want to hold the babies—
each new great grandchild—
and play with them like you
did our son. He'd cry
for a half hour when you'd leave.

Did you get enough of this planet
when old and bent and sick
you decided not to eat?
Sweet brown eyes,
radiant daylight smile,
I love you.

Our differences—religion—
whatever—seem tiny
like little playhouses
seen from the sky.

Two-Step

We're dancing
My father and me
This isn't the dress
I planned to wear
That one was pink
This one is green but
the pink one tore
when I was washing it

I don't feel very pretty
at this fancy wedding
But my father and I
are shuffling along
He's not good at dancing
I always thought
I could have been
but didn't get dance lessons
and turn to stone
when anyone looks at me

He's shorter
like he is with my mother
We're banging toes
like our lives that only bumped
didn't match smooth
didn't reach deep
into each other's language—
foreign tongues

He'd say football
I'd say poem
He's smiling
So am I
It's our last
but we don't know

Test

The morning of my 50th birthday party
I assist the oral surgeon
extracting my husband's tooth in bits,
suctioning the blood and spraying water
on the drill with a rubber ball,
flaps of cut flesh, surgeon digging
deep with a silver metal hook.

My hand shakes but I know
standing there by the metal chair
I'll do what I need to do
just like my father who had his eye
and part of his face removed
and said, "You never know what
you'll have to go through"
and my mother who changed
the bandage even when she didn't
want to look at the wound,
flushing and cleaning out the cavity.

She'd cry when he wasn't around
about how handsome he used to be.
He'd face the camera without
his eye patch. No complaints.
Her. Him. They're standing with me
as clearly as my mother held my hand
when I learned to walk, my father
sat beside me teaching me to drive.
We're here doing what's required.
Passing life's little pop quizzes.

Yoga

Yoga

I stand on the edge
of the top porch step
balancing on one leg
in a modified bow
Husband stopped below
Arms full of wood
mouth gaping

Be careful he yells
I AM I AM I AM I say
Baby inside echoes
I AM I AM I AM
Be safe he adds
I AM I AM I say

Baby inside center
perfectly centered
Both of us
Round belly
Round baby
Completely whole
together and separately
I AM
WE ARE
I AM YOU
I AM ME
WE ARE WE

And Father Father
makes the Holy Trinity
In a few more days
a hatching
a Nativity

Charles Fort

Charles Fort

Born in 1951 in New Britain, Connecticut, poet CHARLES FORT holds the Paul W. and Clarice Kingston Reynolds Chair in Poetry at the University of Nebraska—Kearney. He is the recipient of a MacDowell Fellowship, the Randall Jarrell Poetry Prize, the Open Voice Award, and the Mary Carolyn Davis Memorial Award. His books include *The Town Clock Burning* (St. Andrews Press, 1985; reprinted 1991, by Carnegie Mellon) and *Darvil* (St. Andrews Press, 1993), as well as *We Did Not Fear the Father, As the Lilac Burned the Laurel Grew, Immortelles, The Vagrant Hours,* and *Afro Psalms,* all Reynolds Chair Books, University of Nebraska at Kearney Press. His poetry has appeared in *Best American Poetry 2000, Best of Prose Poem International, The American Poetry Review, Georgia Review, Prairie Schooner,* and others. He holds the MFA from Bowling Green State University. Fort's newest collection is *Frankenstein Was A Negro* (Logan House Press, 2002).

MARGE: You have a new book. Let's begin by talking about that, and about your other books.

CHARLES: The new book is a book of prose poems, number two of the Darvil trilogy. My first book, *The Town Clock Burning,* was, as first books are, a mixture of so many things. I had originally a thousand pages that I cut down to fifty-three. I had everything I'd written since second grade and I didn't want to put that in. (laughter) The two short stories I wrote as a little lad in second grade. One was the Three Little Bears, my version, and then a Halloween story called "Boo," with twenty-seven O's in "Boo."

I was influenced by Richard Hugo's letter poems and I had thought of doing a book of letter poems. Books of prose poems were rare then, and still are. Darvil is the character based on a short story I had written many years before. Darvil, part evil, devil. I took that character for the entire trilogy.

Years later, during an AWP panel on the prose poem, Robert Bly and others mentioned Darvil; that was a good moment. When I sent the poems off in 1985, I got some back from an editor saying, "What is this?" The poem "Frankenstein was a Negro" went on to be in *The Best of Prose Poem International.* In a recent article, I talk about the dismantling of someone, "the other," putting him back together. I'm taking ownership of the invisible man.

I like the cover of the new book *Frankenstein Was A Negro*. My mother may not like it, but she'll understand. She's my best agent. Mary Shelley, in creating Frankenstein, the contemporary monster, gave him Negroid features. The poems in the book are unlike anything I've written in a long time. I have a section on a blues musician, "In Memoriam for Robert Johnson." I take his titles and write responses. There are jazz and blues rhythms throughout the whole work.

As far as the third book in the trilogy, I told a reporter recently that I was going to title it "The Negro of the Rings."

MARGE: You mentioned some stories you had written as a child. Could you tell us about your

In Charles Fort's office, the walls are covered with posters advertising readings by poets and writers he has brought to the University of Nebraska-Kearney. Charles tells us about some of the readers and also explains that he keeps his office temperature cool because of his manuscript and photographic archives.

childhood? Something that might show that you were on your way to being a writer?

CHARLES: Certainly my parents were important in my becoming a writer. I tried to read every book in the New Britain Public Library. I was always allowed to write and recite poems. "Wynken, Blynken, and Nod" I recited in second grade. They made me stand up and do such things.

In high school, I lettered in three sports: cross country, indoor and outdoor track. People think because of my size I was a football player, but I was a runner. They called me a jock poet; I'd recite poems all the time on the streets of my hometown.

I might have learned my penchant for the quixotic, picaresque, and the urban surreal as a little lad on bicycle rides, weaving between the factories and tenements of my hometown in Connecticut.

SHELLY: When did you begin to call yourself a writer?

CHARLES: I knew I was a writer. As a freshman I submitted a poem to the college magazine, a poem called "Opened and Closed." I received second prize, $5.00. I thought I should have gotten first, of course. (laughter)

It was an important time, those creative writing classes. I founded and edited a college magazine, *Eclipse*, still being published there, an undergrad magazine.

The poem that got second prize ended up in my first book with a new title, "For Mailer and Jack." Strange how things are reinvented and come back.

MARGE: You've already mentioned some influences. Are there others?

CHARLES: The teachers I had in elementary school and junior high noticed something and kept me going. Books, poems, poets. *The New York Times* published a poem every day for years, right in the middle of the editorial page, and I read those. Housman's "Loveliest of Trees" probably turned me into a poet. Later, James Baldwin was very influential to my work. I found myself always attracted to Frost and Baudelaire.

SHELLY: Did your family think it odd that you were interested in poetry?

CHARLES: Our culture thinks it's odd, prefers the M.B.A. to the M.F.A. Even university faculty thinks it's odd. They don't understand what poets do.

MARGE: I'm looking at the posters and fliers here on your walls. Would you talk about your series of readings at UN-K?

CHARLES: I try to bring in all levels of discourse. There are also student readings; students are encouraged to read all the time, fiction as well as poetry. Having the students become poet-observers is my intent, to see the world more clearly and think more clearly.

The Reynolds Series is ongoing; originally it was for five years, and now it has a permanent budget. I brought in all kinds of folks and have others in mind: Alberto

Rios, Fred Chappell, Kelly Cherry, Seamus Heaney. People I've met over the years. I haven't even started bringing in my southern writers. I had a series in North Carolina, different voices, unusual voices.

SHELLY: Could you tell about the neighborhood where you grew up, the place you would call home?

CHARLES: I told people when I first landed here I felt I was in exile. I didn't mean that in a political sense, but in an imaginative sense, being here and connecting to memory and imagination, to my hometown. New Britain is between Boston and New York, right in the middle. We lived in tenements, a three-story house, three attic apartments on top. One of the factories where my father worked was half a block away. In the poems "We Did Not Fear the Father" and "The Worker," I refer to my father's life and work. He barbered from 9:00 to 5:00, then the 11:00 to 7:00 night shift and then landlord twenty-four hours a day in our tenement. Nine of us and a dog on the first floor. There was a factory on every street back then. They call what's left after factories are abandoned "brownfields." I've used that image in several poems, like "Ploughing the Brownfields."

SHELLY: How do you think you are like and unlike your father?

CHARLES: In the work. I probably send more work out and write more than any human I know. In lifestyle I am certainly different from my father. Unless they grew up in a factory town, few people know that lifestyle—going on strike, for example. Few people know about factories and strikes and families receiving mere dollars a week, the union, and the barrels of fire keeping them warm in snowfall. I am forever working class.

MARGE: How do you think this place, Nebraska, has influenced your work?

CHARLES: Many ways. It's isolated. I think it makes the imagination thrive even more.

I've been called a North Carolina writer, I've been in a Connecticut anthology, a Southern anthology, New Orleans, and Nebraska now. These are things publishers and editors tag on. They don't mean as much as publishers think they mean. It takes a while to adapt and I've incorporated Nebraska while I've been here because I'm here; it's where I live.

I consider myself a poet, primarily. If Eamonn Grennan can be an Irish poet, I can be an Afro-American poet, but the implications change. Race in America is much different from Ireland. What I mean about ownership is I'll call myself whatever I want to be called and if someone else responds differently, there are political implications.

SHELLY: What kind of influence did photography have in your life?

CHARLES: My father bought a Polaroid Land camera and later a 35 millimeter. I used to listen to the police radio, jump on my bicycle, and take photos of fires and local demonstrations. Photography helped me to be observant. I published photographs before poems.

In my classes I teach what I call "PhotoPoetics" where students respond to old family photographs. They don't even have to know the names of the people or the places. One of my students has done a whole sequence of photo-poetics for her master's thesis. She has poems based on photos from the 1920s.

Last semester I had my intro class do a three to five page poem based on photo-poetics. I have them research their family name and their family shield. They need three to five photos and 150 lines, minimum. This semester they are doing that in my Graduate Workshop, 250 lines minimum. They come up with interesting images that connect the narrative.

The last few years I've been scanning hundreds of photographs of my own that will be incorporated into a documentary.

SHELLY: What's the focus of the documentary?

CHARLES: The factories that were once there, interviewing the factory workers, some former and some at the one factory left. New Britain used to be called the "Hardware City of the World." Everything in your house was built there, including the family tools. "Hardware City of the World" and now it's nothing. The work is gone. The family farm disappeared; so did the factories. Since the 70s, 80s, gone, devastated.

MARGE: It seems that poetry is a form we use when we want to talk about loss, and those are certainly losses.

CHARLES: Poetry as a kind of recording. I've gone back to my hometown newspaper and looked at many different articles and my own photographs. It's an ongoing project; I'll do the documentary with or without grants.

SHELLY: Do you see your own poetry coming into that?

CHARLES: In fact, the poems in *Frankenstein Was A Negro* are specifically hometown poems that can be used, combining everything, the visual and the poems.

MARGE: Would you talk more about your teaching?

CHARLES: I teach my students what I know and what I do. I show them various prewriting and freewriting strategies that I use and they can use. I've taught a course I called "Freewriting," which means directed freewriting where they write in prose.

I write my poems in prose first, using 8 by 14 legal pads. At a sitting I can do fifty single-spaced pages, trusting intuition rather than reason, and then cut back. Five pages become four sonnets. Fifty pages become one poem. The freewrites can be based on one image or subject or the imagination.

I taught prosody here a few years ago. It's a rare course. I was doing what is called "new formalism" before the term even came out. *The Town Clock Burning* and others had a sense of form. There are great wars and fistfights at AWP, new formalism versus free verse. There are interesting developments in poetry. You just have to keep writing.

In my classes I teach the sonnet and the haiku. I give more specific topics in beginning than I do in advanced, help them create that narrative voice. I have them write about hometown, neighborhood, worst job, and looking into the window, which is looking into a place and describing everything in detail that might lead to metaphor and craft.

Haiku, as simple as it is, can be useful. Richard Wright, the African-American novelist, wrote nearly 7,000 haiku. Imagine, a novelist being influenced by the form. I found it fascinating how he was attracted to simplicity and imagery.

In my advanced classes I have students study the medieval echo verse, call and response. I introduced the students to it and they've done pretty well with that. They always do the prose poem and a poem of witness, sonnet, villanelle, and sestina—the mighty sestina. When they choose the six images for the sestina, they can do that at random, which I advise them against, or they can use related images.

I use a technique in my graduate advanced class I call PoetaFicta. I come in and put an image on the board, such as "Fool's Gold" or "Lie." That one image can become a poem, short story, novel, or film. They fill the page for about ten minutes. Then we read portions of what they have written. That has worked well.

SHELLY: Do you have a regular regimen for your own writing?

CHARLES: Right now my life is so haphazard, but usually I write in the morning and anytime after that to get something done. I write every day. The act of writing is thinking about it. Revising is writing. I'm constructing poems and ideas all the time. It's the curse of writing.

SHELLY: A lot of the struggle in poetry is to keep writing, to do the work, but also the mental part where we ask ourselves: "Gee, am I good enough?"

CHARLES: I've never lacked confidence, which I think is probably the greatest tool a writer can have. Writing can be taught. Confidence cannot.

So many myths young writers have about what it takes to be an artist and writer: the artist in the garret myth and the idea that a lifestyle of smoking or drinking or whatever promotes writing. They get into traps. They get into a lifestyle rather than the work.

I was fortunate that, before I graduated with my B.A., I attended Cranbrook Writers' Conference at the Cranbrook Art Academy three summers in a row. I went to Breadloaf twice. I got support like that. Breadloaf in 1972 for a little lad and again in 1974 was a remarkable experience. Talking with John Ciardi, Mark Strand, Robert Hayden under the oak tree, Isaac Asimov on the porch. It's a much different place now, much more diverse than it was then. In '72 there were only four or five blacks and I was the youngest.

I heard Robert Hayden read there. The other black writers were not kind to him, started laughing, making fun of him, said he wasn't political enough, even though his "Night Death In Mississippi" is one of the most horrifically beautiful poems about lynching you could ever imagine. They misread him. I never said anything to him. I never wrote him; I felt bad when he passed away years ago, but in my first book I do have a poem called "For Robert Hayden."

I have a line in one of my long poems "the only black man on the green mountain," but I made it there, which was remarkable for its time, having little of nothing, but I knew where to go somehow, how to get there.

SHELLY: Do you have poets that you recommend to students?

CHARLES: I have anthologies that contain everyone from Robert Hayden to T.S. Eliot to Hopkins, Etheridge Knight, Robert Frost. The list is so long.

SHELLY: Do you have a poet that you return to for renewal for yourself?

CHARLES: Well, Eliot. Housman, Hopkins, Hughes.

SHELLY: Are there goals you are pointed toward in the future?

CHARLES: I'm starting the Wendy Fort Foundation for Dance, Literature, and Film, providing scholarships and performances. That's coming in a formal announcement, to support literary events, music, dance, and art. Wendy worked with children and intergenerational groups.

I'm working on a book called *Poet's Wife* and a CD book of poetry and jazz, my earliest work transcribed into a CD. I want to get these done, so I can move on to the blank page.

I am always interested in the creative process, how we don't understand and can't control it, how poems do different things on the page that aren't necessarily clear to the reader or the poet. To me, words are magical. They do things beyond the page.

All language is political, I believe, in the sense of who has access to it, who doesn't, who's able to read, who isn't. I'm not talking about Democrat/Republican; I'm talking about the uses of language to determine who we are, who others think we are. Some of my most pastoral poems are my most political. "The writer writes what he has to write," as James Baldwin said when I interviewed him at Bowling Green.

And I think of the writer in Russia who wrote poems in prison on soap bars. Don't tell me that poetry doesn't connect through cultures, Carolyn Forche's *Poetry of Witness,* for example. We are fortunate to be in a culture where we can write without censorship, at least overt censorship.

MARGE: What advice do you give your students? Perhaps you got some advice from somebody sometime about writing or publishing or life in general. What kind of thing do you pass on to them?

CHARLES: Keep writing as if your life depended on it; of course, it does.

Rain Over the Brown Fields

Rain Over the Brown Fields

There was rain over the brown fields
And long knives thrown over the cliff
Into the hollow and a river was born.
We stood under the arc of human color
Two dreams, one heart, imperfect pairs
In winter and the winter light.
We found the sanctuary of thieves
Gathered behind the cathedral doors
The smoldering rocks inside the family pit
And nightbirds blown about the chimney.
There was one sighting of a miracle
That happened between two people
Three miles from hell's border
In a peasant's sword served to the world.

The Worker

The Worker

My father was a barber-surgeon
for thirty-nine years from nine to five,
a factory worker on the night shift
from eleven p.m. to seven a.m.
for thirty-eight of those years,
and a landlord in our three-story
tenement twenty-four hours a day.

On Saturdays it seemed as if
the entire Negro section of town
had grown long hair.
The sounds of shears still vibrate my ears.
I swept clouds into the wastebasket.
The back room contained hard whiskey
bookies and hidden magazines.

When my father came home at seven a.m.
lifting his black aluminum lunch box,
we seven children met him at the door,
knelt, and untied his shoes.
His tired eyes burned lines
into the side of that box.
Each of us wanted left-overs;
we grew older and took turns.
Steel ball-bearings turned in his hands
given to us as marbles
and the largest on the block.

They made my father a supervisor.
His white friends for thirty years
now turned from his voice.
Years before the U.S. army
broke his legs in basic training
and fused them for life.

When dust began to fill my father's bones
I learned how chronic arthritis
can lock together any old man.
From the back room I heard my name
and a razor being slapped against leather.
With magazines thrown into place
I carried out his clean towels.
I picked up clouds.

The Poem Found in Darvil's Back Pocket at the End of the Plains

The Poem Found in Darvil's Back Pocket at the End of the Plains

They lifted his belongings a bundle on a willow stick
and a poem about his father broad shouldered
and young on a fence post with his arms stretched along
the horizon. Was this how the poem skimmed
the Platte River like the sandhill cranes ankle deep
driven into a poisoned well and how they merged
half-alive with the land and marbled sky? His son
boarded a freight train from the Chicago rail yard
to Lincoln with its serpent eye collapsing into the bad-
lands and winding through a reservation for the dead
as he watched the lightning leave his father's flared
shadow a constellation across the plains.

Sonnet for Shelley

for Shelley Hutchinson Fort
born March 16, 1989, 11:07 a.m.

Sonnet for Shelley

One half of our lives is complete and brown.
Is that a paper bow tied to our newborn's neck
or the pink coffin kiss left by the devil's tongue?
Birth is twelve hours of fire and ash falling to the snow
and we curl our fingers and toes before we climb the ivy
and latch onto tumbleweed, tether, and pony tail.
Shelley is asleep in her mother's breath and water
and daughter Claire holds her plum crown and stares
into the dark and living blood of her sister's cord.
Shelley is asleep in her father's pulse and tambourine
and we gather to hear how the sounds of birth and death
merge and how a false start becomes the unexpected triumph
bound in spirit, flesh, and bone, and beauty, if it speaks,
is the other half of our lives complete and brown.

Prose Poem for Claire Aúbin Fort

(Born January 7, 1985, 3:23 a.m.)

Winter brings my wife a child, and your birth arrives with the morning tide like wings alive in a jar. The sunflower seeds and thorns bloom in your hands, Claire, and we walk in the mist and draw circles in the sand. I read your palms like a map, and there are small islands and mountain roads rising in your summer eyes. Is my daughter the dancer, actress, artist, gifted in language or song? I search the form and proper length to write one impossible verse to place into your hand. The unspoken metaphor falls like a meteor into this simple throne of time I've built for you, and your birth arrives with the morning tide like wings alive in a jar.

Hilda Raz

Hilda Raz

HILDA RAZ was born in Rochester, New York, educated at Boston University, and moved to Nebraska in 1963. She is a professor of English at the University of Nebraska-Lincoln, where she edits *Prairie Schooner.* Her poems, essays, articles, and reviews have been published in books from University Press of New England, Scribner's, Longstreet Press, Story Line Press, North Light Books, and the Bench Press as well as *The Colorado Review, Kenyon Review, Women's Review of Books, Judaism, North American Review, Literature in Medicine, Ploughshares,* and elsewhere. She has served as editor, scholar, and fellow at the Breadloaf Writer's Conference, and is a past president of Associated Writing Programs. She has also worked as an artist in the schools. Her books include *Trans* (Wesleyan UP, 2001), *What is Good* (Thorntree Books, 1988), *The Bone Dish* (now out in a second edition from State Street Press), and *Divine Honors* (Wesleyan UP, 1998). She is the editor of several anthologies, including *Living in the Margins: Women Writers on Breast Cancer* (Persea Books, 2000), and *The Prairie Schooner Anthology of Contemporary Jewish American Writing* (1998). In 2002 she received the Outstanding Research and Creative Activity Award from the University of Nebraska.

Hilda Raz has chosen The Mill for her interview. I've met her here many times to write, but today I have my tape recorder, not a notebook, on the table by the window when she arrives. The Mill is a lively place with coffee customers coming and going around us, and Hilda's husband, Dale, roasting coffee at the huge machine in the corner.

MARGE: I'm learning the work of an editor. It seems to take me longer to do the work than it should. Could you talk about learning to do that work?

HILDA: It appalls me to look back on my early days of editing *Prairie Schooner.* Now I can do in a good day's work what it used to take me at least three days to do. I used to go to the office and camp out with my cans of tuna fish and fresh fruit and carrot sticks. I saw no end. It took me that long to throw the material into the air, juggle it around, and let it filter down. Now I know how. Part of the change is knowing when to push myself, when my focus is dissolving and I'm getting tired, and when to let the sorting go on.

Editing uses the same energy my writing uses, and the writing is something I love to do too.

MARGE: What do you point to as influences on your writing?

HILDA: I love the apt phrase so when I read for example the *New York Times Book Review* on Sunday my pen underlines phrases that catch my ear; anything will influence my writing, from a line in a TV show to a cartoon legend, or a novel or short stories, or informational bytes that seem evocative, metaphoric, ironic. The quirky pieces fall together into poems.

My literary influences are varied. Because I studied with Robert Lowell when he was writing *Life Studies,* early influences were local, that is the Boston area, and the details of everyday life in the sixties, details that opened up into other people's lives in a way that seemed interesting; I look for those same details in other people's poems. The literary influences have more to do with Lowell's own reliance on collaboration, for example with his students Anne Sexton and Sylvia Plath and others and his interest in the ways they were writing.

The other influence at the time was, of course, Elizabeth Bishop. Bishop was the example for women who aspired to write candidly but guardedly. Also Adrienne Rich who was writing very formal poems. They and others were literary mentors who, through their work and life, counseled an openness to subject, to approach, and to life. Also an internationalism I admired.

MARGE: Has your writing process undergone changes?

HILDA: I have always written in a notebook, often in prose but often in line, depending on how difficult the material is. Maxine Kumin says form allows us to expand and venture into dangerous places, held by the form. Sometimes in a journal I'll find myself falling into lines.

I write everything in that journal, as many people do. I wrote an essay, "Junk," the title I took from Rita Dove's ironic calling of her notebook, the notebook that caught everything, her "junk."

My journal is not a diary. I don't write down everything or even a lot, but I do begin where I am at the moment and then proceed. When I have time I re-enter the notebooks and revise from the material there. Once it's on the computer, I work deliberately at forming the poem.

Prose is more difficult for me to write because I don't feel comfortable with only the margin to hold me. I'm working now on a prose book. Fortunately I have a leave, so the time will be there. Grace Bauer, a wonderful poet, is writing a novel. I admire poets who write prose. Bill Kloefkorn and Ted Kooser have both written memoir, wonderful prose embodiments.

MARGE: Do you set yourself tasks in writing?

HILDA: You and I have written together and you know that sometimes together we'll choose a subject. In writing the poems in *Trans,* I wanted the material to cover the transgressions and transformations of a time in my life when Sarah had come out to me as Aaron, and I slammed into the wall of my own assumptions, my politically correct assumptions about enacting gender in contemporary American society, my politically correct feminist assumptions about my experience and the experience of friends that suggested gender was enacted by choice and by birth in one way or in a myriad of ways but all on the same side of a division between male and female.

I knew that Aaron would pull me, push me, catapult me into a confrontation, not with him but with myself and my assumptions and the comfortable assumptions of my place. I thought, What can I do with this material? It's going to require Merthiolate and iodine and antibiotics. What can I do with this crisis? That was one of my tasks. I thought, I will not write what I would prefer to write. I will write about this and I will do it in good company. Much of that work I did in your company and felt safe doing it.

MARGE: What was your process in writing *Divine Honors*?

HILDA: Having had breast cancer and treatment, I knew the language others were using to talk to me and I was using to talk to myself and others about the experience I had come to consider toxic. The charge in writing *Divine Honors* was quite different from the charge in writing *Trans. Divine Honors* is about language. The enemy in that book is language, not cancer, the language of illness and especially cancer and particularly breast cancer, which is the site of the maternal and erotic at once for women. *Divine Honors* took its epigraph from W.H. Auden who was the great mentor/god/teacher of poets of my generation, and I cherished its ironic twist, that tumor may come to be a fit subject for poetry.

Trans is a meditation on experience rather than language. Language is much less difficult to approach. Language was a cinch compared to the change of gender that Aaron was acting out, although he's quick to make clear that his gender has not changed. His body has changed. It's now more congruent to his gender than it was.

Crisis, both societal and personal, prevails in any life. The different ways we can talk about crisis may provide openings, opportunities, for art. I can talk more freely about *Trans* as a book than I can about Aaron as my son. Because the subject of the book seems to be my life and, in some ways, isn't, often in response to questions about Aaron I have nothing really to say. And of course I'm not an authority about breast cancer, a subject of *Divine Honors.*

Imagine the crisis of experience World War I must have been. World War II, the Holocaust, all these things seem to be unspeakable. But the privilege of changing gender is not something to pass over, because the shock of new experience is always the occasion for art, or can be, I hope, because what else can you do with the thirst for violence and folly and hope of the human creature?

The question might be: what experiences and activities foster creativity? Catastrophe. Forget that walking in the country. (laughter) I look forward to a peaceful old age, lots of walks on Nine Mile Prairie. I remember the two of us walking there one day. I had to ask you the names of the plants. I was writing carefully in my notebook—

MARGE: Lespedesa, indigo, lead plant...

HILDA: And remember the time we wrote about jewelry we'd lost? We each have a poem that began with that task. My students had a good time with your visit and with those two poems, yours and mine. Afterward they wrote their own poems on the subject.

MARGE: How did you balance family and writing?

HILDA: That's an interesting question. If you live long enough and breathe in and out, they grow up and go away. (laughter) I don't know if we ever balance the two. Maybe getting the kids off and then rushing to the Village Inn before work to write?

MARGE: That was indeed balance.

HILDA: And then the days I brought the computer into the living room and just hung out there and would write when I was so moved, and the kids managed, the family managed.

I remember reading an article in which Kent Haruf, a friend to us all, says that he writes with a woolen cap pulled down over his face. Gerry Shapiro writes facing the wall, looking straight ahead. We didn't have that opportunity, did we? We had to be watching out for mayhem.

MARGE: Lacking the woolen cap option, we moved the computer into the living room. (laughter)

HILDA: Now there's a poem we both might write. We did that job. No laptop luxury. I have a laptop now; it has its own room. (laughter)

I think the writing became part of a full life for us. If we had made a list of our activities as young parents, writing would have been only one of those activities, as was making huge batches of chili.

MARGE: I'm glad we didn't leave the writing out, or the chili out...

HILDA: Could you have left out the writing?

MARGE: I don't know the true answer to that question.

HILDA: I don't think I could have stopped writing. I certainly didn't want to, but I don't think I could have. Easier to give up cooking.

I remember seeing Jonis Agee, after attending a poetry reading not long ago, sitting with a tiny notebook, scribbling like mad. Judy Slater does that too; she writes in every little space. Judith Ortiz Cofer has a wonderful essay in which she talks about the writing room of a young parent being the hip pocket of her jeans, where she carried a small notebook. Fiction writers often write continually, at every occasion. Do you do that as a poet?

MARGE: I get drawn away by projects, but always come back to that idea of writing continually. Projects that use up creative energy cause me to need to the spend some time alone somewhere.

HILDA: Haven't you gone on retreats from time to time?

MARGE: Yes, and even going to cafes to write is a retreat of sorts for me.

HILDA: I found out about cafe retreats in our writing together. My retreat is at home as well, when the last body is out the door, the last door closed.

MARGE: You mentioned studying at Boston University with Robert Lowell. What was next after that?

HILDA: After I graduated from B.U., I immediately went to work, hired by the Planned Parenthood League of Massachusetts during the time we were working to change the blue laws of Massachusetts. Then I stayed home and had a family. We moved to Nebraska. My life at *Prairie Schooner* began happily when I was asked by acting editor Hugh Luke, in exchange for a box of review books, to read some manuscripts and write some book reviews. Robert Lowell was still very productive and I knew his work so I wrote some reviews of Robert Lowell's books.

MARGE: You are not only writer and editor, but teacher. Could you talk about your teaching philosophy?

HILDA: I don't think I have a teaching philosophy. I know the kinds of things that help my own writing so bring to the classroom books and exercises that work for me. I read, write, and talk with my students. What a privilege.

I've always been interested in criticism. I grew up as a student during the most fertile part of the poetry publishing expansion and the expansion of women's poetry in the sixties. I was there and it helps when you're there, to read both the new work and commentary on the work.

Creative writing as a discipline is fairly new in the academy and the good textbooks are few and far between. So I teach six or eight recently published books of poetry with little or no teaching apparatus.

MARGE: What makes good writing?

HILDA: Although I'm not a great Ezra Pound fan, I understand the change his criticism made in our sense of what good writing ought to be. I love his definition of art as "news that stays news." Any news that is not discussed is the fit province of poetry. All good writing begins with the body; it's sensory in nature and meditates on what isn't sensory. And many points of view. For new perspectives and points of view, empathy is the softening technique that writers can use to carry news from one culture to another.

Revising is constant. I think of Cynthia Ozick who said it was torture not to be published when she was a young writer. Her advice to a young writer is publish, publish, publish, as soon as you can. It's true that the text may not be fixed, it may not be finished, it may only be abandoned, but publishing your work is important for writers to do. It's important for readers. The mind at work is always interesting, so I don't believe in the fixed polished text but the text on the way.

Small Shelter

Small Shelter

The needful things have been done:
sugar in the cupboard, honey, sweet
bacon in the smokehouse; buckles
done up, pines felled by lightning
shored against the flood bank.
Nothing to do now but wait.

I go to a tin box, remove
your ring, bed it for some long
season. Oh love, we have risked
our lives for this and still
it is over, long shadows crossing
over us. Fold, hands, be still for the sake of memory,
for our sweet sake who have done
the needful things, who have been true
to our hands, to our hard shoring up.
No floods can take us now.

I braid up my hair, our tent,
that sweet shelter.
Now winter.

Accident

for John

Accident

High summer heat.

Here clear storage bags
from a strange kitchen
hang upside down
from chrome hooks
high in the air over a bed
where someone I know
who resembles someone precious
is lying naked. It wears blue
hoses in its throat.

Air makes a sound it makes
nowhere else. What is lying
on the bed is breathing,
surely now absorbing
red threads at all
the body's openings.
I can't stay here very well.
I can't stay here long.

No flowers allowed.

They go in
they come out of the far room
where air is frigid.
They say *rigid*, they say *fluid*
they say something
I can't hear.
I'm not listening.

Light comes and goes.
I go into the room, I come out.
I say something again and again.
His toes are cold.

Road Trip

Going away coming back
trees unfurl
in an arch over some oval.
My hands and feet move together
and I move
into the arch
as the oval moves out.

He smiles
around tubes.
I smile.
He is sitting up in a cage.
He can't talk. He has a hose
in his throat.
His dials leap.
"Is this the worst from now on?"
he writes on a board.
Now he is sleeping more deeply
than I can say. Surgery.
Now he is rescued.

Is he breathing?
Yes, quietly. He is sleeping,
breathing alone.

Now he is beginning to walk.
He is more tall than my womb,
but very bending.
He leans on something chrome.

Now we are going home.
He is buckled into his seat,
dressed
he is sitting beside me.
I am buckled too.
We are going home.

I have been scrubbing his room.
I can polish its wood
I can shine its windows;
it has food. He enters it.

He is very thin.
He is slow down the hall.

Behind him, I can't see
he is breathing
and moving.

Twenty-one years ago
I panted and bore down
into scarlet and dazzle
between my thighs
in order to release him
to the shiny air

that tick-turning cord
still pulsing.

You,
lift up from the bloody ditch
and watch
what's whole and dripping
come again into the world.

Diction

"God is in the details,"
I tell the kids
in the public school
at Milligan, Nebraska.
They wonder what I mean.
I tell them to look
out the window
at the spring fields
the mud coming up
just to the knee
of the small pig
in the far pasture.
They tell me
it's not a knee
but a hock
and I hadn't ought
to say things I know
nothing about. I say
the light on the mud
is pure chalcedony.
They say the mud
killed two cows
over the weekend.
I tell them the pig
is alive and the spring
trees are standing in a green haze.
They tell me school is out
in a week and they have to plant.
The grain elevator at the end
of Main Street stretches out
her blue arms. The kids say chutes.

Hilda Raz

Mutation Blues

Mutation Blues

Got blues so harsh they take my breath
Got blues so strong I'm on my head
with your fussing and praising and denying and saying
sweet honeybun you're the mystery of my life.

Each day I wake up praying you're gonna stay.
Each day I raise my nose up to the sunny sky
sighing God above you gave me what I wanted
Sweet God above I begged you for a chance.

My breath comes up goes down my cinnamon throat
breath clangs hard in my head and in my ears.
Sweet honey stick I gave away my heart to
what's natural is what I give to keep you here.

Close to me you watch my eyeballs swell.
Far from me you turn your head away.
I wear a rag and screwturn on my skullcap
but you never notice me at all until I'm gone.

Oh lord above please tell me what to make up out of
Oh lordy above I don't know what I know.
I'm a honeybun that's used her days for nothing
and now I'm going home I don't know where I've been.

Aaron at Work/Rain

Aaron at Work/Rain

By the light box propped in the window,
bare chested, scars rosy in artificial sun,
he crouches over his workbench.
Dental tools in their holder at hand, silver discs,
his torch, the tiny saw. Light flares, breaks on
his earring as he turns his head,
frowns, dark eyebrows almost meeting.
He takes a watch from his jeans pocket,
rubs it absently over his beard, electricity.
The braid clinks its beads as his head
turns, reading something. Now he rises, goes
to the cupboard, mixes wallpaper paste with water.
The pile of miraculous papers, shot metal
threaded with linen, he sorts to start
a papier-mache hypodermic needle he's building on the table,
matches to the real one he used this morning,
adds it as a detail to the mask to change the meaning:
a revolution: what he's about. Out the window the black car
beads up rain. He never drives it. An emblem, but of what?
A memory of pain, his slouching walk just home from hospital?
Where is the child whose shoes I bought? Where the bread
we kneaded? Where our kitchen? Our dead?

Ron Block

Ron Block

Poet and fiction writer RON BLOCK was born in Gothenburg, a town of 3500 that lists thirty-four entries for *Block* in its phone directory. After attending the University of Nebraska-Lincoln, he moved to Kennebunkport, Maine, where he lived in a barn, and then to New Orleans, where he waited tables in the French Quarter. He attended graduate school in Syracuse, New York, receiving an MS in telecommunications/film and an MA in the Creative Writing Program, studying under poets Hayden Carruth, Philip Booth, and Tess Gallagher. He taught English and Film Studies at North Dakota State University, creative writing and literature at Marquette University, and additional classes at Milwaukee Area Technical College. His book, *Dismal River: A Narrative Poem* (New Rivers, 1990), won the Minnesota Voices competition. His second book, *The Dirty Shame Motel and Other Stories* (New Rivers Press, 1998), was a finalist for an Independent Publisher's Book Award and a Barnes and Noble Discovery selection. *The Bloomsbury Review* noted, "The quality of these short stories far exceeds that of many short story collections—even 'best of' compilations by preeminent authors." Block now teaches at Mid-Plains Community College in North Platte. He has held a variety of jobs besides teaching—constructing a rodeo, binding books, writing film reviews, tooling leather, and farming with his father. In 2000 he won a Distinguished Achievement Award from the Nebraska Arts Council, and in 2002 an individual artist fellowship from the National Endowment for the Arts.

MARGE: I've heard you speak about your writing in connection with your father's voice and your mother's voice. What are those two voices?

Ron Block has come from North Platte to Kearney to give a reading this evening, and he generously gives us an interview in the afternoon instead of taking a nap or a walk near the Platte. The Holiday Inn staffer finds us a conference room and we're all set.

RON: My mother was an English teacher, a very proper person. If you talk to people in Gothenburg, you would know she is someone that many people respected. She taught Sunday school. She's not necessarily a Pollyanna figure; she has a healthy skepticism about what people are up to. She's very careful about what she says, very composed. My father was a farmer and more of a wildcat businessman, an entrepreneur, an inventor. He has an eighth grade education. When he speaks, he speaks with a Nebraska rural folk voice. My mother speaks standard English. I've always been able to switch. It's almost like growing up bilingual, except both of these are English, and one's an extremely folk voice. I guess I go back and forth between these two voices. A lot of what I do with writing has to do with the composed nature of my mother's voice versus the open and more reckless and vivid nature of my father's voice. It's easier to access my father's voice than my mother's voice, because my mother can be a very quiet person. But it's her voice that composes my father's voice; it's my mother's voice that gives it a shape.

MARGE: You're lucky as a writer to have this duality.

RON: I grew up doing work with my father. He talked a lot; we didn't sit down and have reflective conversations, but I could watch him as he interacted with farmers. Once when we were camping in Minnesota, I hadn't showed up yet and my brother-in-law started getting worried about me. My father said, "Oh, don't worry. Ron's had a lot of practice being lost." And he wouldn't even think that was funny. Other people would think he was funny. He was very unselfconscious.

MARGE: What about other relatives or teachers as influences on your writing?

RON: My grandfather was probably an influence.

He sat next to the refrigerator in the kitchen and chained-smoked Camel cigarettes and supervised the women as they cooked the meals. He didn't seem to be a very likable person. The kids would go into his garden and, of course, we were up to no good, pulling his carrots out of the ground to see if they were ready yet. "This one's not quite ready; let's try that one." So he'd come out and yell at us. I thought he was a very grumpy person, but then he would tell stories, and when he told stories he changed. He was tolerant of us because we were interested in the stories he had to tell.

He grew up in Muscatine, Iowa, right along the Mississippi, so his stories had a Huck Finn flavor to them. He had stories about river rafting and finding skulls buried in riverbanks, and one story about being chased by wolves. Whether or not that was a true story we didn't really care, because it was an exciting story. Everyone said the same thing about him; they said they really didn't know if they liked him, but by golly he told good stories. He could relate to people that way.

When I heard stories about his childhood, I understood more about why he was the way he was. Those stories connected the dots for me, and I got interested in people's backgrounds and in motivation and in what makes people more sympathetic. Grandpa's father was a Holy Roller, a Bible-thumping minister. Grandpa's mother was allowed to marry the minister with the condition that he never force her to go to church, so this minister had a wife who would never go to church. We've wondered what the story was with that. My brother, who's a minister, has a theory about it, my sister has a theory about it, we all speculate on it.

Those people are long dead, but there's this human impulse to want to have the whole story, so you can use your creativity to figure out what the story could be. You have to do that with integrity; you have to make it consistent with their time period, with what you know about human beings, and the characteristics that they have in other stories.

Everyone talked about Grandpa's strange ideas about religion, and how he never went to church either. My grandmother was very religious, but Grandpa stayed home and cooked the chicken. There's a theory in our family that atheists make the best chicken. (laughter) He'd stay home and turn it very carefully, and make sure it was all evenly cooked.

SHELLY: Tell us a story about you as a child that might characterize who you were then and/or predict who you became.

RON: The whole idea of who I was as a child is a really scary thing, because I don't understand who that was. Recently I've been working with younger kids in a summer honors program. Some of them—my heart goes out to them because of their creativeness—just don't fit in at all, and no one has a clue about what's going on inside their heads. I don't.

I remember being like that, where people didn't have a clue about what went on in my head. I don't want to romanticize myself, but I was a strange kid. I no longer understand who that kid was. I was a kid who was sent to the principal's office because I bit another kid. I bit him hard and I bit him deliberately. I bit him because I had just read Dracula; I had been inspired. The principal didn't know what to do with me; I mean, what do you do with a kid who deliberately bites another kid because he's read a book?

I bought a hat like Castro's, a military fatigue hat, and I would sit on the edge of the playground and annihilate everyone with my stares. I would wear this cap pulled low down over my eyes, and I would sit there and stare at them. I remember at that point just hating people, you know, just wanting to see them explode. I have no idea what was going on in my head, what I was trying to do with this hat, this disguise that I was wearing. I was around nine years old. I lived in my head, you know. Reading Dracula was a big moment in my life; it changed me. How many kids do you know who read Dracula and cry at the end? Weep bitter tears at how cruel humanity is?

SHELLY: I bet *Frankenstein* was tough for you too.

RON: I didn't read that until I was much older. But vampires for some reason got to me. They are very sad creatures, vampires are. Half in life, half not in life. I suppose that was part of the identification, that I had been half-way born; I wasn't completely born yet. Half of me got to this world and the other half stayed in the last world. The other kids thought I was creepy. After a while, I learned to turn that creepiness against my teachers, which made the other kids like me. If they thought that I could freak out the teachers, then I was cool again, and I was okay.

SHELLY: What would you do to freak out the teachers?

RON: One thing I started doing when I was about 12 was carrying around a copy of *The Communist Manifesto* in my back pocket. That seemed to freak out people pretty well. I remember wanting to write a surrealistic comedy when I was in seventh grade. I know where that came from. It was because I saw something on PBS, a surrealistic comedy, and I thought it was fascinating. I announced to my class that this was a surrealistic comedy. One of the character's names was Sugar Diabetes. She was, of course, a very sexy fantasy for my thirteen-year-old imagination.

MARGE: You've lived and taught in different parts of the country and now are back in Nebraska. What would you say about your rambling around the country?

RON: I grew up in Gothenburg, a medium-sized town in Nebraska terms, a town where my family has been since the 1880s. I grew up in a town where I was related to all these people; I grew up hating the fact that everyone always knew what you were doing and everyone was into each other's business. There's gossip, and I just hated that stuff. Like a lot of kids, I figured I was successful based on how many miles I was able to put between myself and that town. That would be the measure of my success.

I went off and got interested in writing, and then I all of a sudden found that this was the stuff that I used. Actually, I don't want to live in small towns, I really don't, but I can't shake it. It made my character and it's how I look at the world. I could write about sophisticated New Yorkers, but it would not have a ring of authenticity because that's not how I see things.

Especially in graduate school in Syracuse, I thought, Oh, I should not be writing about Nebraska. I don't live there anymore. I should write about what I'm experiencing now, and I tried, but I found people were always more interested in what I had to say about Nebraska, working from a more rural perspective and writing about small-town character, writing about the absurdities of small town life and the incongruities of life on the plains. I go back there because that's what I seem to be able to write about.

I didn't come back to Nebraska because I couldn't live without it. I came back because, when I was living in Milwaukee, a couple of things happened. It was almost like the stars started lining up. You hear the little clicking mechanism of the universe setting things up, forcing you to do something. I was teaching with a three-year contract at Marquette. That contract ran out and I applied for teaching jobs, but I wasn't finding any, so I went to work for a consulting agency.

I knew I couldn't work there much longer, so I started putting out résumés and all of a sudden, this job in North Platte comes up. The second thing that happened was that my wife and I started hearing stories about my folks and their ability to be live independent lives. My wife went on a reconnaissance mission to check out how things were. I couldn't go because I had to work. She came back and said it's worse than you could ever dream.

So we started wondering, well, how can we help them? The job in North Platte comes up, a community college thirty miles from my home town. I applied for the job. My time back here in Nebraska has been a period of managing my parents as they came to the moment of truth and realized they couldn't live in the house any more. Taking over more and more of the things that they do.

When it got to be the worst, I would have to call my mother every morning to walk her through medications for my father. She was developing Alzheimer's at the same time that he had stroke-related dementia. Every morning I would walk Mom through the medications: "Now take the red pill..." But they've gone into the nursing home now and are planning their escape. (laughter)

SHELLY: To be able to laugh...

RON: When you have two parents who are going through dementia, there are a lot of things that are just plain funny, and you are not laughing because of a coping mechanism, you are laughing because it's just funny. My father doesn't want to give up on the control he's had in his life; he's going to maintain that little bit of control. He wants to be the boss of something. So in the final days of independence, what he's boss of is the thermostat. By God, he's going to get it the right temperature. No one is going to mess with his thermostat. That's the only thing he can control now and he's become possessive of it.

MARGE: Can you talk about your writing process? What kind of changes has it gone through?

RON: I have a lot less time than I used to have. In my twenties I had no family; I didn't get married until I was 36 and I didn't have a baby until I was 37, so my life is backwards. In my twenties, I had a lot of time, not that I got a lot done, but I had a lot of time for writing. At the same time I've gone from writing poetry exclusively to writing longer and longer pieces, and that seems like a paradox, but it's not, because when I have time, I pick up the thread and follow it a little bit further, then I have to drop the thread, then I have to pick it up again.

The biggest problem is that you have a life that's fractured by work, and by children, and by the demands of the parents, the ultimate sandwich generation kind of experience. At the same time you are feeding a baby with a spoon, you're feeding your father with a spoon. At the same time you are changing your baby's diapers, you are changing your father's diapers. There's this period of my life when it became like that. The problem is remembering where I dropped the thread of the story. I can pick it up and I can follow it if I can find it.

It's important, more so now than ever, to make sure I spend even five minutes a day revisiting where I was, to keep it in my head, so when I get time I'm ready, so I don't have to reconstruct where I was in order to take the next step.

Basically I have to use weekends, and thank God I have a wife who sleeps late. She likes to sleep in on Saturday and Sunday mornings, so I get big chunks of time then. It's hard to work on things, to get things done. There's nothing very creative about it, but managing time and finding chunks where you can work is sort of the game now.

SHELLY: Do you remember at what point you decided to make writing a part of your life? Was there something that helped you along the way? A mentor? A teacher? Someone who recognized something? Or was it pretty much your own personal progression?

RON: No one gave me any encouragement. No one ever encouraged me. (laughter) I remember thinking about wanting to write poetry when I was in seventh grade. I found a poem that my brother had written, and I thought this is really odd, because it didn't fit my image of him at all. My brother is nine years older, and his job in the family was to keep me working. He was my foreman. I didn't realize until later in life how unfair that was to him to make him keep me busy. But that was his job.

I found this poem of his that was very reflective and I knew he never meant for me to read it, or for anyone to read it. It was self-communication, something he was writing for himself. That whole idea of writing for yourself, communicating with yourself, which had never occurred to me before, became important. I started writing a variety of things to try to get at something that was bothering me when I was kid. I'm not even sure what that was, I just felt that there was something that wasn't right. There was something bothering me, and I tried to find it by writing.

That kept up. Periodically I would do that when I was a teenager. I had a girlfriend who was interested in poetry. I started to try to communicate with someone else at that point, to impress her that I was a thoughtful person, that I wasn't a thug.

People gave me things to read, so I got more models for ways of writing. My sister was very important for feeding me books of poems. She showed me Sylvia Plath and Ted Hughes, poems she read when she was in college. She's about 12 years older. She showed me a lot of women writers.

When I went off to college, Greg Kuzma was an influence by the role that he had. It occurred to me for the first time that there were people who were spending their lives as writers, not as journalists, but as poets. I didn't know you could do that. Actually, I got into a lot of fights with Greg when I took his creative writing class. I know he didn't like me because I was a smart ass, and I set out to deliberately be a smart ass in his class at times, because—I don't know why, for the hell of it. Just to make his life more uncomfortable.

Winesburg, Ohio was a very important book for me when I was a teenager because I realized that you could write about small towns. I didn't meet anyone in the flesh who was doing that until I took a class from William Kloefkorn. Kloefkorn, using the rural voice, opened that up a bit. Not that he's the only person in the world who's done that, but he was the person in the flesh. He showed me someone living a life and transforming material like that. He had a good sense of humor which made it easy to have him for a teacher.

I studied under Hayden Carruth when I went to graduate school. He was a very tough teacher, but brilliant. He was probably the person who challenged me most in a way that will continue to challenge me long after he's gone.

SHELLY: Why?

RON: I don't know if I can entirely sum it up. For one thing, the way in which he would question metaphor. Sometimes people think that a poem is a poem because it has metaphors in it, and you excuse the use of metaphor, but metaphor always involves a distortion of the truth. The man in fact is not a wolf; he's a man. Metaphor involves something that is ontologically untrue. Carruth's sense of wanting to tell the truth raised the stakes for me. You couldn't get away with saying something because it sounded cool or was creative. You always had to be saying things that were true.

And poetic license? Forget about it. Someone would write a poem in his workshop and they would talk about what they thought was true. They would talk about a still being hidden in an old stone mill by a river and he would tear it apart. He'd say no, that's impossible, that can't happen, bootleggers kept on the move, they would never put bootlegging equipment into a permanent structure. He had that sense of responsibility to make your poems align with the facts of the world.

He'd also say that you have an obligation to understand the tradition of where poetry has been before. He would get a poem, read it and paraphrase it for you, to make sure you knew that he understood the poem, that he wasn't misreading it. He would survey the whole history of the people who tried to do this type of thing and then he would tell you why this didn't work. And by the time he was done with you, I mean, forget self esteem. The self esteem movement had not hit yet. You would say, Yes, that's right, I'll go do something else for a living.

He raised the stakes, and actually for a lot of people it raised the stakes too high; they couldn't continue to write under those conditions and maybe that's a good thing, you know.

SHELLY: Tell us about your own teaching of creative writing, how you approach it now.

RON: It's kind of funny because I almost go entirely in the opposite direction of where I was taken with Carruth. Lots of times I am dealing with people who are so young. Carruth was teaching adults, the time to decide if you are serious or not. Generally I'm teaching kids who are experimenting. In the summer honors program that I teach in Holdrege, ninth graders to seniors, most of the students are not planning to be poets or fiction writers. This is something they do because they like it. They like coming for these two weeks, doing their writing and listening to what everyone else says. It's like a vacation for them, so I don't get very critical.

I once heard that William Stafford would never offer criticism of poems. He would never say anything, and I started wondering, what is he doing? But I understand what he was doing: providing the context for things to happen. And most people correct themselves. I guess I'm more in that framework now. I don't try to push revision on them, not too much. I focus on the things that I like and skip over the things I don't like, and hope the positive example teaches them. Since I don't have to grade them at this summer honors program, I don't have to get serious. I find it very hard to grade creative writing.

SHELLY: Have you found a way that you can live with?

RON: No, I haven't. To be honest, I haven't. I mean how can you grade? The students would say, "How can you grade something that is so subjective?" And I used to think, No, it's not subjective, but it is. I don't have any standards by which to grade it. I suppose that's a horrible thing, but I just don't. But I'm honest about it.

MARGE: That leads us to your own writing. When you are looking at your own writing, how do figure out if it is good? What makes good writing in your own work?

RON: There are certain tests I put things through. The test of imagining. If you can get your imagination to supply the reader, based upon living readers in your life. The best way is to prepare to do a reading of it out loud. You all of a sudden get really honest about things.

One thing I do when I write is to get off into head stuff way too often. I don't stick to the story; I see myself do that time and time again, so that's something I have to correct.

I don't know what makes something good. I really don't know what makes anything good. You have to have a sense of integrity; things have to be written with a good heart, with a desire to tell the truth. The truth, of course, is extremely relative, but you have to want to tell the truth. If people don't love the truth, then there's nothing you can do with them. If they love violence and they don't love the truth, then there's nothing you can do with them.

Now, which truth do they love? Well, who knows? But they have this desire to get something down that doesn't deliberately distort for their own advantage.

I guess the older I get the more I love coherence. Coherence is an honorable goal. It is so easy to be incoherent. Actually, for certain parts of my life I loved incoherence. A lot of things in the twentieth century are written out of the love of incoherence.

The old communities are vanishing. It's all gone; people don't grow up in the same place where they get married and where they die. Our lives are fractured, so it would make sense to learn to love fragmentation. You have a certain literature that grows out of the love of fragmentation. This desire to make fragmentation beautiful, to transform it. Maybe we're in a new era. You can't give up on the sense of things being relative and things being subjective, and yet we desire something that is coherent and unified and beautiful. We desire to be committed in a relativistic world, to be committed in the midst of that.

I keep thinking of the next phase of our human evolution. We've gone through the century of relativity and fragmentation and breakdown, and we've learned how to have fun with even that, by using irony and metafictional representations. We can't go back to the nineteenth century where things were unified through sentimentality. You have to move on. How does one find commitment in the midst of this?

SHELLY: Thinking about your work, what's down the road for you? Your hopes and dreams?

RON: When I find time I have about six books I'd like to write, but I don't think I'll get to them, and they'll probably be replaced by other books that become more important. The book I'm working on is a strange project, an autobiographical novel about the Wizard of Oz. It's a book about a man who uses the Wizard of Oz as a medium to understand his life. Finishing that book is important to me, and I think I'll actually be able to finish that pretty soon.

And I've got poems. I'm not sure about how poems figure in my life. I end up trying to write poems in sequence, where they become a longer narrative, and that's hard to do. It's almost like it's too much work; I don't want to do it anymore, to write poems that add up to a book that has a kind of beginning, middle, and end with more of a narrative thrust to it, more unified than books of poems usually are. A book like *Alvin Turner as Farmer* is one variation of that. *The Book of Nightmares* is another variation of it. I am working on a collection called *Twilight Drive-In*. I'm hoping I can get done with it and someone will be interested in it so I can stop doing that type of thing, because it's just so much work. I think I'd like to write more personal poems if I write poetry.

There's a book I'd like to write, *The Weird Kid*, that plays off the idea of growing up as a strange kid. That's been inspired by working with the summer honors kids.

There's a book I'd like to write about Gothenburg and Cozad and that area about the turn of the century. There's a series of stories; parts of which are fragments from family histories that I'd like to clothe and complete. I'd like to tell a reasonable story based upon the facts that I know. One about the doctor who takes a man with brain fever on this long wagon ride to the only hospital, which is more than a hundred miles away, and what their relationship is. One about the German photographer who takes photographs of windmills and no one can understand why he's doing that—they figure he must be a spy. One about the woman who runs a brothel in a railroad town. Those are all parts of stories I'd like to tell, having to do with family history. I have a couple of other ideas; I don't know which ones will move to the front.

It's so hard to find time to write; I wish I had a job where I had like a light schedule, but unfortunately, because of my wayward youth, I never secured a job like that and so now I have to work hard to find every single moment where I can write.

SHELLY: Are you in a writing group? Do you have anyone to read your work or anyone to send it to for feedback?

RON: My group has gotten winnowed down; I need to develop another group. I have a friend in New York City who takes a careful eye to my things; but sometimes I don't know if it's necessarily good to let him read it. He's got a lot of integrity and a lot of loyalty. The thing is he's so much of a realist that I'm not sure that he's the best reader for my stuff. I used to have lots of people but I have fewer people now.

MARGE: Maybe you need fewer people now.

RON: Yes, probably. When you're in graduate school, you finish a poem and you want to run over and read it to someone right away. If it's two o'clock in the morning, you call them up and read your poem.

SHELLY: Maybe it's characteristic of writers just getting started to need feedback, to need someone to give it validity. Do you remember your first acceptance letter, a great moment when you thought, I can do this, I know I can do this, when you got a poem published?

RON: I haven't published a lot in terms of magazines. I never found it very fulfilling. You have to work so hard to get your poems in magazines. You keep them in the mail and collect rejection letters. Then your poem is published and you never hear about it again. No one responds to it. The purpose seems to be to collect the periodicals as a way of selling your book to a publisher or to apply for an NEA grant because you have to have the required fifteen poems published in the last five years

Who are you really communicating with? You don't know that from periodicals. From books you do. It's much better situation to find a publisher who likes your work and is willing to support it, and to have a personal relationship that goes into the building of the book.

Salvage

When my father went bankrupt, we tried to salvage
what we could, hat forms and the antique tools,
the rip saws painted with the covered bridges
of a sentimental past our town has never known
with its Quonset huts and its temporary buildings.

All day I thought of my father weeping in
his hands that morning, under a reproduction
of an old man praying over bread and soup,
his hands dry and full of stiff veins, perhaps
in shame at what people in that town would say.

In the back of the business, he had a pile of scrap iron,
channel iron, pipe, car frames, I-beams—
and with his welding wand he'd fuse the junk
into something useful that few in town would buy:
cattle gates, stanchions, crowding alleys, calf tables.

If you live in the city, perhaps you cannot imagine
what these objects are. But you can probably imagine
the player-piano. We wrapped it in a log chain cradle.
This was the last work I did for my father while
he was still in business on his own in that town.

For years I helped him irrigate corn, mow hay,
set siphon tubes, drain an interstate lake
into a sandy field, cultivate the fields
with a lister and go-dig, dragging a spring-
tooth harrow through the fallow dirt.

Resilient, he went bankrupt and then built
another business, and I worked with him,
salvaging houses for wood, salvaging chicken wire
to bury in the concrete floors, salvaging drill stem
to sell to ranchers who'd build it into corrals.

We used the offset printing sheets of the town's
only newspaper to panel the walls with a backward
story of the town, and we salvaged center pivot
irrigation pipe for the frame of the building,
and then he took his chapter seven.

Before the sheriff came to change the locks,
I climbed on the tractor, which trembled, lifting
the salvaged piano on hydraulic hoists into the air.
I hauled it home to hide it from his creditors,
and in that small town, our neighbors heard the pot holes

setting loose a drone. They stepped out on their porches
to see a player-piano wrapped in chains and swinging
wildly from a tractor's payload. They nodded at me
and kept quiet. They didn't need an explanation.
They knew exactly what the story was.

My Father's Legs

My Father's Legs

He didn't teach me how to care for tools. We did our work
and left them in the dust or rain. No peg-board with the shadows
of the pliers painted in a silhouette and half our tools missing,
so he taught me invention.
But now he throws his makeshift walker down the stairs.
I see it lying there like someone he's murdered
the legs wrapped with plumber's tape,
the caps replaced by tennis balls.
And now he's modified it with a basket plundered from a shopping cart,
and he pushes and pulls himself, dragging a leg across the lawn.

There is something lawless about him when he rolls up his pant legs,
his syringe and insulin set out on the neat kitchen table,
but now his legs are pale as creatures that have spent their lives in caves,
they are bloated and pale as a drowning victim,
a premonition of an amputation,
they are his ghost legs now.
What's more, they are my own invention,
the figure of the distance that I keep from the facts,
for his legs are the facts, unimaginably pale, they are peerless now,
and all the poisons have gathered there.

In the name of neglect and all too often drunk on sugar,
he lances himself two times a day
still wanting to do for himself. But for now at least
he offers me a pair of scissors nicked and stained by rust,
at least I think it's rust, and he asks me to use them on
his yellowed toe nails, which he's always kept hidden.
At a distance I consider them: they are hooked like beaks
and twisted as the thick bark of cedars and I imagine bending over them
and cutting them back, but then I think twice. I don't want to risk
a diabetic's infections. I don't want to lose him piece by piece.

So instead, I watch him disappear into the doctor's sterile office,
who has the right tools. You might say I am useless.
You might say I might as well be anywhere
as I dream and read magazines others have abandoned there.
For sure I will walk his limp someday myself,
but right now I'm reading of wild rice growing in the alkali lakes
not far from here. It surprises me that anything would grow there,
they're our own dead seas, though not dead yet,
where the far-fetched rainfall comes too seldom,
and when it comes it has no place to drain.

A Painting of Mount St. Helens

The painting used to hang above my mother's sofa, a big amateur landscape,
the stippled brushstrokes of tall ponderosas, putty-knifed mountains, sponges of clouds.
When she moved into the nursing home, I took the painting because I'd grown used to it,
and because the mountain, behind the trees, behind the open lake that economically
occupied half of the painting, was Mount St. Helens before the explosion.

The painting once hung above her head as she sat on the sofa and watched television.
She probably didn't look at the painting that much. Rather, it became a part of the way
I saw *her,* hanging above her head as though it was a thought balloon, a lake
without waves, a shoreline straight and mathematical, with clean divisions between
the earth and the sky that would soon fill up with hot ash, blocking out the sun.

The painting hangs now at the foot of my bed. If your defenses and your irony
and your skepticism are weakened, as when you wake up trying to sort out the dreams
from the memories each morning, you can easily be drawn into the painting on
a brushed band of light meant to give the lake depth, letting your eyes cross
the sometimes choppy waves to the gray mass in the background, about to erupt.

As she began to lose her memories, the painting became more vague and remote,
and if you asked her what that painting represented, she'd say she didn't know.
Maybe nothing. Maybe it was totally abstract to her, the simple mathematics
of its composition, the symmetry and balance, drifting apart into fragments of green,
and smears of blue, and the small, broken triangles of light, and all that dust.

And this is what the painting represents to me—a big empty thought, which is nice
sometimes. I can walk among the trees at the shoreline, everything perfectly quiet.
The band of light, whether sunlight or moonlight, invites me to cross the water.
My thoughts are still in the imaginary winds. Like birds, my memories still gather darkly
in the trees, until I hear a sound deep inside the earth, and everything scatters.

Estate

They were auctioning off the unclaimed contents
of the lockers at the rest home: mostly junk
a surprising number of stuffed animals
and too many telephones as if that's the last claim
anyone makes upon a place. Too many tool boxes too,
as if some old guy still believed he would
never know when he'd need a vise grip or a rasp.

In one box, among the spent batteries and sewing kits,
mostly empty spools, and the kind of junk that
finds itself at the bottom of a drawer, I found
a packet of x-rays of some old guy's skull,
who maybe carried them about until he died,
they being both intimate and costly.
I wanted to buy the x-rays but the sun was too hot.

So I watched the men bid against men for severed
extension cords they thought they could repair,
and women against women for souvenir plates,
stripped of the memories they once held.
I started to wonder why the men would end up
keeping so much junk, while the whys of the women
were slightly more obvious.

And just when I was starting to dream a mystery here,
a clue to a murder or a life exhumed
from the bottom of a steamer trunk,
my wife showed the plastic bag of linens.
At first, I was too stupid to know them for what they were
as she bid them up from a dollar to six as tense
as if it were a thousand, this being her first auction.

Only after we watched the fierce revenge bidding
of two grand-dads over a Tonka truck
did we examine my wife's linens, discovering there
an elaborate embroidery of cardinals and bluebirds,
the stitches close and small and with a clever counter stitch
visible only from the back to keep the design from puckering,
and in the design, we saw many years of a woman's life.

We saw the small room, her hunched back, the stiff
fingers of the dimming light, the day's eye lost
in the daisies and tulips and elaborate flourishes
and all of it anonymous, a shadow work, and unclaimed
by whatever family that remained after she had died.
We followed the stitches to the common grave of keepsakes
and the almost useful junk you keep because you-never-know.

And there we discovered the roses and asters,
the hummingbirds and bluebells lost among a sad list
of the junk left over, among severed cords and telephones,
among cuff links and receipts and x-rays that withhold
their stories, a place where a life can be purchased for a song,
the ancient stuttering poem going—
going, going, gone.

Eamonn Wall

Eamonn Wall

EAMONN WALL is a native of Enniscorthy, Ireland, who emigrated to the US in 1982. He lived in Milwaukee and New York before moving to Nebraska in 1992 to take up a teaching position at Creighton University. Since 2000, he has lived in St. Louis where he is Jefferson Smurfit Professor of Irish Studies at the University of Missouri-St. Louis. He has published three collections of poetry: *The Crosses* (2000), *Iron Mountain Road* (1997), and *Dyckman-200th Street* (1994). *Iron Mountain Road,* an exploration of Nebraska and surrounding states, has been cited by the editors of *Irish Writing in the Twentieth Century* as one of the most notable collections of poetry published by an Irish poet in the Twentieth Century. *From the Sin-é Café to the Black Hills,* a collection of literary and personal essays, was the co-winner of the American Conference for Irish Studies award given to the best book on Language & Culture published in 2000.

Eamonn Wall lives and teaches in St. Louis, but because of the Western Literature Conference, he is back in Omaha where he and his family lived while he taught at Creighton. We want to ask him about living in Nebraska, as well as about his youth in Ireland.

SHELLY: Tell us a little bit about your family—your parents, siblings, and their influence on your writing.

EAMONN: My family is associated with County Wexford in the southeast of Ireland, as long as anybody can remember. I grew up in the center of Enniscorthy, right smack in the middle of it. A town of 5,000 people. My mother worked as chef and manager in the family business, a small hotel on Main Street which had been started by her parents. This hotel was the center, in many ways, of life and of family life. It was a very exciting place to grow up because the house we lived in was right beside the hotel. It was possible to walk from the house into the hotel, into the dining room, into the kitchens, where it was very lively. It was interesting as a child to be living among a lot of adults. There were parents, but there were all of these other adults as well, a rich source of life and humor and oral tradition.

My dad worked as a journalist for about forty years and then retired early and went to work in the hotel with my mother; she had taken it over from her parents. So the two of them worked together, side by side. My mother is a great business woman. My dad is a good business man but also a dreamer.

When I was fourteen I started working in the business, doing different things, working in the yard, cleaning, taking the empty buckets from the bar down and sorting them all out. Doing all that kind of stuff.

My parents come from diametrically opposed political viewpoints, taking different sides in the Civil War. It was very interesting to live among that ongoing dialogue. Even still you find that the war, which ended seventy years ago, is disputed with great vigor at the dinner table.

And it was also, of course, a time before television. Television didn't come to rural Ireland until Kennedy's visit. That was the reason to bring TV to rural Ireland, so people could see Kennedy.

There was a lot of time to fill and we filled that time in a number of ways. One was rambling. We could go where we wanted to. After school every day we would do something outside. Then on

Saturdays, especially, we would wander into the woods and head off across the fields. It was a Huck Finn childhood in some ways. That was one way to fill the time.

The other way was reading, and my dad, in particular, was a great fan of reading. He read a lot himself. My mother didn't read so much until the last ten years or so. That's because in addition to running the business, she had eight kids. There were only so many hours in the day and so much energy.

I read a lot, and my dad put no limit whatsoever on the amount of money he would spend on books. He would put limits on lots of things but on books, anything went. I was a voracious reader, but I had fallen into bad favor in the local library for not returning books, so I had to buy them.

Another thing that was a part of this early life, of course, was narrative and oral tradition, which was very very strong then and still is in Ireland despite television and media. There was always a rich vein of dialogue and narrative.

Enniscorthy was the center of the Rebellion of 1798, the only real peasants' revolt in Ireland's history. These events that had happened two hundred years before were very much a part of folklore. History was very important. The other thing that was important in childhood was the Catholic Church. At one end of town you had Vinegar Hill, which is where a great battle was fought in 1798. It was the large presence on the right, and the other presence was the Catholic cathedral, which was a powerful symbol, you know, which many people were interested in and many people were kind of fighting against. A lot of Irish writers have talked about the importance of Catholicism and writing in terms of ritual. You see these elaborate rituals in the church so this becomes a kind of framework for poetry or fiction.

SHELLY: What about your siblings? You were from a large family.

EAMONN: Right. There are eight of us and I'm the oldest. Everybody lives in Enniscorthy still except for me and my brother Michael who lives in the west of Ireland. My sister Annette teaches French. The two oldest are involved in education and the others had more sense, you know—they went into business.

My people are involved mostly in business but it's still a family interested in music and reading. In Ireland it's somewhat different because people who are involved in business also read a lot of literature. They feel involved in it in some way. It's a very close family, still. The people in Enniscorthy see each other all the time, and then we get over there in the summer every year.

MARGE: You said it is important for your children to have that connection.

EAMONN: It's much more important than I thought it would be. I was inclined to think that it would just be something that would be interesting for them. But it's very important—having a sense of family. I think particularly because the places that we've lived in America are places where there's been no family, but in a strange way they get this in Ireland.

SHELLY: How is it that you are the only one in the family who left Ireland? Can you tell us how that came about?

EAMONN: I was always curious about America through books and through movies and through music. I grew up listening to Bob Dylan. As a teenager, I was a big fan of Steinbeck and of Jack Kerouac. These got me interested in America.

Movies were important. When I was a kid there was one movie theatre in town, and at that time there was no such thing as an Irish film industry. All the movies were American movies, so I got a visual sense of it.

When I finished college in '77, we were in the middle of a recession that came just at the end of the oil crisis. Many of my graduating class emigrated because there was no work. I decided that I would go to graduate school over here. Even if I'd gone to graduate school in Ireland, I would have had to come over here anyway, to look for work or to go on more. I wanted to spend some time in a creative writing program to see what I could learn and to see what it was all about. That's the reason I came and have never gone back except in the summer.

SHELLY: Tell us a little about your schooling. What teachers do you remember? Maybe some that were either positive or negative influences. Was there something that inspired you to become a writer? Did you think of yourself at all as a writer?

EAMONN: My education was interesting in some ways. The very early part of it in kindergarten was with Loreto nuns for three years. They were gentle people. And then everybody in the town went to the Christian Brothers. At the Christian Brothers, it depended on what teacher you had. In some years we had good teachers and other years we had—I don't know if they were bad teachers, if *bad* is the right word. We had teachers who used a lot of corporal punishment. We were beaten frequently in primary school and we all emerged with a lot of information because we memorized stuff. We learned all the basic skills, but I think mostly we survived.

When I was fourteen, I went to boarding school. I spent three years in County Tipperary in a boarding school run by monks. The school was on one side and the monastery on the other. We didn't have to be involved in the monastic rituals, like vows of silence and all that kind of thing. It was a very good education, though a very lonely time.

It was an all-boys school. A couple of teachers were very helpful, encouraging to me in different ways. I wrote some fiction when I was in high school. At one point, the teacher made me read this out loud to the class because he liked it so much, and the kids were impressed by it because it was funny. From something like that, you get a sense of encouragement. You have permission to do something like this and maybe you can do some more of it.

Near my hometown there was an annual Arts Festival with a literary component. They published a magazine every summer. It started off as a broadsheet, one big sheet with poems on the front and the back, so I sent some poems to that publication and some of those were published. I became great friends over the years with James Liddy, the editor of the broadsheet, and then of the magazine. Eventually I became a co-editor of the magazine. It was James Liddy who made it possible for me to come to America to graduate school.

He said, "You are thinking of coming to America. Why don't you come to my place, and I'll see if I can get you a T.A.-ship?" So he did all that. That's what made it possible. He's been very encouraging over the years. In education in Ireland there were people who helped me both inside and outside of school.

Certainly to be a writer was considered a kind of dangerous occupation, because it wasn't like you could make money or anything. But at the same time the writer still has a certain status in Ireland.

MARGE: Why is poetry important to the world? Perhaps after September 11, particularly?

EAMONN: I grew up with the notion that poetry was important. It was considered part of the ongoing dialogue of everyday life. For me, from the beginning poetry was important and I never had to establish this myself. I never had to try to convince myself, argue to myself on this question. That's not really an issue. In Ireland, even people who don't read poetry would consider it important and part of the national narrative.

The issues were much more practical: try to write good poems, try to learn as much about poetry as possible, try to get more into the nature of poetry, and how to create it. I think in America, maybe, poetry is a little bit more marginal. I am not sure of the reasons for this because it would seem to be as much part of the national narrative here as any place else. Of course, it's ironic, because American poetry is so good. Nothing really can stand up to twentieth century American poetry. It's a kind of marvel, so it seems strange to me. There are certain things about America that I still haven't figured out and this is one of them. I can see this to some extent as being a fact, but I don't understand why it's like this.

MARGE: Thinking about terrorism in all parts of the world, any part of the world, I hear poets asking: what's the role of the poet in a difficult time?

EAMONN: This has always been an issue in Ireland, particularly for the poets in the north of Ireland. Not so much for people like me from the south, which has been peaceful for the last sixty or seventy years, but Seamus Heaney, for example, has been attacked from people from his own community, the Nationalist community, for not writing about the plight of the Nationalist community. And then people from the other side, the Unionist community, have said, Well, you know he is supporting violence and all that. But what Heaney has said is that poetry can't become propaganda. When poetry becomes propaganda it loses its value and it loses its weight. Poetry has to reaffirm the other things of the world. The good strong continuing kind of things. That's an issue but at the same time, poets shouldn't be remote from the kind of events that happened in September in New York.

In Ireland it's been true that poets and writers have spoken out on these issues, particularly when events happen as in Ireland last year when thirty people were murdered in Omagh. People have spoken out and condemned these, and in writing.

But more particular, I suppose, in music. The Irish rock musicians are very good on all this, like U2 have "Sunday, Bloody Sunday." It is important for poets to be involved, and writers to be involved, in what's going on in the world in which they live. I don't like poetry that's solipsistic, poetry that's totally removed from contemporary issues.

As a result of what happened on September 11, I think writers should speak out and I think there should be poems and essays. Each day *The New York Times* has a whole page of pen portraits, about twenty each day on people who were killed in the World Trade Center. I read those very carefully every day. Some people can't read them because it's too painful, but I read them because I think that we have to take note and we have to hear a little bit of their stories. Each piece relates one anecdote of that person who died. In terms of what they're trying to do, they're very close to lyric poems.

People should respond in some way to what happened. What poetry does is to put into words things that would otherwise be lost. It's a kind of duty to record what happened but I'm not certain it will be recorded, because American poets seem to shy away from these issues. It's not all their own fault; they are made to feel unwelcome perhaps in that kind of realm. It's perhaps something to do with what happened with America in the sixties—divisions that were created that are still there.

Obviously this event has changed America. It's made it a little bit more like Europe, in a sense. It's been like that in Ireland for a long time, but it's not very comfortable. I was in Dublin in 1974 when Dublin was bombed. I wasn't near where anything happened, but it's a scary thing. Once you've been around that kind of tragic event, once you realize that this could happen, you will always be aware of it. I think you have to be, just for your own welfare.

MARGE: A little bit ago, you referred to the good poem, and wanting the poems to be good. Would you talk about how you tell if it is good writing, that of your own or others?

EAMONN: There are times when I buy a book of poems or stories, and I read them, and they reveal something different and something that's very, very exciting. They would elicit in me a kind of feeling that's way beyond words. I would have to leave it and come back to it later on, it would be so overpowering. I read with the anticipation, the expectation, that every book will be like this. With poetry it doesn't have to be a whole book. It could be just one poem or one part of a poem.

There is a quality of voice in this kind of writing that is distinctive and that hits a kind of nerve. It's hard to isolate it in terms of technique because everybody knows what the techniques are; everybody does things in a similar kind of way, more or less. But there's a sense of voice, of a kind of urgency, of having something to say—that's what I find in the work, the writing, that hits me the hardest. You are never going to be hit by it the same way again. But you realize that there's some quality there that is really important.

MARGE: A lot of us have responsibilities with our families—writers trying to balance time for writing, time for family. How do find yourself managing that?

EAMONN: I don't think I have too much trouble with that, for a number of reasons. First of all, the main reason I came to America is that I couldn't get a job in Ireland, so the idea of having a job to me is not a burden, because the alternative was to live without a job. So for me, work doesn't seem to be a burden in any way. I mean, obviously it's time consuming, and it is a matter of making time, but it's not a problem. I grew up among a family of eight children so I was used to a kind of organized chaos at home. I understood from an early age that you did things when you could do them, rather than creating wide open spaces of time for yourself. What I have tried to do was to make writing part of the rhythms of ordinary family life. When my kids were very little, I would write when they were asleep, for example.

What I've always tried to do, because it makes sense to me, is to have all those things working together rather than separate. Not to think of trying to escape from family life to do some writing, because I think that wouldn't work for me. That's why I've never applied to go to a writing colony. I have tried to make writing part of family life. That's my way of organizing things.

I learned a lot unconsciously from my parents, particularly from my mother, to be able to do a lot of different things simultaneously. That was very helpful to me. And also she's a very calm person, so I have tried to be calm like her.

There's a danger there will be too many things to do and there won't be enough time to write, but from my upbringing and from my experience, what would be more difficult for me to do, perhaps, would be to have too much time. I work much better with shorter periods of time. I think it's just one way of dealing with it.

MARGE: You've taken students to Ireland. Would you talk about that?

EAMONN: I have taken students to Ireland because I think Ireland is an interesting place for young people and it's a popular place for young people nowadays. They know a little bit about it from music and movies. Also I've taken them because Ireland is part of the European union and very much a part of the global economy.

What's particularly interesting is taking students from Nebraska and neighboring states to Ireland—taking people from a rural place to another rural place, because the main industry in Ireland is agriculture. It's important to travel and it's important to be able to negotiate other countries, other places. It's always been a great experience; the students have enjoyed it, they've learned a lot, they've socialized a lot, maybe socialized too much. I've had good experiences. Kind of a working holiday for me.

It's also interesting that most of these students would not be English majors, but what they would learn in Ireland primarily would be literature and history. They would understand very quickly that literature is something that is important in Ireland and a way of engaging with the culture, in the way that something else might be important someplace else, like surfing in Hawaii, or whatever. Get into what the local people do. For literature students, Dublin is great because they can go to places where Joyce was, and Yeats, and all these people. They can get a sense of literature, walk in the footsteps of great people.

SHELLY: In *Iron Mountain Road* there seems to be the juxtaposition of the sea and the Nebraska prairie. I've got an excerpt here from "The Waves, The Waves"

Listen, she whispers. Listen. Last month and

years ago. Nothing ever changes, everything changes

too much. On these quiet Nebraska streets you hear
your heart beat, when you drive west the prairie sky

becomes the sea.

How does the landscape and how do the people of the Great Plains enrich your writing? Do you think that's brought another perspective to your writing?

EAMONN: It was very important. We came into Omaha in 1992. To see this whole landscape for the first time—it's very much a primal kind of engagement with place and time and landscape. It was an adventure into the unknown because I didn't know much about Nebraska and the surrounding states. The more I traveled, the more I read, the more I learned, the more interesting it became, and I found over time I was able to bond with the region and to develop a kinship to the place.

There were some similarities in terms of where I grew up. Living in Omaha you live by a river, and I lived by a river in Enniscorthy: the Slaney, which is only a little river, considered a big river in Ireland. But in that sense, the river being important.

From New York to Nebraska, I felt I was moving away from the sea. Where I grew up it was only twelve miles from the sea, so seeing the ocean has been very much a part of life. My parents have a small house on the beach, where we spent a lot of time as kids, so the sea is very important and the landscape of the sea. To go to the sand hills, you would see a landscape without the sea, but which looked like the terrain of the sea. Obviously the vegetation is not the same, but the shape of the hills and the mounds were similar, and it brought back the notion that the sea was there a long, long time ago.

It was interesting to be able to come to a place that you know very little about and to become a part of it, psychologically, physically, and emotionally. I've been able to adapt to different places I've lived, but being in Nebraska was a more creative time, in terms of interacting with place. Before that, we'd been in New York, but everybody's been in New York; it's a different kind of a thing. Being in Nebraska was important, and a lot of the *Iron Mountain* poems are about that sense of discovery.

SHELLY: The sea is a touchstone for you, or the prairie as sea. Are there other themes or other touchstones, that you go back to, or you see as a thread throughout your writing?

EAMONN: The sense of place is very important, but that's a cliché for Irish poets because, in a way that's what Irish poetry is all about: where you come from, how you interact with the landscape, where you were born or where you settled. It's very important, still, to write about place in all its different manifestations. Maybe that's the most important touchstone.

Another one that's important is travel and movement; of going from one place to another, whether that be for an afternoon or for ten years.

Also a sense of displacement is important. Although I've lived in the US for twenty years, and I like living here, I always feel at some level a sense of displacement, and at the same time, when I go back to Ireland, I also feel a kind of sense of displacement there, because I've left and I'm only there for a couple of months.

SHELLY: Do you see an evolution in your writing? Tell us about your books. Are you moving in any different directions?

EAMONN: I try to do that, but to what extent I succeed, I don't know. A lot of people said that the poems written in Nebraska are longer and have longer lines, as a result of engagement with a place. That may or may not be true. Like a musician, I have my style. I started to learn a little bit better, writing the *Iron Mountain* poems, about what I could do and how I could do it, and not to be worried too much about getting everything right, about being perfect. I felt more confident.

I'm interested in all kinds of material, so I try to cast a wide net. What I'm doing at the moment is trying to write poems about my home town, or about my home county, different aspects of it. The poems are inclined to be much shorter and they appear to be more organized. If you look at one of the pages, it looks highly organized. I really don't know the reason for that. I can write to a kind of a plan. I can have a list of things to be done. I can do it that way, other times I can just have material, or something can pop into my head. And I suppose, what pops into your head develops over time and has a shape of its own, takes a direction of its own.

When I started to write, I'd always been nervous writing, whereas now I just consider it fun. It's a great way to while away the hours, fooling around with poems or correcting this and correcting that. I could spend an hour, or half an hour, and it would be real good work, and I'd be happy for a couple of days. I find myself happy when I'm sitting down writing, engaged on that kind of level. I suppose that's because of experience maybe, but I also think it's because if you publish a couple of books, you begin to become more comfortable with yourself as somebody who is a writer.

My publisher in Ireland has been very supportive of me. There's no real uncertainty now. The uncertainty, of course, is the whole operation could go bankrupt. That could happen with any poetry publisher. There's a sense that the books sell pretty well in Ireland. You get a feeling that somebody's reading them. Who they are I don't know. Somebody's reading them. I suppose the key is confidence. To be confident enough to be able to write and feel comfortable with yourself. This is something that came to me slowly. It comes to some people in their twenties, but it didn't come to me until later. It's a product of time, of effort, and also of encouragement.

MARGE: What do you think good teachers of writing should do?

EAMONN: It's a difficult question. When you work with writers, you work with people in different stages of development, so at some points the most important thing you can do is to offer encouragement, possibility, ways of doing things: did you consider doing this, or did you consider doing that? Or offer some kind of advice on that level.

Then when people have been writing for a while, a good teacher of writing would be able to offer good, pointed criticism . Some would be tough on the writer, but they have to hear that, and they have to learn. Even with writers who have been at writing for a while, you always have to balance this sense of encouragement with pointed criticism, because you want to assure the student that he or she is moving forward.

Mentoring is important. A certain number of students continue to send me work, continue to contact me, and so this a long-term, ongoing thing. People who are interested in poetry, or writing in general, if they are serious and if they are showing talent—a good writing teacher has to take these people aside and say, "You are good at this."

Most young writers are so uncertain, so unsure that, even though the work in a workshop is being praised, they still don't feel that they are good at it. Students who are serious, who are into it, I take them aside and I say, "Look, you are good at this. Do you understand that?" They get kind of bashful, but it's very important to tell people that.

It's easier then to offer constructive criticism because you've already said you're good at this. It's not easy for writing teachers in big classes to get all this across, but a lot of the students who are serious, even if they are shy, will seek you out in one way or another, and you will have an opportunity to talk to them. Writers need to have permission to be writers because they may not be getting that from their families, who might think it's weird or time wasting or a beat thing to do.

MARGE: Looking over your years in the classroom, what do you see that you are doing differently, that you have changed?

EAMONN: I used to start with and spend a lot of time with poetic form. Nowadays, it's the last thing I do in a class. The forms are very useful but as I've learned more, I find how regimented education is, in terms of assignments, and points for this, points for that. I think the college students need a little bit of space. We start very loosely. We read other poets. I start with completely non-prescriptive point of view, and so we learn from the ground up.

Later on we get into different kinds of poems in a casual way: well, there's also these sonnets, you know, let's have a look at what a sonnet is, let's see if you can write one of those.

I think it's important that people have something to say. Start with that notion, that it's important to have something to say, and then find a way to say it. That's what I've changed, my perspective. Of course, that's for undergraduates. With graduate students that wouldn't be an issue. It would be on a different kind of a plane.

SHELLY: Who are some writers you like to use in the classroom on the undergraduate level? Who are some of your favorite writers you always go back to or writers you've just discovered?

EAMONN: Well, different writers for different things. I'm a great fan of Frank O'Hara, so we always have some Frank O'Hara poems. Students generally enjoy them because they're so casual and they're fun. They're lively and they're funny. Poems like the Billie Holliday poem, "The Day Lady Died" or "Steps," the love poem, material like that. I use "Diving Into The Wreck" because it is a great poem by Adrienne Rich and it is also a great example of following through with one thing the whole way through the poem, the different images from the sea and ships and wrecks.

I use William Stafford poems. Particularly, I used them in Nebraska because they spoke to people, the Kansas poems and poems with animals, that kind of material.

Each class I use some Irish poets because they're poets they haven't heard of, and I feel it's my job to promote Irish writing every chance I get. Some material by Heaney, for example, and Eavan Boland. I bring in poems in Irish with the translations.

One I think is good for writing is Seamus Heaney's poem, "Digging." The speaker in the poem is watching his father digging for potatoes, then switches around to the idea of the son as a poet who is digging with the pen. The implication is that the poet, the speaker, wants to be as good at working with the pen as his father was with the spade.

SHELLY: What are you working on now, as far as your writing?

EAMONN: I have about half of a book of poems done. I'll see where I am by the end of next May, but it probably won't be done until Christmas or so of next year. In one way there's no rush, you know, because you don't want to rush these things, but in another way, I didn't do very much the last year or so because of moving and having a new job.

I've started to be more serious and consistent about sending poems out to magazines, and doing that end of it. Most of the poems are about Wexford. I call the book *Riabhach* (land of spotted fields in English), but people pronounce it "Reebok," like the shoes.

I write essays and articles as well. I have about a half a book of essays on Irish writing, so I have to decide whether to finish that book in a consistent way, which I'm reluctant to do, or to go into this other project which is a book of essays comparing the Irish and the American views of the West, the West of Ireland and the American West. That's a more interesting project, but it would be harder to do. I have bits and pieces done in terms of the more personal narrative end of it, that's not too difficult, but there's a lot of reading to be done of Western American writing so that's the thing that would involve a lot of time. I'll have to see if I really want to do that or not. As long as it is interesting to do and I felt at the end it was decent, then it would be okay. There's no real rush with it. At the moment I want to get the poems in order, to have at least the bones of a book completely done before I would commit.

The western book could be interesting; there are many areas for comparison. The myth of the west in Yeats, the myth of the west in the American material. Very important in Irish writing in the last fifteen years or so is the role of women. In the last twenty years a brilliant generation of women have taken over Irish poetry. All of the most interesting poets now, particularly under the age of fifty, generally speaking, would be women, and a whole lot of those from the West. That would be something to think about and spend some time on, which would be fine, because I enjoy writing essays, even doing literary criticism. It's enjoyable enough for me, not too painful. I want to continue with it.

I always do reviewing of books, mostly of Irish fiction and some poetry as well. I've been doing articles for two encyclopedias, one in Ireland and one in America, that will be coming out next year.

MARGE: You've spoken about a childhood that's rich in the outdoors, rambling, and in books and language. What do you think might be the effect of TV and video games?

EAMONN: I think that on the surface it looks bad. People are watching videos and they're watching MTV and they're playing Play Station, and they don't seem to be that interested in reading. It looks bad, but I think in the long run it won't make much difference because people still like to read. People still have a need to read, and people still can discipline themselves to be able to enjoy books. This media is addictive but I think books have also been addictive. They're never seen as being addictive; you know, you could curl up with a book for two or three days and just let the world go by, just as you could with media. Through the last century, the new media had a very good effect on writing. Film was very important on poetry and fiction. I don't think it will have a terrible effect. There's a certain passivity involved in it, but I suppose that a lot of people understand that eventually, and they go on to do other things.

A lot of the criticism is a result of a generation gap. People who grew up without technology really don't understand it. I have faith in young people. I know they spend a lot of time with video games, but I don't believe they are bad people. I think in lots of ways the young people of this generation are completely admirable. They seem much more tolerant, much more open minded, more interesting, much more likely to talk about things, to be less introverted. Less hung up. In an overall way, the generation of people growing up with it seem to be fine. It's their parents that I have difficulty communicating with. I do okay with the young people, but when they get older they get more set in their ways. Then I sometimes get frustrated.

The Waves, The Waves

It's five o'clock in November in the final
final hour of light in the large prairie sky, this

morning the first frost on the roofs I watched roll
into the gutters and drain onto the concrete pathways

where no one walks. A neighbour says each day
without ice and snow will make the winter shorter and

so I try to be an optimist too. The weather it matters,
it doesn't matter. Tomorrow at dinner I'll say

that I saw the Irish sky in late October, the tree
branch on the sand, the sunken boulders, and Uncle Paddy

on a towel counting heads bobbing on the water. Driving
home I trained my eyes on a falling wave, scrunching

stones and ebb and flow, his white sideburns and navy hat.
I was there again at season's end—the climbing

car, you don't believe it's there until you see it
slate blue and wilder now. But the sea again.

Listen, she whispers. Listen. Last month and
years ago. Nothing ever changes, everything changes

too much. On these quiet Nebraska streets you hear
your heart beat, when you drive west the prairie sky

becomes the sea. With my beads (Red Willow People &
Catholic), snow shovel, and radial tyres I'm ready

for the winter. Spring—red red evening on a backroad
the radio plays the children to sleep gently swaying

eternities of corn on this uncertain journey home. Kiss
me on the prairie. Kiss me on the beach. Summer bride.

Junk Food

The pumpkins are piled in a trailer
outside the 74 St. Albertson's, the
kids waiting in the car for happy meals
to appear through Window 2 of Burger
King—the fading October light, blowing
leaves, the ugliness of Dodge St. west
of 72nd makes me want to cry, and the
song on the radio is so good it makes
me want to cry, but the children are
so happy with their disgorged bags &
Cokes it makes me want to say a prayer
and drive around again to order a bunch of
Whoppers and my son reminds me of the
first time I drove into a fast-food
joint when I was 37 years of age I
didn't know you had to order at the
metal hole in the wall and drove
straight up to the window and told the
greasy kid what I wanted and he couldn't
believe I didn't know the etiquette of
ordering and that was the Mickey Dees on
Dodge so now I stick to the Home of the
Whopper across the street.

I know I'm
slow—I was 28 before I learned how to
ride a bike and that was due to the fact
that (as the NYPD says) I was on the Aran
Islands where there is no public transport-
ation system. You have to turn the radio
down to hear yourself when you order
junk food and the greasy parrot always
shouts it back to you and when you have
an accent it takes a few tries to
get it right. But you see the children's
faces in the back of the car and
you drive on envious because it's
so fucking hard to find pleasure
in the simple things nowadays.

Soon
we'll be buying pumpkins, cutting
horrible faces, burning candles
and the neighbourhood will be full
of magical stories, milk and
pumpkin pie and the snows will
follow and they will sled and I
will shovel & whistle and
parallel play before cooking
some dinner but it won't be junk
food because I can't cook that good.

Cahore

Standing as we were, there was no getting beyond the surfaces
of Cahore

in mid-pier against the railing, a small boat chugging
angular towards

the slipway at the setting out of the Irish autumn, at
full tide

on an August evening, as towards the Blackstairs our muffled day
fell away.

We had driven out from Enniscorthy and wondered as we sat
what hours

lay ahead for us, as heavy, still, winter barley was dragged from
shorn field

to frantic town. Our children fish for crabs, hand lines hooked
with bacon

as youths leap from the pier's end, as across the cove the final waves
cover the

stony beach, smooth & salty, cool as aluminium, this intense
brightness before

the tide turns and the light fades, how cool it is to be alive
I think

heart on my sleeve, freed crabs running busily down the slipway
for seawater.

The Country Doctor

He is standing at his door talking with the world as it crawls up Main Street to church, dogtrack, hurling game, and he tells me to stop smoking, and that Redmond was a greater Irishman than Pearse.

We sat in his waiting room and they sat up late in cottages on the side of the mountain waiting for his car: the ascending car lights throwing odd shapes on cups, plates, and walls, jars of jam, cornflake boxes, and honey. Dr. Bowe rode out into the night's romance to heal the sick to talk and talk and talk, beating his knuckles on your chest and bringing you back to life. You learned the history of County Wexford with the glass jammed under your tongue.

Hurling players walked down from Bellefield with cloths on their wounds and they lay on the doctor's couch while he threaded the gut slowly through, a fraction above the eye, as the soft voice droned on about the Black and Tans marching through Kiltealy. My brother as a child went to Dr. Bowe with the five pound fee, was given back a pound, told to keep it for himself, and to say nothing to our mother.

Like Samuel Beckett, another great Irishman, he slept by day and worked by night. He visited our houses when the work was done and made the family part of all examinations, gathered round the sick like Rembrandt's students, in The Hollow or out in Bree, all leaning over the doctor's shoulders as he explained.

His skeleton in the final embraces of air danced round the ballroom floor at my brother's wedding. I watched the parade come to shake his hand. He burned like Paul Klee's fire as we waltzed around him, all odd-shaped heads and organs. A one man welfare state, who valued talk more than he did the time. A Jesus come to heal us and teach us how to live. In the ballroom that last night. Walking towards the cathedral looking for your face.

How You Leave

Begin with lake water in summer when you have
gathered instruments of memory on your trestle.
Paint & paste. Brush some movement to hill &

river: rain is washing across a bridge though the
forecast remains favourable. If you walk an hour
beyond our town, the old people say, you will meet

fine weather & a ceilí at the crossroads. A lake is
central to your continent. Now, add tall buildings,
underground stations, a woman at a coffee counter

holding forth on the history of cattle and native
grasses, that form of talk you heard on the dry
prairie. Here, you came to know the lore of

doorbells & children who counted cats as paid-
up members of households. Each lodging place
provided one lesson. Snow must be shoveled

before night falls. So much is added, one old day
is buried. You have times of arrival, time line,
routine, your pencil marks of children unsteadily

drawn on a nursery wall. Then, one Sunday morning,
these empty rooms became holdings of people who
cannot know them as you do. They cross from Iowa,

good life to fill from new shades: the dining room's
too dark, the upstairs carpets faded too flat-footed
beige, too stained by slow Sunday breakfast-in-bed.

On the road dodging landmarks of migrating geese,
a big rig motors southward to Kansas City & such
are sundry details that must be added to record, with

notice, of how you leave Nebraska. Your flight
from this street which suited to a T follows your
possessions. You must think of silver maples, caves

birthing into daylight, this core of weakness under-
lining breath, stroke & sigh. What wind can gather:
hand-tied, you must observe passing days discarded.

You will frame fables of locked rooms with light arms.
Now, face East where hills range full of our late season:
the highway on cold nights will remember your hands.

Twyla Hansen

Twyla Hansen

Raised on a small farm in northeast Nebraska, TWYLA HANSEN is a creative writing presenter through the Nebraska Humanities Council. She received her BS from the University of Nebraska-Lincoln, and has worked as a horticulturist for over 25 years.

Her latest book of poetry is *Potato Soup* (The Backwaters Press, 2003). She is also author of *Sanctuary Near Salt Creek* (Lone Willow Press, 2001), *In Our Very Bones* (A Slow Tempo Press, 1997) and *How to Live in the Heartland* (Flatwater Editions, 1992). Her poetry has been published in *Prairie Schooner, Crab Orchard Review, The Laurel Review,* and in the anthologies *Woven in the Wind* (2001) and *Leaning into the Wind* (1997), both from Houghton Mifflin, and a *Contemporary Reader for Creative Writing* (Harcourt Brace, 1994), among others. Twyla and her husband Tom have a married son and two granddaughters. They live in Lincoln and maintain their yard as an urban wildlife habitat, winning the Mayor's Landscape Conservation Award in 1994.

SHELLY: Can you think of a childhood memory or something you did as a child that characterized who you would be when you grew up? Not necessarily grow up to be a writer, but grow up to be Twyla Hansen?

Twyla's yard in north Lincoln is an official wildlife habitat with prairie flowers and beautiful trees around the house that she and Tom have shaped and continue to build and modify. Twyla shows us through the huge new kitchen into the sun room. We settle in to watch the goldfinches, cardinals, and nuthatches in her back yard.

TWYLA: I think I've always done things backwards. For example, I first had a family, then I went to college. I never set out to be a writer by any means and didn't start writing until I was thirty-five. I took a class at Nebraska Wesleyan University because I got free tuition as an employee, a horticulturist. I never thought that I could write; I had never tried it. Although, I must say I was interested in writing, and poetry in particular. I read William Kloefkorn and Ted Kooser's *Cottonwood County*, and I said, Oh my gosh, people write about ordinary things. It was a revelation, an epiphany. I thought maybe I could try this some day.

The first class I took was Kloefkorn's. We read short stories and did a little writing about them. The next fall I thought I could be brave enough to take a poetry writing class. I didn't stop writing after the class. I had a lot I wanted to say, I guess.

As a child, I never once thought about writing. My dad was a storyteller who would tell stories to the point I got sick of hearing them. Now I wish I had recorded them because, unfortunately, I don't remember them all. He would tell stories about his parents who came over from Denmark, and what they went through to make a life on the plains in farming.

What made me what I am is the experience of the farm. More than anything, the life on the land and the connection to the land. My grandpa came over in the 1880s and farmed with his uncle in Burt County. They lived in a dugout for a couple of years, going back to Omaha in the winters. One spring they came out and they couldn't find the dugout. The creek had risen; there had been so much snow. These are the stories I heard.

My grandpa went back to Denmark and brought over his first cousin, my grandmother, and they got married in this country. She was sixteen, I believe, and he was in his 30s. They lost the first three children to typhoid; the oldest one was four when he died. How could you live after your first three children died?

They had three more children. My dad was the youngest; his mother was in her forties when he was born. My dad was in his forties when I was born, so we have this close connection to the old world. Those were the stories I grew up with, the old world and Denmark and what it was like in this country for them. It was so lonely.

My grandmother's sister came over with her husband. They were going to live here and farm, but her sister didn't like it so they went back to Denmark. That left my grandmother, again, alone. As I understand it, my grandfather was not an overly warm, effusive person. The land is so different here; Denmark was wooded and hilly. When they came to the treeless plains, it must have been mind-boggling. I can't imagine her loneliness. That kind of shapes my thoughts.

SHELLY: Did you know your grandmother well?

TWYLA: I was five when she died. I didn't know her really, but my father had such great respect for his mother. He was thirty-one when he married my mother, who was eighteen, similar to what his father had done. My father had to quit school when he was in tenth grade to start farming and he resented that all his life. He didn't like farming; he was asthmatic and had hay fever, if you can imagine. He didn't want my brothers to farm. None of them are farmers, but I'm a horticulturist by training, so I have that connection with the land.

If we hadn't moved to Lincoln, I would probably be married to a farmer up in Lyons right now. I can imagine that would be my life, but my dad quit farming in the 60s, learned to be a meat cutter, sold the farm, and moved to Lincoln. Those are the experiences that have shaped me and continue to shape me.

SHELLY: What about the influence of your mom?

TWYLA: My mother is not a storyteller at all. In fact, I have to pry stories out of my mother. She grew up in a big family during the Depression, lots of mouths to feed. Her father was not a real successful wage earner, I guess you'd say, so at one point he picked up the family and moved to California, like the Joads in *The Grapes of Wrath.* He actually worked cutting down the redwood forest in California (laughter), but the work was there. I didn't grow up with stories about my mother's family but we had big family gatherings, huge deafening family get-togethers.

SHELLY: Growing up, did you ever think you were different from other kids or other people in your family?

TWYLA: Not having television when all of our neighbors did was a huge source of embarrassment for me. I was fourteen before we got a TV. My parents were conservative and didn't spend a lot of money. Growing up without television, growing up on a farm with three older brothers, I didn't have any playmates, so I spent a lot of time alone. I think that's what shaped me, finding things to do on my own and observing things. I've put a lot of those details in my poems.

I did a lot of watching. I don't know if it was because I was the baby or what, but my mother didn't make me do anything. I remember watching my mother chop off chicken heads, render the lard, gather the eggs, and I tagged along. I don't think they expected me to do the work. When I got married it was as if I didn't even know how to wash the clothes. My mother-in-law had to show me how to separate the colors.

I don't know if I set myself apart. I always thought I was special in some ways, but maybe it was because I was the baby, you know. My dad treated me differently than my brothers. They had to do the chores. There were very few expectations of me. My dad expected my brothers to go to college. He'd say, "Get all the education you can" and that rubbed off on me, but in an indirect way. I think the expectation was that I would get married.

MARGE: What was your school like?

TWYLA: I went to a one-room country school. It actually had two rooms, but there were not enough students for two rooms. We had one teacher, kindergarten through eighth. I had a huge grade—we had five. A lot of the grades had two and there weren't any kids in some of the grades. There were teachers that were kind of mean to some of the kids and weren't very good teachers, I can see that now. I got along great with my teachers. Eighth grade was the best year because my friend Anne and I studied for the spelling contests. What that meant was sitting out in the hallway with a huge dictionary and learning words.

The state didn't believe that country kids were taught as well as town kids so we had to take what they called the eighth grade examination. We were the top scorers in the county, so we did okay.

SHELLY: As a country kid, were you treated differently when you went to town to high school?

TWYLA: No, I had friends there, and it's such a small town anyway, everybody knew everybody. There were probably 1,500 people in town. I went to high school two years and then we moved to Lincoln, so I went from a town of less than 2,000 to a high school with more than 2,000. It was hard, but you find your little group within the big group. I don't feel as close to the classmates in Lincoln as I do to the ones back there.

MARGE: What do you think makes good teaching?

TWYLA: My first writing experience was in Kloefkorn's class, so how can you go wrong there? What I've noticed about the way he teaches is—and I think it's admirable—he just lets you start. You just do it. That's how you learn, by doing. You start writing, at whatever level, and learn by your mistakes. He didn't emphasize so much what didn't work as what did. I think that's good teaching. Having someone say the positive things. "Let's build on this."

I try to do that as much as possible when I am teaching. I think it's good to have a writer as a writing teacher. There's theory, and then there's writing. They don't always jive. You can find shelves of books on how to write, but it's interesting to note that I'm always more interested in ones written by writers.

SHELLY: Tell us about some of your teaching experiences in your workshops.

TWYLA: I have always liked the junior high workshops. I've liked to get the kids talking. I feel like I'm being this crazy cheerleader, I'm talking, I'm getting them to talk. These kids are gathered from all the different middle schools in Lincoln. They don't know each other and they really don't want to look stupid in front of their peers. I'm writing with them, and I say this is our chance to do something wild here.

I like working with the Platte River Trails trip. It's been a good one. The last few years, more science teachers came along rather than just English types, and science teachers don't write (laughter) so the trick was to get them to journal about what we saw along the Oregon Trail.

Getting them to write about what they're experiencing is a way in, like a wedge, to get them to write. Most of them don't feel they are writers. It's fun doing some writing exercises and journaling with them. I have them do a timeline: here's what we did at 8 o'clock, and then at 10:00 and noon, little entries all the way along. I have them write about one entry and encourage them to keep the others in mind for later writing.

On the trail we stop at two pioneer graves, one by Kenesaw and another by Scottsbluff. A participant who was nervous about writing was touched by being at the graves and wrote a powerful, emotional piece about it. That kind of writing is close to the heart. Those have been good experiences. I'm hoping to do more. There's the Mari Sandoz workshop, which I've done, a week-long session at Chadron. That's maybe more of a challenge, with high school kids you have for the whole week.

SHELLY: Do you remember the first poem you fell in love with? Or the first book?

TWYLA: When I talk about my first writings, I always point to *Cottonwood County* and I say, that's where I learned it was okay to talk about dirt and cattle. I went back and read it the other day, and there isn't any dirt or cattle in it. (laughter) There wasn't ostensibly dirt or cattle.

I remember my first impression of Ted Kooser was that he wrote a lot about death. All poets write about death, but at that time I wasn't ready for it. I was ready for the dirt and cattle, I guess, but I appreciate his poems more now. It's funny, you go through those phases.

SHELLY: Do you remember any books or poems influencing you in your earlier years?

TWYLA: I don't remember studying any poetry in high school. Certainly not in horticulture. When I was an undergraduate, I took Roger Welsch's folklore. That was the best class, because everything is folklore. He would have us keep a journal and bring in examples of folklore. And, of course, Roger is a showman, so he just sat up there and was Roger. (laughter) The class was doing exactly what poets do, observing, making notes, seeing what is folklore all around you that is not written down. Those are the kinds of things that make poetry, too.

SHELLY: How do you think your poetry has changed or evolved since those early days in Kloefkorn's class? Subject matter or form, for example?

TWYLA: I started writing about my farm experience. My first book contains a lot about the farm and those early experiences. Some of the first poems I wrote were kind of easy, had an easy emotion, maybe just about one thing, and I know now that doesn't grab people too much. Everything is connected to something else and I see how far I can push that kind of thing. You've got to keep making new challenges for yourself or you get bored. What is that saying: *No surprise for the writer, no surprise for the reader.* I want to surprise myself every time I sit down to write. I get there sometimes.

SHELLY: What helps you get there? What inspires you?

TWYLA: I read. I tell young people you need to read and, unfortunately, kids don't spend much time reading. I think if you want to write, you need to read, so I sit down with a book of poetry or some writer I've heard. If I'm interested in that writer, I'll try to get their book. That gets me in the frame of mind. If I'm stuck I'll give myself an exercise, sit down with a challenge in front of me. For instance, I have to use these words and this situation, now write something. And let the words drive it. The poems might be a little unusual and it doesn't always work.

SHELLY: When it does work, why do you think it works?

TWYLA: There are lots of ways to go about writing, no one way or right way. I'm interested in this whole concept of creativity. Where does it come from?

I want my writing to be interesting to myself as well as someone else. Writing about a thing or a situation doesn't always make good poetry. You have to find some surprises somewhere along the way. That's what I try to do. It doesn't work every time you sit down, but as Jack Nicklaus said, "The more I practice, the luckier I get."

SHELLY: We tell our students and we tell our children: dream big. What are your dreams now?

TWYLA: Everyone wants recognition. I'm not so much driven by any sort of ambition. I'm happy when my poems touch someone in some way. If a poem gets out there and someone reads it and likes it, that's a reward. I don't think, for myself, poetry will ever be a career. It's a life choice; it's a life style. It certainly isn't going to make me rich. It's a good thing I'm not worried about that.

I'm an environmentalist and try to do things with the earth and for the earth and I'm into community service here and there. I'm not single-minded about writing. I love writing but it's not my whole life. I have a family and a home and I have other interests. Writing is definitely part of my life, a big part, but it's not everything.

SHELLY: How is your poetry distinctive from other poets in this state and elsewhere? What do you think it means to say "Twyla Hansen's voice"?

TWYLA: I think Midwest writers and Nebraska writers have solid values from which to build. We are honest and hardworking. There's not much phoniness, I would say. We are pretty free of that around here. I think my poetry comes out of that kind of thing. Most writers in this area are not looking for the cheap shot or something for show. There's something solid behind most of the writing, and I don't know how mine differs, but an individual's writing is different in the way you express yourself. You don't think about voice when you're writing.

SHELLY: How would you complete this sentence: If you are really going to teach kids to write...?

TWYLA: I think you need to read to them. Prompt writing by reading something first. It's amazing how that works because it affects what they write. You can't be sure they will have good models so you need to bring those into the classroom.

If you really want to teach kids to write, you have to give them paper and pencil and let them write. Nebraska poets are really under-appreciated; I was never taught Nebraska poets in high school. We're missing the boat there, a little bit. There are all these great writers right here in this state.

SHELLY: I'm glad you brought that up because no one has mentioned that about our own Nebraska poets, teaching and bringing them into the classrooms.

TWYLA: I grew up thinking poetry was something that was British and hard to understand. If I had known that poetry could be about ordinary things, I would have been more interested much earlier in writing. When students are studying Nebraska culture and history, I know there are lots of things to teach, but wouldn't it be great if they could study a couple of Nebraska writers? They have a lot to study in fourth grade now, I realize. My granddaughter's in fourth grade. I doubt if they've ever seen a poet, if they even know what a poet looks like. It would be kind of cool to have some resources available.

SHELLY: Is there a question we didn't ask or a subject we didn't hit upon, that you'd like to comment on?

TWYLA: I think the questions were interesting because childhood and your early experiences affect your whole life.

I find it difficult to write unless I'm sitting in this chair. That's how I write now. I have a certain place. You didn't ask the usual questions, like how often do you write? (laughter)

SHELLY: Okay, tell us about your process.

TWYLA: Lately I think I'm becoming a hermit. I sit right here and write. I give myself a certain time to do that. It's usually right after a weekend. Mondays are writing days, like Mondays used to be my mother's wash day.

I think regular attention to writing is important because it's so hard when you've had a dry spell for a while to get back in the saddle. Sometimes you need that time, though, to think. I go in waves as far as writing goes. Sometimes I'll have lots of ideas and every poem I write, I like something about it. Then you feel very lucky. It doesn't always work that way. I go through dry spells, too.

MARGE: Is there something you've always wanted to do?

TWYLA: With writing?

MARGE: With anything.

TWYLA: Well, I always wanted to be a rock singer. (laughter) I thought if I could get up in front of an audience and sing, that would just be the perfect thing.

SHELLY: So when are you going to start music lessons?

TWYLA: (laughter) Yeah.

MARGE: Not on Mondays.

Planting Trees

Humming an old hymn,
I shove my spade deep
and turn over rich earth.
Good soil, good ground for
growing trees that alone
I'm planting this Good Friday.

As did my grandfather, who,
looking over the homestead,
uttered in Dane: *Augk! No Trees!*
and set out to correct the
godless plains. And my young
father planting oak, elm, pine,
and cedar, maple, spruce, and
hackberry. I learned those
stories later, worshipped among
the limbs of their labor.

Now these hands and feet
tire, wish they were finished
yet never quit. Like my
father and grandfather before me,
I pray to the soil, to the sky
for strength, for good planting
weather, to continue. Each
shovelful now a sacrament:
Take eat, this soil my body
crumbled for your roots; drink
of this water, my blood, shed
for you now, and ever more.

And I sing the hymn
again and again,
knowing there is no end,
knowing no end.

Just Before Dawn

Just Before Dawn

Just before dawn the great blue heron
glides its bony frame into the dusty light,
flapping slow above the russet field,
giant harvester inching through the rows,

its operator my father, perhaps,
pulling an ancient combine
behind an even older John Deere,
thin brown arms propped over its wheel,
his lungs wheezing, wiping his nose
with a rolled-up sleeve.

I can see his seedcap and work denims,
this scene replayed slowly ten thousand times,
following him after dark into the kitchen,
milking and feeding and fixing complete,

at the sink stripped to his boxers and undershirt,
washing with Lava the day's grit off
his leathery face and arms,
aroma of supper and sweat and soap,
his old-fashioned wire-rims and old country
references, hold-over from the last century,

not embarrassing me now—
flying above it all,
settling down onto shallow water,
body erect, senses alert, all alone.

My Husband Speaks of Wood

My Husband Speaks of Wood

It's all there he says
In the grain
The story of the tree
Its stresses
Its imperfections
The thick of rain
The thin of drought

Burl and pattern and knot
How some woods age smooth
Filled with grace
How maple sometimes goes
Birdseye
Others split and pockmark
Beyond salvation

Feel this he says
It's walnut smell it
Juglans
This pine
Resin
Or this cherrywood
Call it sweet

Wine aged in oak
Taste it
The tannins
Wood and beer
Their grain their
Pigment their
Texture

I'll rip these two
Plane them to hear
A distinctive resonance
Show you bookmatching
With tung oil finish them
Wait!
I'll show you

Twyla Hansen

The Snowball Sisters

Behind me, behind the sofa
two little sisters stand styling my hair—
combs, bands and barrettes—
their tools put to serious use,
their voices from somewhere far in the back
of their blameless throats.

The Snowball Sisters

Reading the news, I try to picture it:
Earth, once a gigantic snowball.
There's now evidence our planet turned
so cold, oceans froze from pole to equator.
Half a billion years ago, for some ten million years.
Thawing then in a sudden greenhouse effect.

Their breaths, uttering tiny dictums, are cool
and sweet. Today the sun bears down,
a scorching sphere. Concrete a willing
and absorbing heat sink. Have we decided finally
more is better? The ozone shrinks.
I obey their every command.

Volcanoes, however, keep belching
carbon, the runaway glaciation cannot last.
I read faster. *Then, all hell breaks loose,*
The scientist says. *The meltdown is rapid.*
Evolution, we are told, speeded up, defining
everything: complex species.

In a few short months it will be winter,
the onward march. Glaciers wait patiently
on mountain slopes. Days shorten.
We will be cozy around the fire, or throwing
snowballs. Youth, as it was meant to be,
perfectly wasted on the young.

Worms and snails, meanwhile, burrowing
into the ocean floor, stirring up gases.
The younger one swipes at my bangs
with a brush. I am frozen in place. The older one
pauses, swatch of my hair in her hand, whispers
This will only hurt a little.

Backyard

It's that place after
I've gone everywhere,
seen everything,
I can't wait to return to,

trumpetcreeper and sumac and
bluestem,
prairie small enough
to be taken in—

and I sit at dusk
with a fatcat on my lap
watching blue in the form of jay
become red in the form of sunset,

my back yard unable
to contain itself, already
a half moon nesting atop the ash,
and I'm like that myself, I guess,

at home but not contained, already
my wild heart beating
as if those wings
sufficient to have brought me back,

in spite of all
that's so secure
to lift me somehow far,
far away.

J.V. Brummels

J.V. Brummels

J.V. BRUMMELS is the descendant of pioneers who first came to the region in the 1870s. His great-grandfather, Peter Brummels, served as a fireman on the first train to cross Wayne County. His great-grandmother, Augusta Stark, was brought as a child by her uncle and aunt to the area in the 1870s. When the uncle and aunt died, neighbors raised Augusta. She met Peter Brummels at the newly-formed railroad town of Hoskins.

J.V. Brummels was educated at the University of Nebraska-Lincoln and Syracuse University. He teaches at Wayne State College where he directs the Plains Writers Circuit. His poems have appeared in *Chariton Review, Quarterly West, The Midwest Quarterly, Prairie Schooner,* and elsewhere. His work has been anthologized in *A Geography of Poets* (Bantam, 1979). He has also been published in *Rolling Stone.* His books include *614 Pearl (*Abattoir Editions, 1986), *Deus Ex Machina* (Spectra/Bantam, 1989), and *Sunday's Child* (Basfal, 1994). His most recent books are *Clay Hills* (Nosila Press, 1996) and *Cheyenne Line and Other Poems* (Backwaters Press, 2001). He lives in Wayne County, where he and his family run a horseback cattle operation.

SHELLY: Could you talk about your early life and possible influences on the writer, teacher, rancher you later became?

J.V.: At home there were seven kids and not a lot of books in the house. For a while Mom got those condensed books from the Reader's Digest, and later my older brother joined a Book of the Month Club. There were enough kids so that if I kept my head down and my mouth shut, I could maybe get away from chores for a while, so reading made all kinds of sense for me. I loved it. I would sneak away and read whenever I could.

Part of the reason I became a poet was that I loved falling into the worlds those authors were creating. My world seemed bland and boring by comparison, and I was looking for a way to fill up the time. Television wasn't a big thing; we got one channel on the TV, so I was always looking for something to do.

The country school I went to got books from the Lincoln library by the crate every six weeks or so. School was always easy for me, so I would read a lot there. I got into the habit of reading early on and read pretty adult things. (laughter) We had a dictionary, which was good, because there were a number of words that I would run into that I didn't know.

Darrel Krei was the teacher at that country school for four years when I was a first grader through a fourth grader. He was nineteen, with a two-year certificate from Wayne Normal. He was probably the first educated person I was around much. He spoke very well and his grammar was flawless. I was interested in that. He had a big impact on me because he suggested another way of looking at the world when he spoke. He was different.

We went to a big Lutheran church, and when we would sing, there were good voices. That had an impact on me. I liked the sounds of it. If I looked real hard, I'm sure I could find those sorts of rhythms at work in my poems.

When I was a freshman in high school, we had a lot of etymology. There was something about that science of words, where words came from, that

As we pull up in front of the ranch house, J.V.'s black dog puts up a ruckus. We know we are being announced and, sure enough, J.V. comes out to receive us. We take a side trip to the corral to look at his horses, and then go into the kitchen for good old-fashioned coffee from an honest-to-goodness percolator.

interested me.

Clearwater was a tiny town, no paved streets, a big old wide main street. People parked on the curbs and people parked in the middle, and during the spring thaw, you could get a car stuck on main street. Probably the biggest influence was Ralph Frakes, who came to Clearwater to take a teaching job and to avoid the draft. He had an MFA in drama from Denver University. He didn't have any experience and was teaching by the seat of his pants. He was a dramatic, skinny fellow, dark-haired, which was sort of special in that place where everybody was pretty much blonde. He would read to us, which was his way of teaching. He did accents and dialect. Every reading was a dramatic set-piece. He dumped a carton of paperback novels in the library and let us use those. Ralph Frakes had all the kids in that school reading, which was an amazing thing in itself.

It was a bad winter, and our place was eighteen miles out of town, so my brother and I stayed at my grandparents because we couldn't get back and forth. We partied with Ralph. He asked me one time what I was going to do, and I had decided English looked pretty good. He looked at me and said, "Well, you know, studying literature might be good for you." I think he was trying to steer me away from acting, because he could see I didn't have any talent there. So that got me started on an English major, which I dropped and then came back to.

Off and on I had written ever since I was a little kid. I didn't do it steadily and I didn't keep journals or diaries, but I would think of an idea and scribble it down. When I was small, I thought I'd like a job with *Mad* magazine because it would be great to work with those guys. (laughter)

I ended up in a workshop in Lincoln where the poems were handed out to the rest of the class anonymously for comments. The first poem I turned in, the students' responses were: Oh, yeah, this is good, and I kind of like this. It went around the table like that. I was feeling pretty cocky, and then the teacher said when they got done, "Well, this poem demonstrates all that is wrong with early poems," and he tore it apart line by line and sentence by sentence and punctuation mark by punctuation mark. I guess there was something in me that wanted to continue writing because rather than drop it and get out of there, I thought, well, I'll figure this out. I took it as a challenge.

I got to the point where I was going to graduate, and Greg Kuzma asked me what I was going to do after graduation. I didn't have a clue. I was just waiting for my student deferment to run out and the war to run out. He said, "Well, if you want into grad school someplace, let me know and I could probably help you with that." That seemed to make sense. I decided that, like all good Western boys, I should go East for an education and I did.

I met some great poets at Syracuse. Two poets working there at the time were W.D. Snodgrass and Phillip Booth. Phillip Booth, a great craftsman, was good at looking at a poem and saying, "You know, if you just change this a little bit, it would be a much better poem."

W.D. Snodgrass had won his Pulitzer fifteen or twenty years before. While he was looking at students' poems, he would say, "Look at these two or three lines here. Man, if I had ever written anything that good, I would just break the pencils and throw them out the window." I thought, "Wow, that is high praise." It turned out he said that on the average of once or twice a week. (laughter) He was generally supportive of what we did.

Phil Booth was picky, and he taught us a lot of things by being picky. Snodgrass didn't much care about that sort of thing, but he was incredibly encouraging. He did tell us a lot about poetry. He spent half of each workshop talking about a poem that he cared about, you know, Whitman, Frost. He set a high standard and that was good.

As helpful as Phil Booth was, it was what Snodgrass said, in the most off-handed manner, that kept coming up in our minds.

MARGE: His use of language? His ideas about poetry?

J.V.: I think his ideas about poetry. If I was going to give it a quick and easy label, I'd say that what he did was celebrate poetry and celebrate language. He was an emotional poet. He was a poet who worked in form. The book he got the Pulitzer for was *Heart's Needle*, a first sort of confessional. The poems were not free verse, which is what I expected from a guy who was writing confessional poetry. There was a rhythm and a rhyme scheme involved. He exposed his emotions. *Heart's Needle* was a story of his divorce and the pain of losing his daughter through this divorce. There was not much oblique about his approach to emotion nor was there anything obscure about his pain. If I hadn't been before, by the time I got out of there I was a confessional poet.

SHELLY: Did you always know that you would come back west? Was it in your bones?

J.V.: I was just looking for a way to make a living and to work in a place where I wanted to live.

I did my program at Syracuse, and Lin did hers, so we were there for about four years. We were tired of the weather, for one thing; Syracuse has very overcast days, high humidity in the summer, not particularly cold, lots of snow. It was a crowded city. We had had enough of cities. When we left, we decided we would at least cross the Missouri River. We got that far and not much further and settled first in Wayne and then we moved after about four years onto this place.

At one point after I had gone through my program, I gave up writing. There was no money in it and there was no job in it. It was a huge disappointment; the world was not knocking at my door waiting for my next poem. (laughter) Off and on through that time I did various kinds of social work. We got here and I talked myself into a job at Wayne State. The first few years, I spent half my time doing poets-in-the-schools, using grants from the Nebraska Arts Council, spending time in old folks' homes and schools.

About 1980, my students became more career-oriented, more interested in the correct placement of a semicolon than in the world's greatest poem. At present, we are again in one of those places where young people are interested in the arts generally and poetry specifically. It is a good time to be teaching poetry.

Another thing W.D. Snodgrass said was, "If you can do anything else, do it. If you can quit, quit." I thought that was one of the silly things that he would say but that turned out to be true. I tried to quit and, after a month or two, I found myself writing an eight-page poem. People who are poets don't really have a choice about it.

MARGE: You have touched on teaching. Is there anything you might want to say, J.V., about what makes good teaching?

J.V.: Yeah, I'll say a little bit. I've got a few weeks left and then I am on sabbatical until next August. I'm pretty excited about that. I had a sabbatical about ten years ago that gave me a chance to think about a lot of things, including teaching. One of the things that hit me then is that students and teachers end up in adversarial relationships. I want to make that not true. I want to make sure, if possible, that we are not in an adversarial relationship.

I often wondered what is really important about what we are doing here. I thought, if my students are reading books, I'm happy. In my general education lit classes at the freshman and sophomore levels, I stopped having them write papers. It was supposed to be a literature class and what it got to be about were those doggone papers. I would point out all the things that were wrong, and guess what—pretty soon I was in an adversarial relationship with my students.

I tried to go into those classes with the idea that we are all on the same side, and we are looking at some books, some novels and poetry, creative nonfiction. These books, with luck, will inform us or address matters of the spirit as nothing else does. That is the territory literature has to stake out if it is going to have any sort of validity in an academic setting. If you don't talk in terms of spiritual matters, I don't think you can defend its inclusion in the catalog except as a kind of intellectual history.

If we are going to talk about literature, we probably really need to talk about what is immediate and close to us. That was natural for me because I have a regional look at the world. When I approached it that way, I could jettison the big fat anthologies and bring in those small press books.

We got rid of the papers and we read out loud. I gave them variety; I would have sixty titles in the bookstore. They would select so many points' worth. They read a lot.

If you have a long list of requirements, students spend time trying to circumvent them, so I made it real simple: you have to come. (laughter) You have to be here, and you have to read what you say you're going to read. Students occasionally came in, and they hadn't read what they had contracted to read. I was drinking a lot of coffee then and I had it worked out that I could get red; it was a nice acting job. I could raise some veins. (laughter) I did it for a class one time and raised veins in my neck and forehead—

SHELLY: You have more acting talent than you thought.

J.V.: I would practice doing that. I would teach one or two of these sections every semester, and in each of those I would have to have that conversation with a student, the poor schmuck. (laughter) I would tell him, if you don't get the book read, you don't get the book read, but you are a lot better off just telling me, "Look, I didn't read the book." It's okay. But when you lie to me, it becomes personal. There was always one poor schmuck in there who would try to sneak through and that would give me my opportunity to be outraged. Lying is a personal thing.

I would tell them to read what they say they're going to read and be able to talk about it, and then read us a page or a poem out loud. We spent a lot of time in those classes listening to people read.

Early on when I was getting the system going, I was careful in my explanations: if this isn't good for you, go do another section. There are probably sections where you don't have to read anything or pretend to read anything. If you have trouble reading out loud, maybe this isn't the section for you.

In one of the sections, I had a student who had this incredibly bad stutter. At first, to listen to her was alarming, but the students were very patient. After a while it took on a sort of beauty and you started waiting for this to work when she read. It was obviously difficult for her but she was committed to doing it and she would get through it. What it meant was that we had a little longer than usual to sit and listen to somebody read in her own technically flawed voice, but what the heck. It was still a fine voice to listen to.

One of the things that I tell students is that we can talk about anything you want to talk about. The only rule is that we have to talk about it together. That means that we are not going to have a little dyad talking over here and a little triad over there. My notion is that while we are in class we can take on any topic, but we are a group and we will work together.

We started doing readings by young poets. The audiences for those readings are much bigger than for a famous poet. We don't have a good place for readings. There will be people standing in the halls because there is no place to sit. There is something about those young poets speaking more directly to that young audience. If we don't do everything we can for young writers and young poets, we will lose them. They need an audience and they need to get their poems out in front of people.

SHELLY: Do you think the performance poetry, the rap poetry, the poetry slams, have been a component of that?

J.V.: I think poetry slams have been great, but there is a kind of delivery when you are doing a slam. It sometimes becomes more delivery than substance. It doesn't make any difference if you are talking about the cat who fell off the roof or you are talking about your mother's illness, it all sounds the same. I think that is a little bit of a problem; I wonder about that with slams. They do value performance and delivery maybe more than substance.

On the other hand, the first poems were oral. Early on when somebody was scratching little horses on a cave wall, somebody grunted, and somebody else said, "Hey, that's good. I like the way you did that. Tell us that grunt again." (laughter)

So poetry is first oral, and poetry is, I think, best oral. I love the page. Clearly, I don't want poetry not to have books and magazines, but I think it needs to start with the breath and the heartbeat, and you do that out loud. If you're lucky, that transfers onto the page. Somebody can pick up the book and get that breathing right and get that rhythm right and make it work, but the page is just a convenience. It's a way of communicating something a longer distance than you can shout.

I like slams. We used to ask young folks to do a reading, and they'd become very nervous. Somehow—I don't understand this quite yet—somehow to read at a slam is less nerve-wracking for some of them. It may be this generation of poets, the amazing nerve of folks to get up in front of fifty or sixty people in a bar. We always have them in bars, and it gets loud. You can cut the smoke with a knife, and there are people yelling, and there are people out there who can barely sit in their chairs by the time it's done. You get up there and you lay something out in front of them.

MARGE: Would you talk about what makes good writing?

J.V.: No adverbs. (laughter) I have an anti-adverb campaign going. I don't think the word *quickly* ought to exist. I don't think he ran *quickly*, he ran *quick*, because *quick* is a quick word and *quickly* is not.

There's the old chestnut: write about what you know. Well, that's true, but write about what you don't know in an attempt to figure out what it is. For young poets particularly, it is important to keep playing and keep experimenting. If you can keep playing, if you're engaged with language, crossing out a word here and adding a word there, the poem keeps changing until you get it exactly right. There are some people who don't want to do that.

Try to understand what a poem might be able to explain to you. Literature can make some sense out of things that nothing else can. Literature addresses those matters of the human spirit. Some of those are enigmas that never can be solved or explained or articulated in any way except with a poem.

I like the concrete stuff; give me images or tell me a story. Don't give me a beginning, a middle, and an end. That's a leftover from writing all these essays that they write forever: an introductory stanza, body stanzas, concluding stanza. Don't do that, don't worry about it. A poem has a beginning, a middle, and an end but not necessarily in that order, so just let it stop sometime. You might have a tendency to want to sum it all up at the end. Many last stanzas you could cross off and not hurt the poem.

Do something honest. It doesn't have to be true, but it ought to be honest, as my friend Scott McIntosh says.

MARGE: I like that.

J.V.: Yeah, he is absolutely right about that. Make sure that if you are going to bullshit me, we know it is bullshit. Quality bullshit can make a heck of a poem. Pretend to know some things, and in the pretending, we may actually know them.

There are a number of rules, and any rule in poetry ought to be broken every once in a while. I like to keep it monosyllabic. I like to keep it English rather than Latin and try to avoid the polysyllables, although there are folks, most notably Bill Kloefkorn, who can run those long words out there and they work beautifully.

(Sound of dryer buzzing)

Here's the thing about teaching: Don't teach Mondays. It gives you the opportunity to do the laundry, and in between loads, you can get set up for the week. Mom did the laundry on Monday, so I have to do it on Monday. I am not using a hand wringer, so I can get a lot done in between loads.

MARGE: Laundry as tether, which keeps you from running off from your writing.

SHELLY: When do you write? How do you get inspired? What is your process?

J.V.: I write erratically. Right now I am in a strong blue funk, because there was just enough to do this fall that the rhythm of my writing has been interrupted, and it does make me not as much fun to be around. I would like to think that I'm pretty easy to be around, and I can find a lot of fun in a lot of things, if I am getting a poem accomplished every once in a while. But when the rhythm gets interrupted, then to re-establish it is like moving heaven and earth. I am feeling pretty good right now because I have been thinking poems quite a bit the last few days, so I am getting close to getting something down, and once I can get a poem or two going good, then the rhythm picks up.

I try to work on poetry in the mornings. I get up and do whatever chores and get a cup of coffee and go downstairs and have a draft or two or three that I can look at and play with.

I start with notes in a composition book. When I get a little quiet time in the evening and have an idea or rhythm or a piece of language or an image, I scribble it down. What I find is that they will hold the course. When it is working well for me, I will have a bunch of stuff, usually very short things, and I will think these are different poems. Often I find they are all the same poem. I get from that journal onto a word processing program and then hammer it until it takes some kind of shape that is pleasing and is honest. Some of that comes together pretty quick and some of it takes a long time. I don't really care as long as I am doing it.

I don't know that I worry about finishing a poem. I am a happy camper as long as I am working on poetry, whether I ever get it done or not. I used to get off on keeping them in the mail to the journals and magazines. That was a game I played and it was useful in that it did give me a deadline. When I would get four poems, I'd think now I've got to finish this poem and pack it up and send it to a journal. There were times when I would have six packets of poems out. I haven't done so much of that lately. I have this sense that the journals are not as efficient, not as focused as they used to be in taking care of business, making some decisions and getting the stuff back. I am guessing the average readership for even a prestigious journal is minuscule.

I need to get back into submitting poems. One of the things that W.D. Snodgrass said was when you get poems rejected, just slip them into an envelope and send them right back out. Don't be sitting around looking at them. Get them in shape and finish them before you send them out. Once you have sent them out, keep them in the mail. I was good about that for years.

Several years ago, I had two or three poems in the *Iowa Review* and I was real happy and pleased. About six months later, it occurred to me that of all the writers and poets and readers I know, nobody had mentioned that they had seen my poems in a lead-off spot of the *Iowa Review*, which made me believe maybe we were not reading these journals very much. (laughter) It seems the journals are pretending there is a kind of readership out there for them that I don't think exists. If that's the case it is maybe time to refocus or restructure, re-emphasize, and try for a readership.

In my writing, as quick as I can, I get the poems on a word processor. I love word processors for obvious reasons and I don't know that I would have written any prose if it weren't for those. What I do miss though, is the clack of the typewriter. A keyboard is too quiet. It took me a long time to get used to the quiet keyboard on a word processor. If you're working on a typewriter, you hear the rhythm of the poem as you are typing it. That can tell you things about whether the poem is working or not. You have to just keep running the poem again, again, and again and revise it, revise it, and revise it. Give it some time and finally it seems to come together. Then walk away from it.

SHELLY: If you look back at your early work and where you are now, do you see an evolution?

J.V.: Oh yeah, big differences. Early on I was writing voice poems, but they weren't my voice. I did poems from women's points of view and I did dramatic monologues. I thought these were the most interesting things in the world. I spent several years doing a huge long manuscript. The poems were often published in journals and magazines, and the manuscript maintained a narrative all the way through. I have always loved telling stories, so I was having different characters speak their stories, characters connected in a place and in a time.

Finally, there was too much risk for editors to be doing poems from a woman's point of view written by a man. Poets weren't encouraged to pretend to experiences beyond their own. Part of it, also, is that I just got tired of doing that. I shifted into poems that are much more true to my experience. The speaker in my poems now is me. There is no mask. I love those personas and I love pretending to be somebody else, but maybe I did enough of it that I wore out on it. Now I'll speak for myself. Partly it's an age thing. I am old enough to have some faith in the validity of my own experience and my own perceptions so that I am not trying to lay it off on some pretend-person. I think that is the biggest difference.

Somebody said one time about T.S. Eliot that he started out to write great poetry and then he decided to live an interesting life or a good life. Great poetry is somebody else's decision; you know, they get to call that one, but I want to have a good life and an interesting life. I have lived enough and my life is so much what I want it to be that if I can't address the reader out of that experience, I don't know who else I can pretend to be that's going to know any more than me.

MARGE: You were born near Winside. You have been on this particular ranch for the last twenty years. You've spent a great deal of time on this land.

J.V.: Actually, I was born and raised north and west of here, but I do have family connections to Wayne County. My great-grandmother, Augusta Stark, came in the 1870s with an uncle and aunt from the Old Country. They settled around Hoskins before Hoskins existed. The aunt and uncle died when Augusta was still a girl, and she was taken in by neighbors and raised.

My great-great-grandfather stowed away on a ship, probably to avoid a European war. He got here and settled in Wisconsin. Things were tough enough that he became a bounty soldier in the Civil War, that arrangement where someone who got drafted could pay somebody else to take their place.

One story that I like, true or not, is that at the end of the war when the roads were full of tramps, my great-great-grandmother had told the children to make sure that you leave these tramps alone, these beat-up dirty people walking down the road. Don't bother them or anything. So they were astounded to see her one time standing on the road hugging this tramp, my great-great-grandfather who had returned home.

One of their sons, Peter, was a railroad man, the fireman on the work train on the first railroad that was built across Wayne County. He met my great-grandmother there and they were married. They are buried in a rural cemetery fifteen miles from here. I didn't know any of this—I knew some of the stories, but I had no idea of the location until I took the job at Wayne State. I then found out part of my family was based right here. So I feel real tied to the place.

I sort of stumbled into Wayne State, but having been here and having found that I am sort of from here, I feel a vested interest in the place and in the students, which makes the job interesting. If you are on a faculty and you live too much inside that faculty, you don't get into the community outside that. To run horses and cattle and to live fourteen miles from campus has put us in contact with folks that we would not otherwise know.

I lived on both farms and ranches as a kid. It was the early 50s, and at that time farming was about a half-step removed from doing everything by hand. We had hydraulics and we had a tractor and electricity, but it was still incredibly time-consuming and energy-zapping. On the good side, my folks were making a living on that farm for their children and somehow we were getting by. There wasn't a lot of money; we had $6 or $12 a week from cream and eggs, and that is what people were living on. I remember coming down at 6:00 in the morning in November; it was cold and wet and drizzling, and my dad was having a cup of coffee and had already been out to pick a load of corn. The work year was so long in farming. When we moved to the ranch, we worked pretty hard from the Fourth of July until the time school started. We had to hay the cattle in the wintertime, but it was much more relaxed. The people were different, I thought. For the first time in my life I ran into adult men who joked. (laughter)

When Lin and I moved here, what we had in mind was a kind of little truck farm and we would raise some potatoes. We always wanted horses again so we started with horses. Pretty soon we thought, if we've got horses, we'd better have something to do with them, so we'd better buy some calves. There were people who were interested in the same kind of thing, horses and cattle, and doing it a certain old-fashioned way with ropes and spurs. There was a kind of local horse culture that developed.

One of the things about poetry for years was that it was full of folks who were getting their MFAs and going to work in a college or university. Poetry became very academic. There didn't seem to be any real life to it. Academia is a great place for

poetry if that is not the only place you are. If you can't break out of that in some way, the poetry can be hamstrung. Poetry was probably not as bad as short fiction. For years it was impossible to distinguish among the lives of the characters in short fiction. Everybody was getting a divorce, and everybody lived in Connecticut, and everybody had the same dang blender sitting on the same dang kitchen counter. America was one vast suburban wasteland.

Two generations ago, many of us came from a background that was rural in nature. Now people are coming out of a housing tract life. There is nothing bad about that, but not much of that experience interests me.

Poets tend to live in a campus world, and when they break out of it, they don't go 100 miles, instead they go 10,000 miles to get away, but there are some other things which are a little bit nearer that we can look at, especially the American West. If you want a good survey sometime, check out the poetry journals east of the Missouri. You'll get a list that goes on and on. West of the Missouri there are few journals.

MARGE: But there is much good writing.

J.V.: There is much good writing, but the infrastructure for poetry is not in place on the west side of the Missouri. So part of the job is to provide that infrastructure for poets. That is becoming easier because it so much easier to do books.

I don't think that our campuses are necessarily the place to bring in eastern poets with eastern credentials, when there are so many poets around who would benefit from a reading and the money and the audience that goes along with it. The very fact that the faculty recognizes a name is the reason not to bring so-and-so because so-and-so is also going to cost you your entire budget for the year, right? We need to give support looking in a different direction. Great poets living east of the Big River are well taken care of. Western America is just a different place than the East, and this is the culture that I am interested in trying to find and articulate.

Krei

for D.W.

Some flutter at the end of our reach,
moths we swat away more often than grasp.
Some we cage in hands of will and age.
My grandfather Harry, blind near the end,
saw clearly a neighbor man eight decades gone
drive his team across the near ridge.

Or hands of history and weather:
This winter day I recollect Cedar County.
District 115. Prospect Hill.
A merry-go-round and a giant-strides–
a sort of Maypole; a couple acres
of brome grass on a south-facing slope,
a little brush in the northwest corner;
the barren apple between the outhouses;
the pie we stomped in snow for fox-and-goose.

Each family each week sent its own
tin water glass to stand inverted
on a tray beside a blue-striped crock
the teacher filled each morning
from a tin milkcan toted from home.

Rows of desks with inkwells descending
from the back of the room to the low stage
on which the teacher's desk stood alone
but for the piano bench where we sat
in turn to recite. White cursive loped
across black cards above the board
between the portraits of Washington and Lincoln.
A Nebraska map. A tin locker filled
with aromatic supplies. Curtained shelves
for library books and tin dinnerpails.

A wall clock with a red sweephand.
Krei. Darrell Krei. Mister Krei.
First day, first grade, in those sane days
of post-Labor Day school starts,
I walked the county road in new jeans
stiff as tin. Mr. Krei waited
for us on the step, brass bell in hand.
Nineteen, he had his two-year certificate
from the Teachers College in Wayne.
What hopes for the settling flocks of neighbor kids
whirled and fluttered within the cage of his ribs?

What do I recall? Mr. Krei toted to school
a television set and rigged an antenna
in a near-blizzard wind and sub-zero cold
to show us the President's inauguration.
I still see Robert Frost's frail page
wind-whipped in the poet's hand, winter
glare and ghosts through the snow of poor reception.
Today marks the ninth inauguration since, and still
I picture Mr. Krei more easily than any President.
How, after recess, he'd study the mirror
beside the water crock, comb his hair just so,
a spiral of spitcurl over his forehead.
And how well he spoke! A flawless grammar.
One star-filled arctic night,
between stacks behind the hayrack,
I confided in my older brother my ambition:
I want to talk like him. He laughed.
Now he wonders if the laugh is on him:
Of the four of us Mr. Krei taught only he
is not some brand of language teacher.

*

The older I get, the nearer frontier
my childhood seems, as if by
some law of relativity
or artist's trick of perspective.
I see it now as a heavy wagon descending
a long slope, the team reined by a gentle hand.

Krei

Mr. Krei boarded in our home, then,
the bad winters when the roads closed.
After the morning swarm of chores and breakfast,
he led us out into the wind, busted the drifts
with his thin legs, toted books and papers
and gradebook and lesson plans and the cold
tin milk can of drinking water.
Through the day he kept us at our desks learning
while the red hand of the wall clock
swept its tidy face hundreds of times.
At night, after chores and supper, grading and planning
he would brush his teeth at the cold water tap
at the kitchen sink, drink from our family's tin
drinking glass, lie down to sleep
on our old busted-down davenport,
his glasses resting upon the arm.
It must have near broke his back.

*

But always a day came when winter's back
was broken. I recall the day after Mr. Krei's
fourth school picnic at Prospect Hill.
The last book was stacked away,
and each desk was emptied and scrubbed.
The red sweephand moved so slow
that some physical law seemed broken,
until Mr. Krei looked up from his desk
on its low stage, smiled and released us
into the swirl of that spring and the coming summer
and the winter and the summers after.
He stood upon the step to watch
us disappear in a rush up a hill,
almost climbing into the sky,
little pigeons bound for home.

Did he wait to see if any of us looked back?
Did he cry out after us? And did we turn?

Letter to New York

Letter to New York

Those big storms on the news brought you to mind.
The weather on the wide side of the Big River
is seldom reported, except locally, and here
it's hardly news. All last summer we flirted
with record highs set in the dirtiest years
of the thirties without breaking a single one.
What's funny is that along in late September
some chilly nights snapped the old record lows.
Despite that cool weather, '95 turned out to be
the warmest year on record. Around Christmas
we had twenty-seven days–one full moon
to one day shy of the next–without seeing the sun.
Blue skies in January, and a couple of record highs.

The day before this Arctic cold rolled in
Zeke and I rode out to sort a few open heifers
from the herd. There's always a bunch-quitter
that makes the task a chore. We brushed up
in some willows. It took half an hour of cussing
each other before those heifers popped out.
The sun dropped behind a ridge, and I looked around
and saw the darndest moon I ever recall.
Though just one day off new, the outline
of the whole globe of it was perfectly easy
to see. Only the slimmest crescent was lit,
and that was at the bottom. It looked for all
the world like somebody giving the slyest
of smiles. It made me smile to see it.

Later, crossing the last ridge to the corrals,
I looked up to see it again and thought of New York.
Though there was no other human but Zeke
for a mile in any direction, I could imagine
millions of people and tons of tons of snow
all trying to occupy the same space. I'm not sure
why. I guess it was just the ground beneath
the horses' feet frozen hard as any concrete.

The American Heart

constitutes its own country,
and over each our particular weathers range–
lightning strike and cyclone, hot wind
and blizzard drift, three-day blow,

long light and a deep bowl of blue,
ragged clouds and a shower of rain,
taste of salt, tactile night air.

The American heart sits out its time in cheap
motel rooms of its own making while outside
the wind scours streetlights with sand.

A stark shadow on a bordertown street,
it stands in heat measured in degrees
not of Fahrenheit but eye-stinging bright.

It drives some Cadillac of need
over a highway of hard-packed ice,
with faith that a turn of the wheel
or earth will keep it well.

The American heart travels alone, feeling
its way along vague and inaccurate maps
of a common frontier where rumor says
some other impatient heart might wait.

Its every beat expresses a simple hope:
that other heart might echo its call.
The American heart drives the blood of us all.

—For Jim and Linda

Ted Kooser

Ted Kooser

Born in Ames, Iowa, in 1939, TED KOOSER is one of Nebraska's most highly regarded poets. He earned a BS at Iowa State University in 1962 and the MA at the University of Nebraska in 1968. He is the author of nine collections of poetry, including *Sure Signs* (Pittsburgh, 1980), *One World at a Time* (Pittsburgh, 1985), *Weather Central* (Pittsburgh, 1994), and his latest, *Winter Morning Walks: One Hundred Postcards to Jim Harrison* (Carnegie-Mellon, 2000), winner of the 2001 Nebraska Book Award for poetry. His work has appeared in *The New Yorker, Poetry, The American Poetry Review, The Hudson Review, Kansas Quarterly, The Kenyon Review, Antioch Review, Midwest Quarterly, Prairie Schooner, Poetry Northwest, Shenandoah, Tailwind, Cream City Review* and elsewhere. His poems appear in textbooks and anthologies currently in use in secondary schools and college classrooms across the country. He writes fiction and literary criticism and contributes regular book reviews to *Georgia Review*. *Sure Signs* was awarded The Society of Midland Authors Prize for the best book of poetry by a midwestern writer and was featured on NPR's "All Things Considered." He has received two NEA fellowships in poetry, the Pushcart Prize, the Stanley Kunitz Prize, The James Boatwright Prize, and a Merit Award from the Nebraska Arts Council. He is editor and publisher of Windflower Press, a small press specializing in contemporary poetry. He teaches as a Visiting Professor in the English Department of the University of Nebraska—Lincoln. Recent publications include a chapbook from Sandhills Press, *Riding with Colonel Carter* and, in the American Lives Series, *Local Wonders: Seasons in the Bohemian Alps* (University of Nebraska Press, 2002). He recently retired as vice-president of Lincoln Benefit Life, an insurance company, and lives on an acreage near the village of Garland, Nebraska.

MARGE: You grew up in Ames, Iowa. What was that like?

We should be interviewing at Ted's place in the country, in the room where he writes, his dog Alice at his feet or moving about the room, Ted surrounded by windows, art, and books. That plan fell through this morning, so we meet at The Mill to talk.

TED: My father was a retail department store manager, managing the first branch store that Younkers opened in Iowa. My mother was a traditional homemaker. We lived in the older part of town among my older Kooser relatives who were there at that time, an uncle, my father's mother, lots of great uncles and aunts. They're all gone now. I graduated from high school and went right on to Iowa State College in Ames, living at home. I left college in 1962, moved away from Ames, and have not been back but to visit. By that time I was ready to leave. I taught high school for one year, came to Lincoln to go to graduate school, was a terrible failure as a graduate student, dropped out, and went to work for an insurance company in 1964. I worked in the insurance business for thirty-five years.

MARGE: Did you write poetry early on?

TED: My fourth grade teacher, Miss Kirby, got us to writing poems in fourth grade. My mother of course, kept the poems. One of them goes:

"I love my dog, his padded paws.
At Christmas he's my Santa Claus.
At Easter he's my Easter Bunny..."

—and then I suppose the next line ends with "funny." (laughter)

In high school and junior high I had some good teachers that would steer me toward writing later. When you're a student, you're skeptical about your teachers' enthusiasms but some of them were good at communicating enthusiasm to us.

I was like a lot of other kids, rebellious in high school. I had a hot rod and walked around with the collar of my jacket turned up and my hair swept back. I wasn't too much into impressing teachers. I had a real serious girlfriend from the time I was a sophomore in high school until I was a junior in college and that sort of went against the grain, too, with the family. They didn't like that, which was fine with me, because I wanted to do things they didn't like.

MARGE: You dedicated *Weather Central,* in part, to your mother. What kind of person was she?

TED: Mother was a very quiet, very serene person who kept everything in. I don't remember my parents ever having an argument, at least that we witnessed as children. I'm sure they had resentments for one another. They were very formal; there wasn't a whole lot of physical affection in our house. Everybody understood we all loved each other, but there was not a lot of hugging. Mother grew up in a German-American farm family with two sisters and a disabled brother. They were extremely thrifty people. I've written about Mother's thrift, which is quite incredible. She wrote down in spiral notebooks every cent she spent from the day she was married in 1936 until the day she died, every penny including $45.00 for a week in the hospital when I was born. She managed on social security and a tiny little pension that my father had. In the twenty years between when my father died and she died, my mother on social security and this little $239-a-month pension was able to amass an estate of around $400,000.

When the CDs came due, if she didn't get the CD cashed in and moved that day to another place that had a better rate of interest, there was hell to pay. You had to get in the car and get that CD moved across town. She made my sister stand with the senior citizens on drug discount day at the drugstore to save twenty-five cents on her prescriptions. There are a lot of people like that in the midwest.

She was extremely supportive of me. I could do no wrong, even though I tried to. She was always on my side. The kind of permission she gave me to do what I wanted to do was probably helpful to me as a writer. I still have an impulse to finish up something I've written and to show it to her, even though she's gone.

There's been this persistent romantic myth of the artist coming from a troubled childhood. It's true that many of them have, but many of the successful painters and poets I know came from blissfully happy childhoods. They were allowed to do what they wanted to do. We had permission to play with our paints and our words. I said to somebody recently that we talk a lot in this country about being members of minorities; it may very well be that I am a member of the minority among writers in that I had a happy childhood. Keith Jacobshagen, the painter, is an only child. His parents just loved him. I've been around the parents and around him, and you can see it. He is completely self-assured about his work.

On the other hand there is the type of mother who whenever the person would say, "Well, Mother, I'm going to try to sew a quilt now," she'd say "Quilts are really difficult, you know. You have to get eight stitches to the inch, you have to be neat, and you have to get the colors right." You can see that person sinking in defeat.

MARGE: You are a painter as well as a writer. Do you find writing similar to painting?

TED: Imagistic writing, I think, is like painting. My own poetry is very descriptive, so I suppose there are those similarities. One of the pleasures of painting is that it doesn't have words that go along with it. You don't have to explain yourself in the same way you have to with a poem. You don't have to necessarily make sense with a painting. It has its own vocabulary, but it's a different kind of a language.

MARGE: Is there anything in the process of painting that is like the process of writing?

TED: I often build a poem up out of an image, and I guess you find something in a landscape you might fasten upon and do something with. The revision process in both media would be similar: standing back, looking at it, giving it a little time, then going back in, correcting things.

I do extensive revision in my writing. For the small poem of twelve or fourteen lines, there might be thirty or forty versions by the time I'm done. My revisions are toward a kind of clarity and freedom so that—and this would be a parallel with painting—it appears the poem came off the brush like a stroke of watercolor without any effort whatsoever. Good water color paintings look like the artist dashed them off, although it takes a tremendous effort to do that.

MARGE: Does your own painting afford you some energy renewal?

TED: Sort of, but I'm too judgmental about my painting. I'm pissed off about it most of the time because I can't get to the canvas what I see in my head. I can see every stroke the way it ought to be and yet I can't get that on the surface. Sometimes its better than others, but generally I have not played enough in that medium to feel really comfortable with it.

MARGE: What is your writing routine?

TED: Ordinarily what I do is to get up in the morning very early, make myself some coffee, and then sit someplace where it's quiet. My notebook is a combination of a diary and a workbook. I start by making a couple of diary style entries about the weather and what I did last night or what I'm reading. This, that, or the other. Then I break away and begin to let things fall into my mind. Sometimes I might write down a little list of words.

Before long something catches up my interest and I'll pursue that. Then when I get, oh, maybe seven or eight lines written that seem to be going in some direction, I usually go upstairs and start up the computer. I begin to work on it on the screen at that point. I have to do it early in the morning; I can't do it at other times of the day. I think it's because when you are just waking up, your mind is groping for connections. The metaphorical work that I like to do is all about making those connections, and the most startling connections come about at that time of the day. When I've written in late afternoon or evening, the poems seem to me much more plodding and deterministic. They don't have that freshness to them.

I've learned over the years that it's very useful to trust the metaphors that come to your mind even though they seem off-the-wall at first. They are coming from some place that makes sense, and if you look at them long enough and start tinkering with them they will develop into something interesting.

When I used to drink, I would write when I was loaded, write these things that I thought were brilliant. The next morning I couldn't read them or make any sense out of them. Trusting the metaphors that come is very different from that. So how about you, how do you begin to write?

MARGE: I like to write in cafes. Another way I write is to sit propped up in the couch and look out the window before dawn. Something will come to mind. I'm remembering a morning when I looked out and saw a plastic bag in a little breeze, moving low on the driveway, moving slowly as a possum might, and the way it moved made an unexpected connection with me, having to do with grieving for my father. The movement of that silly plastic was a connection that, as you said, I had to trust and write to see what would develop.

TED: I've told students this: your feelings will surface no matter what you are writing. If you're carrying some grief at that moment, and you write a poem about a bouquet of daffodils in a sunny room, the grief will come forward through that somehow. I've told them this because students try to write overtly about their feelings, which is not successful often. Maybe these metaphors are a way for us to get to feelings in a circuitous manner.

I had an email from some students in South Carolina that had read my abandoned farmhouse poem. At the end of the poem it says something went wrong, and they wanted to know what it was that went wrong. I told them it was mainly about indebtedness and failure of farming. They wrote back saying that was far off their idea; they thought it was this or they thought it was that. I wrote back and said, "It's OK that you think it's something else because the poem is only an object I put in front of you. You have every right to do what you want to with it." I think that would probably alarm their teacher, who was trying to find the one meaning. An imagistic poem is like an object I'm pushing across the table in front of you, and you can do whatever you want to do with it.

MARGE: You let go of it when you publish it.

TED: You don't let go of it quite as much when you read it aloud, because you're still hanging on to it, you're imposing your presence or attaching your presence to it. That may be one reason I'm not too crazy about poetry readings. There's an additonal interpretation going on, the modulation of the poet's voice. If the poet emphasizes something that you wouldn't see emphasized in the poem itself by pacing, that is evidence of a lack of control that I'm uncomfortable with.

Once it's set free and on the page, a poem ought to be its own system of controls for the reader, so the reader doesn't have a whole lot of latitude. You want to give some latitude, but the poet's intent should be part of the controlling mechanisms of the poem. If the poet wants to govern how the poem is read, then he or she should do it with meter and pacing and the kind of things that the reader can pick up.

I learned what poetry was from reading it in books, and that's really where I like to think about my work being. I don't think of it as a performance art. Part of that is because I'm shy and I don't like getting up in front of crowds of people. It makes me very nervous, and maybe I'm just excusing that, but I think not. I think I want the poems to be solid things on the page that don't require my presence to make them effective.

MARGE: Years ago I heard you comment that when a person learns to read by silent reading, that affects how they might use words later in their lives.

TED: My wife had been educated during the Kennedy years when speed reading was the thing to do. If you read from the printed word directly into the brain, so that you don't say the word aloud in your head when you read it, you miss something. As a result when we got together, she really didn't understand what poetry was about. I would read a poem aloud to her and she would begin to understand that poetry is something else, something with music in it. I think people who were taught speed reading probably have difficulty writing successful poetry because they don't have that aural sense to it. They are writing in the way that they would think rather than feel.

MARGE: Have you received advice that you have valued, and that you could pass on to the rest of us?

TED: The first creative writing class I took as an adult had a great deal of emphasis on form, and I think that did me a lot of good. The teacher had been to Stanford University and had been a student of Yvor Winters. The first assignment we had was to write thirty lines of natural description in rhyming heroic couplets, that sort of thing. I think that's important.

As far as more general advice, one of the most interesting things that anyone said to me in recent years was when I had written a piece of satirical fiction about the insurance company where I was working. I had written a novel actually, and one day I was reading a chapter of it to an older friend. It was pretty funny, the satire and so on, and when I finished he said, "Don't be too hard on those people, Ted. Almost everybody is doing the best they can." I've been thinking about that ever since. It's true, really.

I went to a wedding a year ago, and during the reception, I was sitting with a man who was a guard at Huntsville Prison in Texas where all the executions are. He was a guard on death row and I said, "Of the people on death row that you've met over the years, how many of them are genuinely evil?"

He said probably less than ten percent. The other ninety per cent are people who have just made bad choices. That's a way of looking at life. I think as a young man when I was cynical and rebellious, I would never have thought of that. I didn't have that kind of tolerance for other people, but that's something you learn.

MARGE: What makes good teaching?

TED: When I taught high school, I made a mistake in trying to be a friend to my students, because they are not ready for that. But in college teaching, I think it works to put yourself on their level and be vulnerable and willing to make mistakes in front of them, willing to say dumb things and to establish some rapport.

That's one of the reasons I'm now teaching one-on-one where I don't have any classes. I meet my students individually an hour a week, each of them, and that allows me to build a rapport that I think has been very useful. They seem to like it and I like working that way. Each student then can work toward a personal fulfillment within the frame of the class that is not interfered with by the other students.

I had last year a young Korean man whose English was very poor. If he had been in a writers' workshop, we would have had difficulty because I would have had to tend to him and tend to the people who were impatient with him. Working with him one-on-one, I called him in and said, "You know, your English is not skillful enough that you are going to be able to write good English poems, so what I want you to do is write Korean poems. Then you translate them roughly into English for me and then I'll help you make better translations." It really worked. I could not have done that in a class.

MARGE: What writers do you recommend that your students read?

TED: I recommend writers as I they come to mind, and as a student has a certain need. I had a young woman this semester whose family members are professional horse trainers. She was writing about race track things, so it came to mind that a friend of mine had written a book about auto racing that I thought was a good model for this. That's another one of these individual things where a book may come to mind to illustrate something. Somebody said to me this semester, "The word in the department is that you are extremely well read."

I said, "That isn't true at all. It's just that I talk about everything I read." (laughter)

MARGE: No, I've seen the walls of books in your house. You live in a very fine library.

TED: Two out of every five of those books I probably have just barely skimmed, but they are there, waiting. I don't want to say we grew up poor, because we were never uncomfortable, but we didn't ever have a lot of extra money, either. We had a little family library, some Balzac and the novels of John Fox, Jr.: *Trail Of The Lonesome Pine* and *Hell For Certain*, but not very many. We probably had twenty books, so the minute I got out on my own, I started collecting books. Now I have thousands of books; I think it has to do with a kind of richness that I wanted. I wanted to have a lot of books around.

MARGE: Did your family tell stories?

TED: My father was a marvelous storyteller. He would go off to the department store and then he'd come home and tell us something that happened there. He was extremely good at describing people. One of his friends told me, "I would rather hear your father describe someone than see that person myself."

We had a dear family friend named Margaret Livingston who was what we would have called in those days 'a large woman, an ample woman,' and he said, "Margaret moves like a piano on casters." I loved that.

Dad had a lively imagination. He'd come home exhausted from working a long day, and after supper we'd go for a ride in the car. There was a pen of sheep at the edge of town and we'd pull over and he'd say, "Look, children, the sheep have faces like people." And then he'd name the women who had been nuisances that day: "Why, look, there's Clara Judisch and there's Lillian Pomeroy" and so on.

There were other storytellers in my family. On my mother's side, a lot of their social occasions were people sitting around talking and telling stories. In my grandfather's gas station, the old guys would come down and sit under the awning on the folding chairs and talk. I would sit and listen, trying to wait until I would get a story of my own that I could tell. Every once in a while I would come up with a preposterous lie and tell it and they would tolerate it. They wouldn't tease me about it. I think they understood that I needed a story, too. I've noticed that there is a time in life for children where they admire storytelling, but they don't have stories of their own yet. That's why they go to the movie and come home and relate the entire movie to you, word by word. They are appropriating that story.

I remember one of my stories because it was so embarrassing and preposterous. We had gone to my aunt and uncle's in Omaha for a couple of weeks in the summer when I was twelve or thirteen. I remember coming back to Ames and telling my friends that I had driven a stock car in a race in Peony Park. (laughter) But I didn't win the race; I didn't push that, only that I had driven the car in the race. I knew to lie just enough to make it sort of credible.

MARGE: What should the poets in this country be writing about?

TED: I can tell you the things that I don't like about contemporary poetry. One of the things that troubles me concerns anecdotes. We have always had anecdotes as a part of our social intercourse, and it seems to me that the only refuge for the anecdote in literature has come to be the poem. I mean, you can use anecdotes in fiction but they are just an incremental part of it . The only place that an anecdote is legitimate is as a poem today, and as a result we have tens of thousands of poems that are merely anecdotes. They don't ever, as the Chinese poets said, "lift their eyes" beyond that. We have somehow accepted this as being a legitimate way of writing poems, just simply to sit down and start swapping anecdotes that never once attempt to transcend that. You could make them up on the spot, just start telling an anecedote, and then at the end of it come up with some sort of "Harumph" that makes it feel like it's concluded. Simply to take an anecdote of how you helped your mother wash the car and to cut it up in lines and put it on a page is not enough for anybody.

I am interested in poetry that might take a personal anecdote and fit it into a rhetorical structure that heightens its energy. There's a kind of prosody that I would call sentence prosody, in which the organization of the sentence establishes an on-going rhythm or forward motion. I have short poems that are one sentence long; if you looked at the individual lines you wouldn't be able to perceive a scanned rhythm, but if you read the whole sentence aloud you can hear under that sentence a rising and falling structure that sounds like speech but has a musicality about it.

Recently I read a book by Ron Rash, and enjoyed it immensely. Later, I realized that it was written in syllabics; every line in the book is seven syllables long, and I had not even noticed it. It was so deftly done.

MARGE: What advice do you have for writers that want to keep writing for thirty or forty years?

TED: To take care of themselves would be one thing. (laughter) That's the most important thing. It can be exhausting physical work. If I write for three or four hours, I'm really tired. You can't be smoking two packs of cigarettes a day and drinking every night and expect to last that long.

Get to the point that you take your pleasure from the process rather than the product, to be able to enjoy sitting there in the quiet of your house writing something down, without any aspirations of recognition from somebody else. You never get enough recognition. You never get as much as you think you would like to have, so you have to find some reason to do it other than that. Just the pleasure of the process, to have that feeling all of a sudden that something's unscrewed the top of your head and dropped something magnificent in. Endorphins burst out of you. You really feel it right then; that's what's good, I think. Publishing poems is fun; it's necessary if you are teaching to have a lot of books on your vita, but the process is what's really important.

I was talking to a young poet the other day and I said, "What are your aspirations?"

She said, "Oh I'd like to get a couple of books out and get a real good teaching job somewhere teaching creative writing." She is not saying a couple of books that people want to read or a couple of books that are of quality or that will endure. They are part of a résumé that she's going to use in getting a teaching job, which is, I'd say, sad.

MARGE: I believe you've made a writing space for yourself in your home.

TED: I have lots of them. I like best sitting in the living room in the morning where it's warm and comfortable, but I have outside places I can go to. As long as I am not bothered in the house I can write. It's so easy to shatter the state of concentration. As you're sitting on your couch in the morning writing, your spouse comes in and says, "Where's the milk?" Then it's over for me. It's very hard to get back. That's one of the reasons to get up very early.

Bill Stafford said that he used to get up at 5:30 in the morning when the children were small. Then his daughter figured out that if she got up at 5.30, she could have an hour with her dad before the rest of the family. So Stafford began getting up at 4:30. He's the person who really showed us how to do this early morning writing. It's worked for me and I guess it's worked for you and a lot of other people.

MARGE: For one thing, it takes writing time from the top of the day.

TED: It is a kind of meditation that feels good, a peaceful quiet concentration, no radio, only bird sounds outside maybe. It has a spiritual feeling, let's say.

Then also there's the idea that by breakfast time you've already gotten something done. You can't get to the end of the day and say you wasted the whole day. I'm much more sensitive to that than I used to be.

After I was seriously ill a few years ago, I got to thinking how precious time is, so I have a hard time reading novels because I'm going to have to spend four or five hours reading, and I'm not sure that's the best use of my time. I can read a short story in half an hour, and I feel that's all right, but commiting myself to big heavy books, I can't do that any more. Kathy can sit down and read through David McCullough's biography of Truman from the front to the back, get completely absorbed, and learn a great deal. I even resent good TV movies because they might take up a couple of hours.

MARGE: Anything else about current publishing?

TED: Personal recounting of sexual adventures is not very original. There is all kinds of it in contemporary writing. I had a good friend, a well-educated attorney who had gone to Harvard Law School, who said to me one day, "Why is it that poets feel they can write about sex as if they were the only people who had ever had it?" I've thought about that a lot.

A friend of mine published what might have been a pretty good novel before the editors at this big press in New York got hold of it. It started out to be a novel about the life of an artist. Then standard sex, kinky sex, oral sex, bondage, all these things appear in sequence as if it were necessary to include everything in the Kama Sutra. None of it was necessary to make this a good story but, I fear, some editor wanted it in there for marketing purposes. I am also uncomfortable with other kinds of personal revelations that don't seem to be any more than somebody trying to get something off their chest. It doesn't seem to me that is what art is about.

MARGE: Do other kinds of art besides poetry renew you? What is it that renews or gives you energy? For instance, I personally need time alone to recharge. After socializing or giving a reading or teaching, I have to draw back because I'm depleted. Some of my friends get energy from that kind of thing, but I have to get energy back by taking a walk or reading.

TED: I'm exactly the same way. I don't like parties because they absolutely drain me. I don't know if it's because there's so much data coming at me from all directions or what. I used to drink heavily at parties. After I quit drinking, I began to understand it's because I hated them. I didn't want to be there. It was a way of anesthesizing myself against being there and chatting with people.

I need to get away and be very quiet and by myself, and then sometimes I get this hunger for being around people and want to just yammer at them for a while. You led into this by mentioning art. It is pleasurable for me to be in art galleries by myself when no one else is tugging me along to the next picture and I can spend as much time as I want to.

Here's something you ought to try. How long has it been since you've been over to look at those dioramas in the basement of Morrill Hall? There are buttons you can push to hear the magpie or the meadowlark. When you push the badger's button, you hear the badger go *bup bup bup* down in his burrow in the bank. The thing to do is to go over there in the middle of the afternoon when no one is around and push all the buttons and stand there in the middle with the buffalo noise and badgers' noise and birds singing. (laughter)

So This is Nebraska

So This is Nebraska

The gravel road rides with a slow gallop
over the fields, the telephone lines
streaming behind, its billow of dust
full of the sparks of redwing blackbirds.

On either side, those dear old ladies,
the loosening barns, their little windows
dulled by cataracts of hay and cobwebs
hide broken tractors under their skirts.

So this is Nebraska. A Sunday
afternoon; July. Driving along
with your hand out squeezing the air,
a meadowlark waiting on every post.

Behind a shelterbelt of cedars,
top-deep in hollyhocks, pollen and bees,
a pickup kicks its fenders off
and settles back to read the clouds.

You feel like that; you feel like letting
your tires go flat, like letting the mice
build a nest in your muffler, like being
no more than a truck in the weeds,

clucking with chickens or sticky with honey
or holding a skinny old man in your lap
while he watches the road, waiting
for someone to wave to. You feel like

waving. You feel like stopping the car
and dancing around on the road. You wave
instead and leave your hand out gliding
larklike over the wheat, over the houses.

Abandoned Farmhouse

Abandoned Farmhouse

He was a big man, says the size of his shoes
on a pile of broken dishes by the house;
a tall man too, says the length of the bed
in an upstairs room; and a good, God-fearing man,
says the Bible with a broken back
on the floor below the window, dusty with sun;
but not a man for farming, say the fields
cluttered with boulders and the leaky barn.

A woman lived with him, says the bedroom wall
papered with lilacs and the kitchen shelves
covered with oilcloth, and they had a child,
says the sandbox made from a tractor tire.
Money was scarce, say the jars of plum preserves
and canned tomatoes sealed in the cellar hole.
And the winters cold, say the rags in the window frames.
It was lonely here, says the narrow country road.

Something went wrong, says the empty house
in the weed-choked yard. Stones in the fields
say he was not a farmer; the still-sealed jars
in the cellar say she left in a nervous haste.
And the child? Its toys are strewn in the yard
like branches after a storm—a rubber cow,
a rusty tractor with a broken plow,
a doll in overalls. Something went wrong, they say.

November 17

November 17

Clouds to the west, clear in the east.

Older this morning, the moon
hid most of her face
behind a round gray mirror.

In a half-hour's walk, I saw
six shooting stars. Celestial notes,
I thought, struck from the high end
of the keyboard.

March 13

Overcast and still.

High in an elm, a red-bellied woodpecker
rattles a branch, rattling and resting,
rattling and resting, each flat dry burst
like a single extended sound. It's the creak
of the painted wainscot ceiling
of my grandparents' porch, under the strain
of the chains of the swing. Somehow
it has carried this far, four hundred miles
and more than fifty years, the sound
of my Uncle Elvy watching the highway
and swinging, the toes of his good shoes
just touching the floor.

For Jeff

On the morning of your wedding
I walked alone in the little park
where sometimes we ran and played
when you were small. My father
was living then and would walk
behind us as we jumped and laughed,
his step already cautious, his eyes
on his everyday wing-tip shoes
as they parted the grass. It was
as if he had begun to sense
that the world is less than solid,
for he stepped out so thoughtfully
onto each day: hands in his pockets,
jacket zipped to the neck,
his brown felt hat, brim up,
on the back of his head as if
a wind were blowing into his face,
and such a wind was surely blowing.

This time it was I who walked there,
buttoned against the wind, alone,
my hands in my jacket pockets,
a ball of Kleenex closed in one fist.
Under a spreading tree by a stream,
I shaded my eyes with my father's hand.
Through swirls of diamonds I saw you
run swiftly ahead, looking back
to encourage a boy with a kite
as he clumsily followed, tugging
the string. And as I watched
from my place at the back of your life,
the kite bounced along on its tail,
then shuddered and lifted itself,
and shook off its own surprise.

CREDITS

Cover photo by Randy Barger
Photo of editors by Matt Riley

Photos of Jonis Agee, Eamonn Wall, Hilda Raz, Ron Block, Charles Fort, Twyla Hansen, and Ted Kooser courtesy of the writers.

Photos of William Kloefkorn, Barbara Schmitz, Don Welch, Brent Spencer, and J.V. Brummels by Shelly Clark.

Cover and book design by Chris Bristol.

E.L. Doctorow quote used by permission of E.L. Doctorow.

ACKNOWLEDGMENTS

JONIS AGEE

"Earl" reprinted with permission from *Acts of Love on Indigo Road,* Coffee House Press, 2003.

J.V. BRUMMELS

"Krei," "Letter to New York," and "The American Heart" from *Cheyenne Line,* The Backwaters Press, 2001.

CHARLES FORT

"Rain Over the Brown Fields" from *Afro Psalms,* University of Nebraska at Kearney Press, 2001.

"The Worker" from *The Carnegie Mellon Anthology of Poetry,* Carnegie-Mellon University Press, 1993, and *A New Geography of Poets,* University of Arkansas Press, 1992.

"The Poem Found In Darvil's Back Pocket At The End Of The Plains" from *Frankenstein Was A Negro,* Logan House Press, 2002.

"Sonnet for Shelley" from *Plein Chant,* Chateau-neuf-sur-Charente, France, 1989.

"Prose Poem for Claire Aúbin Fort" from *Words And Witness: 100 Years Of North Carolina Writers,* Carolina Academic Press, 1999, and *St. Andrews Review,* 1989.

TWYLA HANSEN

"Planting Trees" from *How to Live in the Heartland,* Flatwater Editions, 1992.

"My Husband Speaks of Wood," "Just Before Dawn," and "The Snowball Sisters" from *Sanctuary Near Salt Creek,* Lone Willow Press, 2001.

"Backyard" from *In Our Very Bones,* A Slow Tempo Press, 1997.

WILLIAM KLOEFKORN

"#13" from *Alvin Turner As Farmer,* Windflower Press, 1974.

"Easter Sunday" from *Where The Visible Sun Is,* Spoon River Poetry Press, 1989.

"Last of the Mohicans" from *Dragging Sand Creek For Minnows,* Spoon River Poetry Press, 1992.

"Epiphany" from *Going Out, Coming Back,* White Pine Press, 1993.

"My Love For All Things Warm And Breathing" from *Cottonwood County,* Windflower Press, 1979.

"Love Song at Midnight" from *Loup River Psalter,* Spoon River Poetry Press, 2001.

TED KOOSER

"So This is Nebraska" is reprinted by permission of the author from *Sure Signs,* University of Pittsburgh Press, 1980.

"Abandoned Farmhouse" from *A Local Habitation & A Name,* Solo Press, 1974.

"November 17," and "March 13" from *Winter Morning Walks: One Hundred Postcards To Jim Harrison,* Carnegie-Mellon University Press, 2000.

"For Jeff" from *Weather Central,* University of Pittsburgh Press, 1994.

HILDA RAZ

"Small Shelter," and "Accident" from *What is Good,* Thorntree Press, 1988.

"Diction" from *The Bone Dish,* State Street Chapbooks, 1989.

"Mutation Blues" from *Divine Honors,* Wesleyan University Press, 1997.

"Aaron at Work/Rain" from *Trans,* Wesleyan University Press, 2001.

MARJORIE SAISER

"The Pelican's Dive" first appeared in *Prairie Schooner,* Fall, 2001, used by permission.

"My Old Aunts Play Canasta in a Snow Storm" from *Lost In Seward County,* Backwaters Press, 2001.

"Calling Cardinals," and "Road Trip" from *Moving On,* Lone Willow Press, 2002.

BARBARA SCHMITZ

"Yoga," "Test," "Gift," "Two Step," and "I Kiss You" from *How to Get Out Of The Body,* Sandhills Press, 1999.

BRENT SPENCER

"Save or Turn to Stone" reprinted with permission from *Are We Not Men?,* Arcade Publishing, 1996.

EAMONN WALL

"The Waves, The Waves," and "Junk Food," from *Iron Mountain Road,* Salmon Publishing, 1997.

"Cahore" from *The Crosses,* Salmon Publishing, 2000.

"The Country Doctor" from *Dyckman—200 Street,* Salmon Publishing, 1994.

We are grateful to the editors at Salmon Publishing for the use of Eamonn Wall's poems. (Salmon Publishing, Ltd., Knockeven, Cliffs of Moher, Co. Clare, Ireland)

DON WELCH

"Funeral At Ansley" from *Inklings: Poems Old and New,* Sandhills Press, 2001.

"June" from *In the Field's Hands,* University of Nebraska at Kearney Press, 1998.

"Poet In Residence At A Country School" from *The Rarer Game,* Kearney State College Press, 1980.

"About Your Classrooms" from *Fire's Tongue in the Candle's End,* University of Nebraska at Kearney Press, 1996.

"Letter To Aanya, Two Months Old," and "Note To A Young Writer" from *Fire's Tongue in the Candle's End,* University of Nebraska at Kearney Press, 1996.